# STUDIES OF EXCELLENCE IN TEACHER EDUCATION

## PREPARATION AT THE
## *graduate level*

**BANK STREET COLLEGE OF EDUCATION**
BY LINDA DARLING-HAMMOND AND MARITZA B. MACDONALD

**UNIVERSITY OF CALIFORNIA-BERKELEY**
BY JON SNYDER

**UNIVERSITY OF SOUTHERN MAINE**
BY BETTY LOU WHITFORD, GORDON RUSCOE, AND LETITIA FICKEL

Linda Darling-Hammond, Editor

# STUDIES OF EXCELLENCE IN TEACHER EDUCATION

## PREPARATION AT THE
## *graduate level*

**BANK STREET COLLEGE OF EDUCATION**
BY LINDA DARLING-HAMMOND AND MARITZA B. MACDONALD

**UNIVERSITY OF CALIFORNIA-BERKELEY**
BY JON SNYDER

**UNIVERSITY OF SOUTHERN MAINE**
BY BETTY LOU WHITFORD, GORDON RUSCOE, AND LETITIA FICKEL

Linda Darling-Hammond, Editor

The American Association of Colleges for Teacher Education is a national, voluntary association of colleges and universities with undergraduate or graduate programs to prepare professional educators. The Association supports programs in data gathering, equity, leadership development, networking policy analysis, professional issues, and scholarship.

The opinions, conclusions, and recommendations expressed in this monograph do not necessarily reflect the views or opinions of the American Association of Colleges for Teacher Education. The AACTE does not endorse or warrant this information. The AACTE is publishing this document to stimulate discussion, study, and experimentation among educators. The reader must evaluate this information in light of the unique circumstances of any particular situation and must determine independently the applicability of this information thereto.

*Studies in Excellence in Teacher Education: Preparation at the Graduate Level* may be ordered from:

AACTE Publications
1307 New York Avenue, NW, Suite 300
Washington, DC  20005-4701
Tel: 202/293-2450
Fax: 202/457-8095
Web site: www.aacte.org
Single copy: $20.95 AACTE members/$25.95 nonmembers

This three-volume series also includes:
*Studies in Excellence in Teacher Education: Preparation in a Five-Year Program*
*Studies in Excellence in Teacher Education: Preparation in the Undergraduate Years*

> National Commission
> on Teaching & America's Future

The National Commission on Teaching and America's Future, initiated in 1994, was created to identify the implications for teaching embodied in current school reforms; to examine what steps need to be taken to guarantee all children access to skilled, knowledgeable, and committed teachers; and to develop a comprehensive policy blueprint for high educational performance. The Commission's work has been supported by grants from the AT&T Foundation; BellSouth Foundation; Carnegie Corporation of New York; the DeWitt Wallace - Reader's Digest Fund; the Ford Foundation; the Philip Morris Companies Inc.; the Rockefeller Foundation; the US Department of Education's Office of Educational Research and Improvement; and the William R. Kenan Jr. Charitable Trust.

Grateful acknowledgment is made to the DeWitt Wallace - Reader's Digest Fund for support of this publication.

ISBN No: 0-9654535-7-X

ABC-7099

# TABLE OF CONTENTS

# TABLE OF CONTENTS

# FOREWORD
*by Linda Darling-Hammond*

This set of case studies about extraordinary teacher education programs is one of three volumes being published by the American Association of Colleges for Teacher Education in collaboration with the National Commission on Teaching & America's Future. A cross-cutting analysis of the cases, published separately, will describe the common features of these seven programs that are distinguished by their success in preparing teachers to practice in ways that we describe as both *learner-centered* and *learning-centered.* By this, we mean that they prepare teacher to meet the needs of very diverse learners—to teach in ways that are responsive to individual students' intelligences, talents, cultural and linguistic backgrounds, needs, and interests; and they prepare teachers to teach for understanding—to teach in ways that support active, in-depth learning which results in powerful thinking and flexible, proficient performances on the part of their students.

These abilities are the foundation of new standards developed by the National Board for Professional Teaching Standards (NBPTS), the Interstate New Teacher Assessment and Support Consortium (INTASC), and the National Council for Accreditation of Teacher Education (NCATE), along with professional associations engaged in developing new standards for students. However, while there is increasing consensus on what teachers and their students need to know and be able to do in order to meet the more ambitious goals of 21st century schools, there is not yet a well-developed knowledge base about how to prepare teachers to do these things. Although teacher education has been much critiqued, little research has been done to examine the kinds of learning experiences that help beginning teachers acquire the knowledge and skills that underlie learner-centered and learning-centered practice.

That teacher knowledge is central to this mission is a new concept in 20th century school reform. After decades of trying to fix schools by changing curriculum packages, texts, tests, and management systems, most reformers now agree that deepening teachers' knowledge and skills is critical to the success of ongoing efforts to reform American education. Only very knowledgeable and skillful teachers who are able to respond differentially and appropriately to students' interests and needs can enable diverse learners to succeed at much more challenging learning goals. These goals include helping students learn to master ambitious subject matter content and to think critically, create, and solve complex problems, rather than merely to perform rote tasks. And teachers are being asked to achieve these goals for *all* children, not just the 10 to 20 percent who have traditionally been siphoned off into programs for the gifted and talented or "honors" track. Furthermore, students are more diverse in their needs and backgrounds and less supported in their communities than in the past. So schools are being asked to take achieve higher goals for a broader group of students with greater learning needs than ever before.

This collection of case studies seeks to answer a question that has not yet been yet addressed by reformers: How can we prepare teachers for this daunting mission? The study, conducted under the auspices of the National Commission on Teaching & America's Future at Teachers College, Columbia University, reports how seven teacher education programs have been able to prepare teachers to succeed at the kind of highly demanding practice described above, and thus to create substantially more successful and powerful learning experiences for students. It provides evidence about the outcomes of the programs as well as the content they engage and the processes they employ. The goal of this work is to provide greater knowledge that others in the field can build upon—knowledge that will help us understand what successful teacher education models look like, what they aim for, what they do, and what their students can accomplish as a result.

One motivation for this study was to counteract the widely shared set of myths about teaching and teacher education. Among others, these myths include the following: that good teachers are born and not made; that good practice cannot really be taught—it can only be intuited through trial and error; that few can ever really master complex teaching practices or attend to the needs of individual learners (thus, teacher-proof curricula should be continued targets of educational investment); that there are no worthwhile teacher education programs anyway so the whole process of preparing teachers should be abandoned. These myths, despite their lack of grounding, drive much policy work and deflect attention from needed investments in high quality preparation for teachers.

To provide evidence about alternatives, we set out to look at teacher education programs that are so noticeably good at what they do that the distinctive practice of their graduates is obvious as soon as an observer sets foot in the classroom. This phenomenon is one that I have noticed over the years of my work in schools and teaching. In my years in New York, for example, I could almost invariably identify the graduates of preservice programs like those of Bank Street and Teachers College, Columbia by seeing them teach and hearing them discuss their practice. Like the graduates of other programs that we discovered by asking practitioners in other parts of the country, these teachers' knowledge of curriculum and assessment, their focus on and understanding of individual students, and their capacity to use sophisticated teaching strategies for engaging diverse learners were immediately evident. Furthermore, I found that in many parts of the country I could find a high degree of consensus among principals, superintendents, and teachers who operated schools that were extraordinarily successful with diverse learners about where they liked to hire their teachers. These excellent practitioners agreed on a very short list of colleges in their vicinity (often only one or two) that they believe prepare teachers from their very first moments on the job to shape powerful learning experiences for their students and to understand their students' learning and how to support it very, very well.

The seven programs in this study are by no means the only ones that fit these criteria and the more formal parameters we ultimately used in developing the sample. The programs were selected from a much longer list of candidates because they represent elementary and secondary programs in public and private institutions serving different kinds of clientele in different parts of the country. The programs were selected through an extensive review of evidence, including national reputational sampling from researchers, expert practitioners, and scholars of teacher education; local evidence from employers about who they prefer to hire and why; and evidence of outcomes from prior surveys of program graduates. To these data about program outcomes, we added as part of the study a comparison survey of recent program graduates and a national random sample of beginning teachers about their preparation and practices; a survey of the principals of program graduates about their views of the program graduates' abilities and practice in comparison with those of other programs; and observations of graduates' classroom practice after graduation.

The sample institutions use very different models of preparation, some are undergraduate while others are postbaccalaureate or five year (combined undergraduate and graduate); some have created professional development school relationships while others organize student teaching in more traditional ways; some use cohort models while others do not; some attract current or recent college students while others attract mid-career recruits to teaching. Thus, together they represent the gamut of possibilities for teacher education currently found in the field:

- Bank Street College in New York City offers a graduate school program that is known for its long-standing commitments to progressive, democratic practice and has the Bank Street School for Children as an on-site lab school. We examined the programs for preparing elementary and middle school teachers.

- The University of California at Berkeley's Developmental Teacher Education Program is a two-year graduate school model of early childhood education that is strongly focused on the application of developmental psychology to teaching.

- University of Southern Maine's Extended Teacher Education Program (ETEP) is a one-year graduate school model that is substantially school-based. Almost all fieldwork and much course work for both the elementary and secondary teacher education programs takes place in schools that are professional development school partners with the university.

- Wheelock College in Boston, Massachusetts is known for progressive early childhood education, much like Bank Street. We examined the undergraduate early childhood education program that is also a pathway to a master's degree program required of all teachers in Massachusetts before they receive a career teaching license.

- Alverno College in Milwaukee, Wisconsin is an undergraduate model that organizes its work around a sophisticated performance assessment strategy tied to its ability-based curriculum. We examined the elementary teacher education program that works in strong collaboration with Milwaukee Public Schools.

- Trinity University in San Antonio, Texas operates a five-year model that extends from undergraduate through graduate school in a blended program that awards both a disciplinary bachelor's and a Master's in Education for both elementary and secondary candidates. Trinity adopted the major recommendations of the Holmes Group and has organized all of its field work around professional development schools.

- University of Virginia in Charlottesville, Virginia is a five-year dual degree program like Trinity's that does not rely upon professional development schools. We examined the secondary education programs in English and mathematics. These programs provide insights into the preparation of high school teachers, an area that we found was problematic nationwide.

The study does three things: First, it documents the goals, strategies, content, and processes of teacher education programs that are widely acknowledged as exemplars for preparing prospective teachers to engage in skillful, learner-centered practice. Using a standard set of observation and interview protocols, as well as survey instruments, a team of researchers examined all aspects of the program of study and clinical practice engaged in by students—by surveying graduates and their employers; shadowing and interviewing students; visiting classes, seminars, professional development school sites, collecting record data (syllabi, assignments, student work, program descriptions, and statistics) and observing and interviewing university-based and school-based faculty about the intentions, processes, and outcomes of their work.

Second, the study documents the capabilities of the prospective teachers who graduate from these programs. This is done through examination of the teachers' own work during teacher education and in the field (direct observations as well as artifacts of practice: portfolios, exhibitions, lesson plans, assignments, and samples of their own students' work); interviews with faculty and administrators in the schools where graduates teach; surveys of principals comparing the knowledge and skills of these candidates to others whom they have hired; and record data from other surveys and accreditation reviews. Finally, the study examines what policies, organizational features, resources and relationships have enabled these programs to be successful, taking into account the university and state policy contexts within which these programs exist.

We sought to study a diverse set of programs because we believe the findings will be more robust and useful if they characterize important features of successful programs that exist in a wide range of contexts with which other schools can identify. The goal of the study is not to suggest a single cookie-cutter approach to preparing teachers, but to understand the core features of a range of programs that make a difference for preparing teachers who understand their students and who can teach in ways that develop deep understanding and high levels of competence. While they conceptualize and conduct their work in different ways, these programs do have many common features. Among them are the following:

- a common, clear vision of good teaching that is apparent in all course work and clinical experiences;

- well-defined standards of practice and performance that are used to guide and evaluate course work and clinical work;

- a curriculum grounded in substantial knowledge of child and adolescent development, learning theory, cognition, motivation, and subject matter pedagogy, taught in the context of practice;

- extended clinical experiences (at least 30 weeks) which are carefully chosen to support the ideas and practices presented in simultaneous, closely interwoven course work;

- strong relationships, common knowledge, and shared beliefs among school- and university-based faculty; and

- extensive use of case study methods, teacher research, performance assessments, and portfolio evaluation to ensure that learning is applied to real problems of practice.

These features and others help these programs productively confront many of the core dilemmas of teacher education: the strong influence of the "apprenticeship of observation" candidates bring with them from their years as students in elementary and secondary schools; the presumed divide between theory and practice; the potential limitations of personal and cultural perspectives each person brings to the task of teaching; the difficulty of teaching people how to enact their intentions in complex settings for practice; and many more.

We hope that readers find the case studies to be generative for their own research, thinking, and practical efforts with regard to the education of teachers. If the illustrations provided here spark an idea or an initiative that enables teachers to learn more productively how to teach more powerfully, our work will have been well rewarded.

*Linda Darling-Hammond*
*Provence, July 7, 1999*

Note: The research team was led by Linda Darling-Hammond, then William F. Russell Professor of Education at Teachers College, Columbia University and currently Charles E. Ducommun Professor of Teaching and Teacher Education at Stanford University. It included Julia Koppich, President of Julia E. Koppich and Associates, an education consulting firm; Maritza B. Macdonald, Senior Research Associate, National Center for Restructuring Education, Schools, and Teaching, Teachers College, Columbia University; Kay Merseth, Executive Director of the Harvard Project on Schooling and Children at Harvard University; Lynne Miller, Professor and Director of the Southern Maine Partnership at the University of Southern Maine; Gordon Ruscoe, Professor in the Foundations of Education at the University of Louisville; David Silvernail, Professor and Director of the Center for Educational Policy, Applied Research and Evaluation at the University of Southern Maine; Jon Snyder, Associate Professor and Director of Teacher Education at the University of California at Santa Barbara; Betty Lou Whitford, Professor of Education and Director of the National Center for Restructuring Education, Schools, and Teaching at Teachers College, Columbia University; and Kenneth Zeichner, Hoefs Bascom Professor of Teacher Education at the University of Wisconsin-Madison.

# Where There is Learning There is Hope: The Preparation of Teachers at the Bank Street College of Education

## BY LINDA DARLING-HAMMOND AND MARITZA MACDONALD

*We believe that the purpose of education is to help
students develop a scientific attitude of eager, alert
observation; a constant questioning of old procedures in
the light of new observations; and a use of the world as
well as books and source material . . . Thus, the most
fundamental clause of my personal and institutional
credo is: While we are learning, there is hope.*

– Lucy Sprague Mitchell (1931)

On a spring morning just before the last week of school, when many students are just biding time, Jean Jahr's[1] classroom of 28 second- and third-grade students is intently engaged in a mathematical investigation. A first-year teacher, Jean teaches at P. S. 234, a New York City public elementary school launched by a Bank Street graduate and staffed almost entirely by Bank Street-trained teachers. The multiracial, multilingual class of students is working in small groups on a single problem. Some children use calculators; others do not. Some have drawn clusters of numbers; others have developed a graphic display for their problem. As they finish, everyone takes their solutions with them as they sit on the carpeted meeting area facing the board. Jean begins by reading the problem with the group: "The problem: In September each person in class 113 brought one ream (1 package) of Xerox paper. There are 500 sheets of paper in one ream. There are 28 children in class 113. How many pieces of paper where there altogether?"

She opens the discussion with an invitation, "Let's talk about how different people solved the problem, and why you decided to solve it that way." Over the next 20 minutes, students show, draw, and discuss seven different strategies they have used to solve the problem. Jane questions them to draw out details about their solution strategies and frequently recaps what students say. With patience and careful word choices, she helps each member of the group understand the thought processes of the others.

As the session nears its end, she asks if everyone understands the different solutions. Three children from one group seem in doubt and raise their hands. Jean asks one of the girls to come up and show "her way." Teacher and the other children observe patiently, obviously pondering the girls' thought process. Suddenly, Jean's face lights up as she sees what they have done. Her response clarifies their work:

> That's how you did it! I was wondering if you had used tens groupings, but you had a totally different pattern. You started as if there were 30 children and then you subtracted the 1,000 sheets that would have been brought by the additional two children from the total number. You rounded to a higher number and then you sub-

1 Most names of teachers and students are pseudonyms, denoted with an asterisk*, unless otherwise requested by the individual. Actual names of Bank Street faculty and administrators are used throughout.

tracted. Wow. I get it. Let me see if I can show it to the others.

The young girl is pleased when the teacher shows the group "her" system. When everyone seems clear, Jean asks, "Does anyone remember where this problem came from?" A girl raises her hand and says: "That was my problem a long time ago." "You're right," her teacher responds. "You asked that problem during the first week of school when all of you were asked to each bring a ream of paper for the year. You saw all those reams of paper stacked up in front of the room, and you wanted to know how many sheets of paper we had. I told you that we would find out some day but that at that point in the year it was hard to figure it out because you had to learn a lot about grouping, and adding large numbers. But, now you all can do it and in many different ways." Another child recaps by noting, "That means that we used 14,000 sheets of paper this year." Jean notes, "You got it!" The problem stays on the board for the day, along with the students' multiple solutions.

Elsewhere throughout the room, children's work is displayed on walls, bulletin boards, and shelves, along with teacher-made charts listing information related to work that is underway. Near the book collections and writing materials, for example, three different charts pose guiding questions to help students meet the expected writing standards for content, mechanics, and personal goals as a writer.

The content standards ask:
- Does the beginning tell what my piece is about?
- Does the order in which I wrote it make sense?
- Did I use examples and details to create a picture in the reader's mind?
- Does my story make sense?

The chart on standards for mechanics asks:
- Have I checked for correct spelling?
- Have I used upper and lower case letters in the right places?

The chart on Being a Writer in a Community of Writers asks:
- Am I willing to share my writing?
- Do I listen to others, share, and give helpful feedback?
- Am I willing to revise my work?
- Can I say why I selected this piece for publication and what do I like best about it?

It is clear in watching Jane at work that she cares equally about the quality of her students' work and about the quality of their experience as learners in a democratically managed classroom. When there is an opportunity to talk with Jane about her practice and her preparation, it is clear that she chose to attend Bank Street because it would prepare her to teach in this way.

> I started to get information about Bank Street about 10 years ago. Finally I decided to just quit my job (in a technology field) and go to Bank Street full time and pursue a degree. I chose Bank Street because I had known many people who went there. My children had gone to a school in Brooklyn (with many Bank Street trained teachers). My son is now a writer. I think having that kind of teaching had a big impact on him.

Jean Jahr's son and her students are among the many thousands influenced by the kind of teaching fostered by the Bank Street School of Education, which has affected educational practice worldwide. Host to thousands of visitors annually from across the U.S. and around the world, Bank Street College and its famous School for Children have been wellsprings for constructivist, developmentally appropriate, and social reconstructionist teaching for over 80 years—long before these terms had found their way onto the educational landscape. Bank Street practice supports the many ways in which children and adults construct knowledge, attends closely to the process of human development and learning, and aims to develop social responsibility and social justice within schools and the broader community. Bank Street's influence on early childhood education extends far beyond its teacher education programs, although these are central to its mission and an important influence on many schools in New York City and elsewhere. Work on curriculum development, school reform, the preparation of school leaders, and the advancement of professional knowledge all contribute to the field of childhood education nationally and beyond.

## THE BANK STREET MISSION

Originally known as the Bureau of Educational Experiments, Bank Street was founded in 1916 by Lucy Sprague Mitchell as a non-degree program for individuals interested in learning about children's development through child study and actual teaching. Formal teacher preparation for degree programs, under the name of Bank Street College of Education, began in 1931. Edna Shapiro (1991), a well known developmental psychologist and long standing faculty member, describes the program's beginnings and its continued commitments in these words:

> The 'School for Teachers' began as a one year program for liberal arts graduates. The faculty was, and continues to be, comprised of people with considerable classroom experience . . . The ethos of the institution was one of belief in education as an ameliorative social force, a means of effecting social change. The teacher was seen as a potentially powerful agent of personal and social liberation, guiding children to become independent thinkers and active participants in a democratic society (p. 6).

Shapiro's description reflects the relationships between school, society, children and curriculum stressed by John Dewey (1900) and voiced more recently by reform groups like the Coalition of Essential Schools (Sizer, 1992), and the Holmes Group (1986). Central to these conceptions is a view of learning that enables independence and empowerment, and of teaching that supports the kind of critical thinking, intellectual and social development needed for democratic life. The educational perspective that infuses the school was summarized by its well-known scholar, Barbara Biber (1973), in a talk to educators entitled "What is Bank Street?":

> We aim for actively involved children acquiring competence and a sense of their own competence. Active investigation, independent pursuit, and learning through discovery are dominant in the learning climate, but we respect and honor the kind of content for which prestructured information or formal instruction may be more efficient and, in fact, satisfying in its own way. The Bank Street teacher uses every opportunity to foster intellectual mastery and to promote cognitive power by creating a pervasive climate of "why and wherefore and wherefrom" kind of thinking. In our philosophy and practice, we feel responsible to nurture equally the intuitive processes, the capacity for feeling and emotion, for reflective as well as goal-directed thinking.

The school as a social institution has broad responsibility for the development of the whole person—his affective and social as well as his intellectual development.

The school is not neutral ground. Educational goals are inevitably value-bound. In our perspective we value effective, autonomous individuality that, in maturity, evolves toward social commitment. We work toward the kind of democratic intragroup functioning that is built on nonauthoritarian forms of control, participation of the governed in decisionmaking, and especially on nonpredatory modes of interchange among people at all stages. We are committed to repeated cycles of innovate, observe, study, evaluate, and revise. There is an organized program of research in which the roster of studies reflects our involvement in probing the depths of the learning-teaching processes. Finally, we are committed to using our private, independent learning environments as laboratories for the development of optimal learning settings for children and adults and as the base for making an impact on the direction of public education. (pp. 1-5)

After roaming its halls and sitting in its classrooms, talking to students and faculty, and peering in at the School for Children, what strikes one about Bank Street is the depth of its commitment to a developmental view of children and learning and a progressive vision of educational goals and possibilities. These views are pervasive in its mission statement and documents, course guides, hallway discourse, and professional endeavors of all kinds. In the Bank Street School for Children—an on-site PK-8 independent school where student teachers are found in virtually every classroom—children are building with blocks, making books, designing architecture and science projects, constructing and visiting museums, arguing mathematics, and collaborating with one another on a kaleidoscope of projects.

In college classrooms, prospective teachers undertake similar kinds of work. They can be seen making picture books for children and curriculum books for teachers, experimenting with beans, sand, water, and other manipulatives for mathematics and science, constructing museum and community trips for themselves and future students, and collaborating with one another on a variety of projects. Their advisors, who meet with them individually and in groups every week and who also teach courses, know them as intimately as they hope someday to know their future students. The prospective teachers see their own development as being nurtured and their interest and passions as being respected and extended.

Bank Street's approach emphasizes teaching for understanding, respecting and building on learners' interests and experiences, looking at individual learners with care and attentiveness, and creating community. These precepts are extraordinarily well integrated in the work of the college and remain identifiable in all of the features of the program: admissions, course work, advisement, field placements, and graduation requirements. Each of these ideals is as carefully represented in the way teacher education faculty nurture their students as it is in the formal curriculum about teaching that faculty seek to transmit. This "hidden curriculum" is, as Barbara Biber (1973) explains, quite deliberate:

> We have assumed for many years that, beyond the structured curriculum that is provided, the students internalize the pervasive qualities of the learning environment we try to create for them, that the qualitative characteristics of their own teaching styles will reflect, later, the qualities of their own personal experience in learning to become teachers. (p. 3)

The belief that teachers must have opportunities to learn in the same ways they will some day be expected to teach appears to develop a strong and distinctive practice, immediately visible the moment one enters a classroom or a school touched by Bank Street training.

## THE BANK STREET ETHOS

Back at P. S. 234, Marilyn Morroca's* kindergarten and first grade classroom, like all of those in the school, reflects the fundamentals of Bank Street practice. To the left of the door is a science area populated by a guinea pig and two snakes (in different cages), a bulletin board covered with pictures of snakes and a real snake skin, and a chart on the wall displaying upper and lower case letters of the alphabet. Students' work covers much of the remaining wall. Handmade pictures include captions that state, "We are the authors." To the right of the door is shelving that separates the block area from the center of the room where small tables are set up to accommodate groups of four to six children each. Straight ahead, a rug and two soft chairs define the reading and meeting area.

Marilyn is reading to the children who are gathered before her on the rug. After reading a page, she shows the students the picture of a flower it includes and asks with a big smile, "How many letters does the word chrysanthemum have?" After they have counted together, Marilyn then pulls out name tags she has prepared with the children's names on them. She asks each child, one by one, to come up to a large piece of newsprint on an easel to her right and post the tag above the number that denotes the number of letters in his or her name. These tags gradually stack up to create bar graphs depicting the number of children in the class with names that have a given number of letters. The title at the top of the chart reads: "How Many Letters in Our Names?"

When they have completed this task Marilyn asks, "Are there any chrysanthemums in the room? Does anyone's name have the same number of letters as chrysanthemum?" This puzzle occupies a few minutes of checking and counting, after which the children agree that no one has a first name that is 13 letters long. Marilyn then asks if they could put two names together to make a name with as many letters as chrysanthemum. She uses small colored blocks to illustrate a combination of letters that equals 13. A student suggests another combination. Once they have realized that there is more than one way to combine numbers to equal 13, Marilyn sends them back to their tables to work together on "making a chrysanthemum"—that is, a combination of names that will produce the number of letters in that word. A quiet hum fills the room as the children work in pairs and small groups combining names, adding and subtracting letters and numbers, and explaining their solutions to one another. For those who finish early, Marilyn has another problem to extend their learning. Some who finish their own work continue helping other students who are still at work.

The idea of collegial learning also shapes the ways in which adults work together at P. S. 234. Jean Jahr notes:

> We're very fortunate in this school that there's a terrific amount of staff support. First of all, we meet on a weekly basis by grade level, so there's a forum to get together and talk with other

teachers about things that are going on. We usually address substantive issues, like how to do book clubs or the kind of writing we are doing. This meeting is run by the assistant principal but she solicits the agenda from us. We had a good system early in the year where we would meet in each others' classrooms. That was a good opportunity to look around and see what other people were doing. People would ask questions and, especially as a new teacher, I found that very helpful. Our staff developer (from Teachers College, Columbia University) was enormously helpful in getting the Writers' Workshop going. I felt like I was taking a mini-course right here in the classroom. Then, we have a lot of teachers who cooperate on their social studies curriculum. In the fall, I worked with two other teachers, and that meant I didn't have to develop that part of the curriculum myself. It was already in place, but I knew there was always room to do what I wanted to do.

Collegial work, ongoing inquiry into teaching, and shared curriculum building are staples of Bank Street practice. So is looking closely at children's work and listening intently to them to understand what they think and can do. When we talk to Marilyn after her chrysanthemum lesson, she speaks in great detail about the learning strengths and progress of individual children, about their needs, and about the puzzles she is working on. One student, for example, writes fluently but is not yet motivated to take care with her work or to improve on it. Another can only produce a single word at a time and has just been diagnosed with an auditory perceptual disability. Marilyn has been interviewing the first child to find out what might change her approach to her writing; she is also developing new strategies for the second student that rely more on visual recognition of words than on aural decoding. Marilyn appears to know a great deal about the learning approaches and needs of each of her students, and chooses activities carefully to maximize their ability to build on strengths while addressing shortcomings.

Another new teacher at P. S. 234, in her second year of teaching, attributes her ability to evaluate individual students' learning and support their progress to the consistency of her experience in courses, advisement, and field experiences at Bank Street. Like many other Bank Street graduates,

Rachel* chose the college for its child-centeredness. "I was committed to making my kids feel respected, and I thought that Bank Street would help me. One of the greatest gifts Bank Street gave me was the commitment to finding ways to accommodate different needs." Rachel attributes the close attention she gives to students and their work in part to the close attention she received from her own advisor:

> I found my advisor so supportive and encouraging and reasonable. First, she saw me every week for two hours in the conference group and then additionally privately for one hour every few weeks and in my placements. She knew me well. She knew what questions to ask to get me to dig deep and to plan better. She also encouraged me to question things that I was learning and maybe not seeing in my kids. I learned to question and to look for evidence. I think the consistency of the person and the depth of the relationship is critical.

To a great extent, the Bank Street ethos shows up in the quality of relationships for which faculty and students strive in all of their work.

## PROGRAM OUTCOMES

These features of a Bank Street education are noted by the many principals in New York City and surrounding areas who hire graduates. Gus Trowbridge, director of Manhattan Country School for the past 30 years, praised Bank Street graduates' abilities to integrate the cognitive, affective, and social dimensions of learning:

> I think they are the best trained teachers in progressive education that I can find. The Bank Street philosophy and methodology is closely connected with ours. Socialization of children always seems to be related to the balance between the cognitive and the affective, as well as between the individual and the group. Our school has emphasis in supporting the individual and also helping him relate to a community.

Tania Kauffman, principal of a public elementary school in Manhattan, emphasized graduates' well-developed curriculum thinking:

I find that the Bank Street graduates have the progressive understandings we need in our school. They use social studies very effectively for developing integrated curriculum that teaches children about society and about themselves as members of a community. I think their understanding of curriculum is very deep.

Suzanna Kaplan, principal of an early childhood school in Teaneck, New Jersey, a multicultural, urban suburb of Manhattan, noted the blend of cognitive understanding, creativity, and a commitment to ongoing learning that graduates bring to their work.

I find that Bank Street graduates are creative and progressive in their views. I have found that they seem to be a more mature group who have either had other careers, are older, or have had a variety of previous life experiences. They seem to have a desire to keep learning and to teach with a cognitive approach that comes from a focused philosophy.

Celenia Chevere, current principal of the Young Women's Leadership School in Manhattan's Community School District #4 and previous director of educational initiatives in District 1 in the lower east side and District 10 in the Bronx, looks for all of these things and more, which is why she seeks out Bank Street graduates:

I have sought out Bank Street graduates in all my positions in the last 10 years. In the mid-80s, I hired Bank Street graduates when I started a school based on principles for gifted education in District 2. My focus was to offer all children the kind of educational experiences that are usually offered to smaller groups that are labeled "gifted" through standardized tests. Some of those teachers are still there and others have moved on to the smaller schools opening in District 1. In district 10 during the last two years we started the professional development school and engaged in a series of curriculum innovations based on social studies. Both the College and its graduates were fundamental to those efforts. Here at this new school for young women, I have hired mostly Bank Street graduates who are strong in development, in understanding multiculturalism, and in subject matter. I hire them for their high level of professionalism and for their willingness to engage in serious conversations about children, their needs, and their potential. For me, it is important that they are able to balance the development of serious curriculum while paying attention to the needs of students in a diverse population. With adolescents it is really important that teachers understand the many issues of development that affect their physical growth, their emotions and sense of belonging, as well as providing them with the intellectual and academic tools for becoming independent and self-fulfilled in a multicultural society.

Carolyn Gear, principal of P. S. 37 in the Bronx, observed that she found Bank Street graduates "very, very well prepared" to work in her multilingual school organized around the multiple intelligences work of Howard Gardner. The school's emphasis on diverse approaches to learning was stimulated by a multicultural and educationally diverse population that is more than 70 percent Latino, about 15 percent African-American, and the rest "other," and includes nine special education classrooms. Having recently hired three Bank Street graduates, Gear declared "They're excellent!" and illustrated with a description of one new teacher she had hired the previous year:

> In terms of her knowledge base, in terms of curriculum, the kinds of approaches she uses and activities she provides for children . . . how she handles the class... in terms of how she teaches children to reason and respond to situations, she is excellent. She teaches them problem solving and logical thinking.

Surveys of principals who have hired Bank Street graduates in the past few years and of recent graduates themselves confirm that teachers prepared in the Early Childhood, Elementary, and Early Adolescence programs seem extraordinarily well prepared in a number of areas. In comparison with a national random sample of beginning teachers, Bank Street teachers felt better prepared than their peers in 33 out of 36 areas, and significantly better prepared in 25 areas (see Appendix B). The differences in

Bank Street graduates' self-reported levels of preparedness were most pronounced (p<.001) in areas dealing with the *development of curriculum* (creating interdisciplinary curriculum; developing curriculum that builds on students' experiences, interests, and abilities; and evaluating curriculum materials); the ability to create a *positive, productive learning environment* for all students (e.g. developing a classroom environment that promotes social development and group responsibility; engaging students in cooperative group work as well as independent learning; teaching from a multicultural vantage point); *teaching for higher order thinking and performance* (helping students learn to think critically and solve problems; helping students develop their abilities to raise questions and discuss ideas; encouraging students to explore ideas from diverse perspectives); and *being prepared to use research and other colleagues to improve their practice* (conducting research and inquiry to inform decisions; working with colleagues to plan and solve problems). The only area in which Bank Street teachers felt less well prepared than other beginning teachers was in the use of technology in the classroom, where a majority of both groups felt less than adequately prepared.

More than 90 percent of principals ranked Bank Street graduates as "well prepared" or "very well prepared" in comparison to those from other teacher education programs, and most found them well prepared in all areas (see Appendix B). Most prominent in principals' responses are the aspects of teaching that distinguish what is often called "progressive" practice: the ability to focus on in-depth learning and on students' needs; the abilities to understand student learning and development and to use this understanding to develop curriculum based on students' experiences; the ability to build interdisciplinary curriculum; the ability to relate learning to the real world; the capacity to teach for social responsibility and collaboration; and the ability to help students learn to think critically, solve problems, question, and see ideas from diverse perspectives. In addition to these areas, principals were virtually unanimous in seeing Bank Street graduates as extraordinarily well prepared in working with parents and families to support student learning, in resolving interpersonal conflict, in working with colleagues, and in assuming leadership responsibilities in their school.

While principals and teachers reported that individuals prepared at Bank Street bring special capabilities to the classroom, Bank Street's influence is felt in even more profound ways in some public schools with heavy concentrations of its graduates and ongoing professional development relationships with the College. At P. S. 234, an extraordinarily successful, extremely diverse elementary school in lower Manhattan, principal Anna Switzer, herself a Bank Street graduate, has built a staff comprised almost entirely of Bank Street graduates. Switzer describes Bank Street graduates as special in this way:

> They bring a way of looking at kids that I feel is very unusual. There is very little negative language about children here and one never gets the sense that the inside of a child is ever attacked. This is a culture of looking at children's growth and strengths, a culture of collaboration and kindness. A distinctive progressive pedagogy—a commitment to intellectually exciting content and to developing high levels of student competence— is part of the Bank Street ethos.

The ability of Bank Street teachers to understand children was also noted by veteran cooperating teacher Lena Hajar* at P. S. 234 who had supervised more than 15 student teachers from various programs over her career. Hajar noted of Bank Street candidates:

> They're really good at interacting with kids—very caring, not patronizing, not condescending, not authoritarian or punitive. I also think they're very, very motivated. They're very committed to this kind of practice and to teaching.

These outcomes of Bank Street preparation and professional relationships are also obvious at Midtown West elementary, a public school that maintains a more formal professional development partnership with Bank Street. Since its beginnings in the 1980s, the school has maintained a professional development liaison person who teaches at the Bank Street for Children three days a week, does ongoing professional development for staff at Midtown West two days a week, and supports linkages between the school and the college, such as the placement of interns and of student teachers. Walking the halls and observing in classrooms, we saw a culturally and linguistically diverse staff and student body at work on a variety of topics: raising animals, cultivating plants, writing books, researching scientific and historical ideas, making murals, calendars, and lists of things learned, and holding classroom meetings to solve problems, discuss ideas together, or decide what to study next.

Teachers describe these meetings as democracy in action. Everyone participates, and decisions made at meetings often guide the direction of, for example, a community project, the study of an author, or the field trip to look at how people use the Hudson River. During meeting time, teachers often sit with notebooks on their laps, writing down children's questions or responses. Later on, they use this information to design further curriculum experiences.

On a day that we visit, Lisa Baumwall, a first year Bank Street graduate at Midtown West, is holding a meeting with her 29 students in a combined kindergarten and first-grade classroom. The topic of conversation is children's author Vera Williams. Baumwall and her students are discussing Williams as an author who writes stories with a social message. They debate whether Williams' stories *always* or only *sometimes* portray children and families saving money for something special or overcoming a family dilemma. The children and their teacher look for evidence of literary style by reviewing her books, characters, plots, and illustrations. The chart in front of the class indicates that author studies are common in this class. Vera Williams' books are cited and listed along with all of Eric Carl's books, which were evaluated by the children months earlier.

As she listens intently to student contributions and guides the conversation along in a sophisticated manner, Lisa has clearly moved past the rudimentary concerns of many first-year teachers, such as merely maintaining classroom discipline. Her students are tackling serious literary questions and creating a genuine intellectual discourse while they interact respectfully and attentively with one another. She credits the help she received from her preservice program, her principal, colleagues, and Roberta, the professional development liaison between the school and College, with helping her learn to pace her teaching and keep her large class simultaneously interested and on task.

In addition, like other Bank Street teachers—and unlike the folk wisdom that suggests teacher education courses are largely irrelevant—Lisa refers often to the skills she learned in various courses. She describes foundations courses that helped her see and understand issues of equity that she now uses in selecting curriculum resources and topics, like the work by author Vera Williams, to help children find themselves in their books. She recalls the value of assignments that asked to find evidence of how children act and think by following a child over a long time and in a variety of contexts. In places like Midtown West, with a strong Bank Street influence schoolwide, this foundation of shared experiences and knowledge has palpable effects on individual and collective practice, and on the overall success of the school as a place where diverse learners are successful. Similar influences can be seen at other public schools where Bank Street has had ongoing relationships for preparing teachers and administrators, such as P. S. 87, Central Park East II Elementary, River East Elementary, Muscota New School, and Manhattan New School.

Another kind of systemic influence is apparent in a number of new public schools that have developed as part of New York City's reform strategy over the last seven years. The directors of these schools, many of them expert teachers who are inventing schools that must survive in a volatile political climate, report that finding teachers who can engage in sophisticated child-centered practices and are willing to stay the course is very important. Judith Foster, director of the Neighborhood School located in the Lower East Side of Manhattan, reflects the views of several new school directors who seek out Bank Street graduates:

> Our teachers have to decide that they want to be pioneers. (Bank Street teachers) are willing to try things in many ways over a long time until they work. We have our first group of sixth graders this year and they can trace back how they began in the school, and their teachers can go back to specific strategies they had tried to motivate different children. They also keep studying and learning. They value the power of integrated curriculum and the role of the arts in learning and in understanding cultures.

That the "Bank Street teaching" we saw among graduates is an intentional outcome of the program is suggested by the description by the College's president, Dr. Augusta Kappner, of the kind of reference letter she would write for graduates:

> I would feel pretty confident saying that most Bank Street graduates are self-starters and strong at taking the initiative, that they

like to question and challenge, that you can probably count on them to address problems and issues in their work setting, and that they will try to find alternative ways to structure those work settings to improve them for the benefit for children.

## THE SETTING AND PROGRAMS

Bank Street College of Education was originally housed on Bank Street in Greenwich Village. It is currently located on 112th Street on the Upper West Side of Manhattan in a single modern building on a quiet street just half a block from the hustle and bustle of Broadway. The nine-story building houses four institutional divisions: a family day care center for infants and toddlers; the Bank Street School for Children, an independent progressive school for children ages three to 13; the Graduate School of Education, and Continuing Education.

Classrooms of the Bank Street School for Children are shared with the Graduate School of Education, and most graduate courses are taught in this laboratory-like setting filled with teaching resources and evidence of children's and teachers' curriculum work. The School for Children describes itself to visitors as a progressive demonstration school where its teachers are educating children and teachers simultaneously. In its multi-age classrooms (each of which combines two grade levels), teachers develop strong relationships with students whom they teach for two years. Older students help younger students learn the ropes in an activity-based curriculum that emphasizes exploration of the classroom and community environment; investigations into the physical and social world; and individual and group production of projects, experiments, models, books, plays, and other evidences of complex learning. During the day, when school is in session, student teachers and interns work side by side with experienced teachers in virtually every classroom. In the evening, the same classrooms are inhabited by graduate students taking courses. They merge theory and practice by constantly connecting what they are learning in their courses with what they observe in these children's classrooms and in their field placements in local public schools.

The College offers six programs leading to a master's degree: Teacher Education, Bilingual Education, Computers in Education, Special Education, Studies in Education, and Educational Leadership. The seven teacher education programs include early childhood, elementary, early adolescence, infant and parent development, museum education, special education, and reading/literacy specialization. The leadership programs prepare early childhood administrators, museum administrators, elementary and middle school principals, and mathematics specialists. Each program has both preservice and inservice components designed by a director and a group of advisors. Many of the advisors in the preservice programs teach courses, supervise students in the field, and work with students in advisory groups. The multiple roles played by these advisors create an unusual level of program coherence that is difficult to replicate in settings where diverse sets of individuals are responsible for these different functions.

This study focuses on the preservice programs that prepare teachers to work with early childhood, elementary, and young adolescent students. These 42-credit programs include 30 credits of graduate level course work plus 12 credits of fieldwork. Students must have completed a bachelor's degree prior to entry. They undertake a full academic year of advisement and practicum experiences which incorporate several student teaching placements alongside intensive course work. In addition to their student teaching and course work, students also complete one of three graduation requirements: a portfolio, an independent study, or a directed essay. Students who pursue their course work in a concentrated fashion can complete the program in 12-15 months. Most students take close to two years to complete their degree. Some begin teaching during the second year while they are finishing the requirements, having already successfully completed the full year of student teaching and core course work. In the 1995-1996 academic year, there were 214 students enrolled in the preservice programs. Of that number, 63 were participating in the required full year of advisement, practicum, and course work. The additional 151 students were taking courses either before entering the full year of advisement and student teaching or after having finished the advisement year.

Perhaps the most striking feature of the Bank Street approach is the extent to which teaching and learning are integrated in every aspect of the program. Program directors and advisors balance administrative roles with teaching, advising, and recruitment, interviewing, selection, and ongoing mentoring of students. There is an institutional belief that participation in these different roles informs courses, advisement, and program decisions. Faculty who engage in field advisement learn the realities of schools and contribute directly to their improvement by taking their needs into consideration when teaching courses and advising students how to teach the children they both meet in the field placements. The involvement of directors in teaching, advisement, and supervision keeps them cognizant of the field and of the kinds of placements where students experience exemplary teaching. Through direct engagement with the work of teaching and the work of schools, they learn what programs need to prepare teachers for.

This integrative approach extends to the work of students as well. After classes, graduate students can often be seen studying the classrooms of the School for Children for evidence of the concepts they are learning about. One evening, for example, we watched graduate students looking at students' work posted in the hallways outside a classroom for 13-year olds. There they saw several handwritten and computer generated letters to senators requesting information on the Federal budget, along with a student-made chart with specific questions about the Federal Budget for Education. Another chart displayed the names, political parties, and addresses of "Our local representatives in Washington." These letters and the accompanying charts had resulted from the semester-long interdisciplinary study of American Government and Democracy, prior to a culminating trip to Washington where students met with their local representatives. The letters and questions had been mailed prior to the trip, and information and responses were included in the final projects.

On another floor, next to the elevators, another group of graduate students seemed to be connecting their observations of children at different ages with the art work that was displayed in the hallways. Children's work showed textured collages representing animals and people. The labels next to the animal collages indicated that they had been made by six- and seven-year olds. Labels next to the collages of people indicated that they have been created by nine- and 10-year-old students. Several graduate students took note of the art work and the labels and questioned whether, if the two groups were put together, the younger children would be inspired to create people or the older ones might deal with animals. When the elevator came, graduate students left, still discussing issues of inter-age grouping that had been raised in their child development course prior to observing the art displays.

On a different night, graduate students taking Math for Teachers were working in small groups solving the same problem. After about 15 minutes of this activity, the instructor, Barbara Dubitsky, who also directs the computer program and serves as an advisor in the preservice program, asked each group to demonstrate how they solved the problem. Eight different solutions were reported. After the groups presented their solutions, the class discussed the different skills each group used in solving the problem and how they would teach students those skills.

At the end of the class, three graduate students, on their way to get pizza before the next class, noticed some graphs on a wall and postponed their pizza run. They sat down on the floor to copy in detail the different types of hand drawn graphs displaying percentages graphically and numerically on the wall. The children's graphs showed the percentage of time each nine-year old had spent watching TV, eating, doing homework, listening to music, reading, doing sports, dancing or doing gymnastics; walking to school or riding the bus, arguing with siblings and sleeping— in a day, a week, and a month. When the graduate students finished copying down the graphs, one of them exclaimed, "I would never have known that kids could think up all these different ways of doing graphs. Did you notice the one shaped like a cake and its different size slices? I wish my day was like slices of cake." The other two nodded and smiled.

This integration of activities is promoted by the use of physical space at the College. In addition to the fact that the School for Children and day care center are in the same building as the College, the library and the cafeteria are shared spaces for children, their families, faculty, student teachers, school administrators from the leadership programs, working teachers from the inservice programs, and the school's many visitors. In the library, it is as common to find graduate students asking a 10-year old the titles of his favorite books as it is to find them checking out books for term papers. The attitude that children know things and have important opinions is evident in the ways these prospective teachers approach children. One gets the impression that there is as much interest and respect for what a child has to say about a particular book as there would be for the opinion of the literature instructor or a curriculum expert.

One late afternoon, several School for Children students discussed their favorite books with a student teacher who was placed in their classroom. Next to them, near the elevators, another graduate student was setting up a video on how to do community studies with four- and five-year olds. The children recognized a school friend on the video and decided to stay and watch. For the next 20 minutes the adults watched, took notes, rewound and reviewed portions of the tape, and quietly discussed what the teachers on the tape were doing. The children stayed with them and pointed out familiar places and people on the tape.

In the cafeteria, we watched parents and children, graduate students, and faculty members at different tables having an early dinner. On the other side of a glass partition, a course on "Music and Movement for Teachers" was underway. Diners smiled at the intriguing scene on the other side of the glass. They appeared to know why all those grownups were playing with a multicolored parachute and crawling though hoops to the fast moving tune of a tarantella. Parents and teachers had seen their children in similar music and movement classes. Children knew that the teachers were learning to use the parachutes and other equipment to prepare them to teach music from all over the world. The instructor later explained that the tarantella was used to invent a spaghetti dance to accompany a cooking unit used by teachers of young children.

At the end of an evening of shadowing graduate students, a newcomer is thoroughly absorbed by the variety of experiences that weave teaching and learning together through a range of social, academic, and interpersonal interactions. This mosaic exemplifies the developmental interaction approach associated with Bank Street from its beginnings. As expressed by its founder, Lucy Sprague Mitchell (1930), Bank Street's commitments are to the development of people who can value one another, work collaboratively together, use their minds fully and flexibly, learn from their experience, and make the world a better place:

> What potentialities in human beings—children, teachers, and ourselves—do we want to see developed?
> * A zest for living that comes from taking in the world with all five senses alert.
> * Lively intellectual curiosities that turn the world into an exciting laboratory and keep one ever a learner.
> * Flexibility when confronted with change and the ability to relinquish patterns that no longer fit the present.
> * Gentleness combined with justice when passing justice on other human beings.
> * A striving to live democratically, in and out of schools, as

the best way to advance our concept of democracy.

Our credo demands ethical standards as well as scientific attitudes. Our work is based on the faith that human beings can improve the society they have created.

## PROGRAM THEMES

Five major themes permeate the commitments and practices of the College. These appear as strong philosophical commitments on the part of the College toward the education of both children *and* adults preparing to work with children. One of the striking aspects of teacher education practice at Bank Street is that the strongly-held progressive views about how children should be educated are mirrored in the processes and practices for educating future teachers. These include:

- **Student-centeredness:** a focus on the needs and interests of individual students and a developmental approach to learning;
- **Community emphasis:** a strong effort to develop communities of learning within which personalized relationships and social learning can be fostered;
- **Social and moral commitment:** a commitment to the moral purposes of teaching and schooling and to the social possibilities for education;
- **Constructivism:** an experiential, constructivist view of curriculum;
- **Continuity:** an expectation of continuity in learning that results in a focus on constructing ongoing, connected learning experiences.

**Student-centeredness grounded in a concern for development.** All of the components of a Bank Street education are designed to support the growth of children and teachers by providing means for understanding children and their learning—as it occurs both individually and collectively—and by promoting knowledge of development and knowledge of self. The theoretical roots of the Bank Street program are described in the following excerpt from a 1992 curriculum guide for the Early Childhood Education program:

Bank Street's approach to education is not limited to any one educational institution . . . . The approach flows from three main sources: (1) the dynamic psychology of Freud and his followers, especially those who were concerned with development in a social context, for example, Anna Freud and Erik Erikson; (2) developmental psychologists like Jean Piaget and Heinz Werner; and (3) educational theorists and practitioners like John Dewey, Harriet Johnson, Susan Isaacs, Lucy Sprague Mitchell and Barbara Biber. However, there are many other psychologists and educators whose ideas are compatible with Bank Street's approach to education, for example, Kurt Lewin, Lois Murphy and Lev Vygotsky. (p. 15)

These moorings lead to a view of education in which cognitive functions are engaged in the course of personal reflective and social processes, in which curriculum and teaching methods are adapted to developmental sequences and patterns, and in which materials, ideas, people, and surroundings are orchestrated to provide sites for learning (Biber, 1973). The grounding in developmental theory that has historically characterized the field of early childhood education extends to Bank Street's programs for older children, adolescents, and adults, as well. A concern for development undergirds a view that takes seriously the individual person's pathway to understanding. Faculty see their students as developing human beings, and look for ways to foster knowledge of self as a means for enabling knowledge about children. Judith Leipsig, director of the Early Childhood and Elementary Program, expressed this view in her description of the program's goals:

> Our goal is to work with students in a very complex and interpersonal dynamic—to collaborate with them in their development, not just as a teacher in the sense that a teacher would be a technician, but as a teaching person. A teaching person is one who reflects on his or her own ability to understand themselves, what their own culture is, what their own context is, what their needs are and what supports they need in order to function effectively, and the lenses through which they they look at children—as well as to develop their greater knowledge of content areas and technical skills in teaching.

The institutional concern with human development is evident in Bank Street's approach to teaching and advising its own graduate students; in its required courses on development and observation of children; and in the developmental component that is woven into the teaching of all subjects. The view that a teacher's personal development is connected to her capacity to support children's development is reflected in the admissions process as well as in the courses and field experiences. In the autobiographical essay candidates write for admission, they are urged to "select and describe those experiences and relationships in your childhood and in your background which seem to you to have been significant for your development as a person going into the field of education" and to connect those experiences to "your present feelings about children and youth." In the application, candidates must also respond to vignettes posing dilemmas about situations raising developmental themes. For example:

> Two five-year-olds are pretending that they are dinosaurs. Down on all fours, the two are hissing at each other and making clawing, scratching movements, until one of the children suddenly stops short, peers somewhat anxiously at his fellow dinosaur, and asks, "Then you'll change back into yourself, OK?" What are the issues in this situation? How would you respond?

In discussing a recent interview, one of the faculty explained how she looks for a desire to learn about children as learners during the admissions process:

> I just came back from a second interview with a prospective student because I had some doubts after the first one. Since our last conversation she has enrolled in one of the courses, so I started to treat her as a student. She said at one point, 'You know, after that session on play, I have begun to think differently about children of different ages.' I observed her reflecting again when I was trying to get at her notions of good teaching. She spoke about a good teacher she had had, and when I asked why was he good, she responded thoughtfully and said: 'He just knew me. I know he really knew who I was.' And to us knowing students well is critical.

This concern for knowing students well carries over to how the graduate faculty studies and reflects on the needs of their own adult students, whose ages range from the mid-20s to early 40s. In the last five years, several faculty members have been studying and reflecting on the contributions and developmental, social and cultural concerns of career changers and older students, who now comprise the majority of students at the College (Crow, Levine', & Nager, 1990). In another study, faculty have been learning about the commitments and concerns of inservice teachers of African-American descent who are in the inservice program (Toppin and Levine, 1992). One graduate, now a supervisor in the State Education Department, noted that, "Bank Street teaches you to value people—not just children or your class in a particular school, but to value the spirit within each individual" (Bank Street Viewbook, n.d.).

**A climate that fosters community and personalized relationships.** Strong communities and personal relationships are fostered in Bank Street's School for Children and in public schools that have adopted its approach by the two-year cycle of students' placements with their teachers. Bank Street teachers use a variety of methods to build community in the classroom, through communal meeting times that serve social and academic purposes, through collaborative work groups, and through the creation of norms that develop students' capacities to participate in decisions, help one another, and share their ideas and skills.

Similarly, the graduate school constructs a variety of close relationships, both one-on-one and in communal groups, that provide opportunities to question and share issues of teaching. In advisement, students are divided into groups of five to seven per advisor. The advisor works with them in three different capacities: supervising their field placement, meeting with students individually every other week, and convening two-hour conference group meetings every week. As one student explained:

> (Advisors) help you develop your program. They focus on your particular situation. It is not just your academic wellbeing. My advisor takes an interest in other parts of my life inside and outside the school. You have an advocate. They know a lot about schools, about you, about finding jobs.

The advisory group provides a setting for collaborative problem solving as well as individual attention. Students frequently stay in touch with their advisors and members of their advisory group long after they've left the program. When asked about beliefs that undergird the program, program director Judith Leipzig returned to the theme of relationships and the program's commitment to model the experiences teachers are expected to enact later:

> Relationships are at the core of everything that we do with students. Relationships are central to the educative process because an important part of that process is getting to know the other person. So much of what we do with our students is modeling and immersing them in experiences like the ones that we want them to have with children. (personal communication, November 17, 1995)

**A commitment to the social and moral dimensions of teaching.** Bank Street provides a strong normative environment within which teachers develop their philosophies of teaching. While prospective teachers consciously work to develop a distinctive personal philosophy, the view that education is a social force and that teachers are moral change agents is evident not only in foundations courses, but also in courses on methods of teaching and child development and the advisement process. An instructor in the Child Development course explained, "I look at issues of a period and their relevance to teaching and educational policy. Right now we can't think about adolescents and teaching them without considering AIDS, diversity, violence, extreme wealth, drugs, poverty."

Issues of diversity, equity, multiculturalism, poverty, language differences, school funding, and reform are evident in assignments, reading, and discussions. Students are repeatedly asked to think about the consequences for students' individual and social development of teaching decisions, means of organizing the classroom, choices of curriculum materials—how these connect to children's family, community, and cultural roots, how teaching decisions support or undermine equity, how they contribute to a participatory society in the classroom and beyond. And student teaching placements provide well developed sites for developing practice that includes democratic forms of community in which antiracist and egalitarian norms are pursued. At the School for Children and in local public schools with strong professional development relationships to Bank Street, prospective teachers work in classrooms that are mini-societies where participation, representation, and the common good are core values.

These experiences encourage prospective teachers to reflect about the meaning of their work for their students and for society. The college culture also models engagement in the larger issues of democratic participation and children's welfare. In June, 1996 one of the last observations for this study took place aboard one of the three buses that took Bank Street faculty, families and students to Washington, DC to the Stand for Children March. At the March, the group stayed together and individuals took turns carrying the Bank Street banner.

**A constructivist approach to curriculum.** An admissions brochure answers the question, "What makes Bank Street a unique place for graduate work?," with this statement:

> We believe that children and teachers learn best through their own experience—and so do graduate students. Here you will find a special blend of theory and practice that will challenge you intellectually while you learn hands-on approaches to help support and develop students and teachers in the learning process.

Based on theory and evidence that people build knowledge from a combination of direct experience, reflection, and guided study, Bank Street's program emphasizes the careful construction of settings for learning in which learners can move back and forth between "book learning" and firsthand experience. Earlier in the century, Lucy Sprague Mitchell took children and teachers on extended field trips across the country to study particular places, themes, and social concerns, convinced that such experiences would enable much deeper learning than intellectual inquiry alone. Today children in the Bank Street School for Children and other schools influenced by these ideas, undertake community studies of their neighborhoods and of local environmental and social issues, while they are reading about them in literature, primary historical or scientific documents, and textbooks. They plant gardens and observe the outcomes while they are studying plant biology. They build and measure structures while they are studying measurement and geometry. Whatever is to be learned is approached from a base of experience with opportunities for reflection rather than only through abstraction.

The teacher education program is also based on a careful combination of experience, reflection, and study. Graduate students are placed in classrooms with cooperating teachers who model Bank Street practices throughout their year of full-time study, while they take courses in child development, teaching methods, and social foundations. Continuous cross-referencing between teaching and study about teaching is made possible by this arrangement, fostering an analytical and practical approach to the development of practice. Teachers develop and try out curriculum in order to understand its goals and effects. They write children's books in order to understand the relationships between literature and experience. They solve mathematical problems in order to understand the thinking and problem solving processes that children undergo. They act and observe the consequences of their actions, interpreted in light of other research and theory, to refine their work in the classroom.

Because teachers understand learning as constructed from students' prior knowledge and experiences, they develop curriculum from their knowledge of students and their goals for in-depth learning. This approach to curriculum is readily apparent at the Bank Street School for Children where virtually all student teachers spend some of their time visiting, observing, and student teaching. There they participate in an interactive process of curriculum building across all of the grade levels and subject areas, one that examines students' progress, ideas, and concerns as part of the process of developing units that will flow from and tap into children's experiences while revealing more of the world to them.

**An expectation of continuity in learning.** Learning is seen as a continuous process that builds upon prior experiences and requires time to unfold. Bank Street practice is patient, both about the processes of learning for children and the processes of learning for adults. Bank Street teachers and teacher educators are always looking for strengths to tease out and build upon; they are willing to look harder, tend new growth steadily, and wait for deep learning to take root and unfold. In organic fashion, there is a quiet but firm insistence on allowing development to occur, not magically without support, but with steady, careful nurturing. Learning to teach is viewed as a continuous process that is transformed by teaching and refined through the knowledge of students, of self, of instruction, and of content (Macdonald, 1991). That process, patiently and carefully nurtured, builds strength in teaching. It cannot be rushed or side stepped.

Many students we interviewed described how they were first attracted to Bank Street both by its philosophy and reputation and by its personalized admissions process. The commitment to students continues throughout the program and into their careers as teachers. In discussing why they selected the Bank Street Program, students often spoke about becoming a member of a teaching community:

> I decided that I wanted to do a career change into teaching. I took the course for teaching reading and I was hooked. I also liked the fact that they help you with job searches. They stay connected with you as long as you are teaching. Your association doesn't end after you graduate.

## PROGRAM CORNERSTONES

There are three major program features that combine to create the signature Bank Street teacher:

- An admissions process that seeks out candidates who are disposed to respect and learn from children in the course of teaching;
- An academic program that focuses on development and learning and that integrates theory and practice; and
- A tightly coupled, learner-centered approach to advisement and field placements.

### Selecting Candidates: The Search for the "Teaching Person"

Whereas teacher education programs have often been criticized for accepting anyone who applies and graduating any who make it through, student selection at Bank Street is a highly personalized and focused process, as is the rest of the program. The admissions process includes multiple forms of evidence that provide indicators about candidates' experiences and views as well as their academic preparation. It reflects the College's concern for individuals and their development as well as for children and society and the role of schools in constructive change.

The formal application process usually follows a series of events aimed at informing candidates about the school: information sessions, catalogue review, telephone inquiries, and open houses scheduled several times a year. At open houses, interested students meet with advisors and directors from the different programs; ask questions about programs, courses, and certification; discuss the nature of field placements; and tour the Bank Street School for Children. Armed with this information, prospective students and faculty engage in a reciprocal selection process. Bank Street students tend to seek a program that is personalized, practical, and child-centered; meanwhile the College is searching for individuals who are thoughtful about education, interested in lifelong learning, and committed to the welfare of children.

The formal process includes an extensive written application form and review of previous academic record and of personal references by the admissions office. The application form includes questions that seek to understand the candidate as a potential "teaching person," as Judy Leipzig put it. Questions range from sentence completions, such as "A children feels unhappy when . . ." or "I do my best when . . ." to vignettes such as the following:

> A conversation between a 10-year-old and a student teacher:
> S.T.: What kinds of things make you mad?
> Child: I get mad when I know the answer and I raise my hand, and the teacher calls on somebody else.
> S.T.: Why does that make you mad?
> Child: Because then I figured out the answer for nothing.
> What are the issues in this situation? How would you respond?

Candidates are asked to write an autobiographical essay that describes events that the candidate feels are significant to her or his decision to enter the field of education. The application form also asks for educational background, references, experiences working with children and adults, thoughts on other careers, reflections on learning experiences, and statements of professional goals.

Ann Morgan, director of admissions, observes that advisement begins at admissions. First, the admissions office reviews all materials to make sure that they meet the school's standards and policy requirements. For example,

> We always looked for students with a background in the liberal arts. In 1993, New York state also made the same change. That means that we do a thorough transcript review to make sure that they have both breadth and depth in the liberal arts and sciences. We look at their previous academic record and at their writing carefully. We do not require GREs, and our reason for

that is we have found that standardized tests don't really tell us anything about who is going to be a wonderful teacher. Since that is what we are looking for, we do look at grades because students do need to read a great deal, and write papers for all their courses, be able to analyze and synthesize, so we look for evidence that they would be able to do those things.

The admissions office generally looks for a grade point average of at least 3.0, although there is no mandated minimum. The average GPA for the group enrolled during the year of this study was 3.4. All of the sources of evidence are aimed at assessing interpersonal skills, empathic attitudes toward children, critical thinking ability, and strong commitment to continued learning and to education as a profession.

The initial screening is followed by an on-site written essay on the date of the scheduled interview with the program director or one of the advisors. The interview provides candidates and advisors with the opportunity to talk about the program, its expectations, and how it might best serve the interests and goals of the candidates and of the profession. In the same manner that teachers will be encouraged to take their students where they are, the first placements usually reflect the interests students have identified in the interview. Thus, thinking about placement begins early in the process. Interviews also provide opportunities for examining attitudes about children, families, and learning. Sometimes candidates who appear to have a superficial or romanticized vision of teaching are advised to find opportunities to visit schools, do some volunteer work, or take a course and return for a second interview later.

This intensive process might be viewed as suitable only for a very small program. Yet in 1994-95, 604 applications were filed and 422 students (in all of the College's programs) were admitted, an admissions rate of 70 percent. Of these, 340 or 80 percent enrolled the following fall. Faculty believe that a thorough and thoughtful admissions process offers the college and the candidates the opportunity to make better informed selections of each other. Leah Gelb, long-time faculty member and current associate dean for academics, explains, "We have a responsibility to children and to the profession. It's better to take time in the selection process and avoid having to counsel people out of programs later on."

This care is one of the deciding factors for many candidates as well.

Many mentioned the close student-faculty connections and personalization that the program, although actually fairly large, is structured to provide. For example,

> I was impressed by the people and how engaged professors and students were. Bank Street was more welcoming and exciting [than other schools I considered].

> The application was so detailed that I trusted I would be taken seriously as an individual.

> They were really interested in who I was and why I wanted to teach. I felt that I had the opportunity to really find out what the profession was about and how I could be part of it.

When we asked, "Why Bank Street?," students and graduates spoke of their interest in serious professional preparation with a focus on developing thoughtful teaching. As one put it, "The whole thing at Bank Street is not only giving kids choices, but making them think and solve problems." Another remembered how exciting and unusual the curriculum appeared to her when she read the Bank Street catalogue, "I was really excited about things like learning to teach newspapers and the museum education program. And, when I saw that they had a program in development for early adolescents, I knew I needed to find out more about it." Several discussed the College's unique blend of theory and practice, "focusing on what you do in the classroom with kids." Some wanted to be able to run classrooms like the ones they had seen at the Bank Street School for Children during their informational tour. One student we interviewed selected the program after having visited The Bank Street School for Children while searching for a school for her own child. When she decided to return to graduate school for teaching, she decided if she was going to teach, she wanted to be able to do it in that way.

Some mentioned as indicators of the kind of practice that interested them the educational programs that have been part of the Bank Street history for decades, such as The Bank Street Readers, The Voyage of the Mimi, The Bank Street Writer, curriculum videos and guides, Follow-Through and Head Start models, and more recently the Center for

Children and Technology. Several students mentioned having done a Web site search that gave them information about the graduate programs, about the kinds of books in the bookstore, and the type of curriculum that teachers design and children evolve at the Bank Street School for Children.

Bank Street students invariably noted that this kind of teaching is complex work that requires intensive preparation. Although many have had other successful professional careers—in fact, most of the College's preservice teachers are entering teaching from other careers (Crow, Levine, & Nager, 1990)—few considered entering teaching without preparation on a temporary license, as hundreds have done annually in New York City. One recent graduate, an African-American teacher now leading a state-funded program for "at-risk" students, described how when she switched from a career in journalism, she was amazed to find out that she could have entered teaching without any background or training, but decided to make the financial sacrifice to attend Bank Street to give herself the best preparation she could find. Michelle* described poignantly the disservice to children she had since witnessed at the inadvertent hands of unprepared teachers:

> (After I graduated from Bank Street), I taught a special education group at a high school in Harlem. That was fun. However, I was also asked to co-teach a social studies class with two new teachers. It was a madhouse for many reasons. One, because these were two teachers who not only were new and not only were they white—which didn't have to be an issue but it was because of the way they responded to the kids—were untrained. It was sad for them because they were trying, but I don't know how much they really truly were committed. It was like they wanted to maybe come to Harlem and do this thing, but really what sort of came out was like, when they got angry they would say things they shouldn't have. And you saw that they were not only anti-child but anti-the whole community, because it was such a different community. And it was unfortunate. In retrospect, it really wasn't fair to them; they truly needed support. And as time progressed, I realized what was really going on in the school, and it was really sad to me that Harlem and the school and the kids were actually being made to suffer from this.

Ileana's* career decision was another typical of many Bank Street students:

> I had been doing arts administration work. I also did translations from Russian into English and had some published work, but I wanted to teach. With my previous degree and knowledge of languages I was able to get temporary certification, but I decided that there was a lot to learn. It would be terrifying to me to be responsible for children and their learning without first getting the right preparation. I made the decision over a one year period. I gathered all kinds of information, talked to a friend who had gone through the program, and took courses as a non-matriculated student. I took Reading and Literature and I was hooked.

This response was frequent. Many students were considering teaching and started out with a single course—Math for Teachers, Reading, or Child Development—and they were "hooked." Once they saw what a rich terrain there was to explore, they entered the path of becoming teaching persons.

## Connecting Theory and Practice in Courses, Advisement, and Clinical Practice

The experience of learning to teach at Bank Street is in many ways seamless. Unlike the critiques of many schools of education (see Goodlad, 1990), course work is coherent and tightly interwoven with the advisement process and students' work in schools. These program elements—along with a capstone project which can be a portfolio, an independent study, or a directed essay—reflect commitments to connect theory and practice, to model desirable teaching practices, and to nurture collegial relationships. Virtually all of the closely interrelated courses involve applications in classrooms where student teaching occurs. These classrooms, in turn, model the kind of practice that is being discussed in courses and advisement.

## Course Work

Required courses are clustered into several broad categories: child development, foundations, and curriculum (see Appendix C). While there are many choices, core requirements include courses in child development, observation of children, family involvement, teaching strategies, and curriculum development. Prospective middle school teachers are as engaged in the study of children as are prospective early childhood and elementary teachers, an unusual feature of Bank Street's secondary education program

During the year of advisement and supervised fieldwork, students take courses from each of these categories. Most courses are taken simultaneously with student teaching placements. Course assignments therefore typically include working with students, observing them, developing curriculum and trying it out, and working with parents. Many students take a course in development and one of the curriculum courses during the summer prior to their advisement year because many cooperating teachers and advisors believe that it is easier for student teachers to start taking on teaching responsibilities in their placements if they have some background in these areas. When students are not yet in student teaching placements, they nonetheless connect their studies to real world contexts by conducting observations in classrooms and interviewing student or parents.

One of our research protocols asked graduates about connections they perceived between what they do in their classrooms and what they learned in their preparation program. Contrary to popular wisdom about teacher education course work, Bank Street teachers frequently cited course work as an important base for their practice, and almost every course was identified by someone. In addition to required courses, graduates frequently mentioned electives from the special education program, such as "Designing and Managing Classroom Environments for Children and Youth with Special Needs" and "Language Development, Diversity, and Disorders: Impact on Reading and Literacy Development." Graduates indicated that most of their courses:

- Modeled or demonstrated the practices they described;
- Developed and explored multiple perspectives on issues;
- Infused developmental theories and concerns;
- Connected theory and field experiences;
- Made constant reference to social contexts and goals;
- Required reflective papers, presentations, and discussions;
- Balanced individual and group experiences;
- Provided extensive feedback with suggestions for improvement; and
- Constantly requested evidence as the basis for making judgments.

Our review of syllabi and assignments found that in almost every course, instructors ask students to relate what they are saying or writing to theory, to developmental issues, and to evidence about children, teaching, and learning from their own settings. Although the work is continuously grounded in practice, it is also intensely theoretical and intellectual. Students read Vygotsky, Piaget, Kohlberg, Gilligan, Coles, Dewey, Montessori, and many other seminal thinkers in their courses on development and learning, rather than encountering simplified summaries of their ideas or even more simplified formulas for practice based on diluted versions of their ideas. Competing theories and research are read and discussed—with additional evidence often pursued in classroom inquiries and observations. It is not uncommon for students and teachers to challenge theories if continuous observation produces contrary evidence about a child's learning or development. In a Child Study project, instructors review students' weekly observations of children, give extensive feedback, and when interpretations of events are confusing or too general, they ask students to make new observations and sometimes to read about the phenomenon under study.

Course sessions are two hours long and include students from different preservice and inservice programs. As a result, class discussions encourage the infusion of multiple perspectives that emerge from personal and professional knowledge of participants who have diverse teaching experiences as well as various cultural and generational perspectives. The setting and class size help increase interaction and model desired practices. Course enrollment is capped at 25 students per section, and graduate students have access to materials and resources in the School for Children classrooms, the computer lab, a math resource room, and a reading resource room in addition to the library and the Bank Street Bookstore located on the corner.

All classes are taught in the evenings and all conference groups meet on Wednesday afternoons for two hours. A typical course session would include four or five modes of instruction that weave together personal, practice-based, theoretical, and academic applications of the subject at hand. Here we review selected courses that are central to the school's conception of core knowledge for teaching: a strong developmental perspective, a set of social and moral commitments, and in-depth knowledge of learner and learning-centered curriculum development.

## Child Development

Developmental perspectives are infused in most courses, but Bank Street's deep culture of connecting an understanding of theory to an understanding of students, recording behavior, and working with families as part of working with the whole child is grounded in a three course sequence that students obviously find very powerful. The three courses are: Child Development (one course for teachers of young children and another for teachers of older children and adolescents); The Study of Children through Observation and Recording, and Family, Child, and Teacher Interaction.

In conjunction, these courses focus on children, how they grow and learn, the influences of societal factors in their development, and how teachers and schools use knowledge of students and their strengths and needs to make decisions about curriculum, instruction, and assessment—and to communicate with families about their children's home and school lives. All of these courses explicitly address concerns for diversity in learning and cultures, including exceptionalities generally treated only in special education courses elsewhere.

Graduate students take one of the two Child Development courses before or during the year of advisement. Observation and Recording of Normal and Exceptional Children must be taken while working with children, either during the year of advisement or when teaching. Parent, Child, and Teacher Interaction in Diverse and Inclusive Settings may be taken after supervised fieldwork while working with children and families. When we asked instructors what they expect from their students, they described attitudes as well as skills, including reflectivity, the ability to synthesize and apply concepts and theories, and a willingness to take children's feelings and thinking seriously. The emphasis on taking children seriously should not be mistaken as an ideology that children always know what they need. Instead, the careful observation of children is a basis for understanding what children are experiencing in order to diagnose how they learn and what will help them progress.

During one of our visits, students entered a session of the Child Development course focusing on older children and adolescents having just read a highly technical article from a medical journal on "the learning disorders of adolescence." Rather than launching into a discussion of the article, instructor Joe Kleinman begins the class by having the students undertake a series of tasks to help them experience what these "out-of-synch" children might be experiencing. First, the students are asked to take dictation with their non-dominant hand. "Keep up," Joe admonishes them as he reads at a conversational rate. "Neatness counts." Some students laugh; others stop and scratch their heads in bewilderment. Beginning a second task, Joe announces, "Now, I'm going to show you a list of words for thirty seconds. Take a look at it." When the thirty seconds are up, Kleinman removes the list and instructs students to write down as many as they can remember. "You can't work with your partner on this one," Joe instructs. After students score their work, Joe asks, "How was it?" Students respond of the first task by saying, "I couldn't keep up," "It was pretty awful—physically uncomfortable and frustrating," and "I just gave up and skipped words."

"I heard laughter," Joe notes, as he points out how some kids might become the class clown rather than dealing with the psychological discomfort they felt. He asks, "Did you wonder how you compared to others?" leading into a discussion of his students' feelings of competence, and how they think their students might feel when they cannot fulfill adults' expectations. Kleinman then moves on to the question of how students compensated. One mentions memorizing words; another created a sentence from some of the words to try to make it more meaningful; a third tried to memorize the words in alphabetical order to bring some structure to the task; a fourth, who used to make up songs as a child, created a litany. These examples become the basis of a discussion of coping and compensation strategies that students may use to make difficult learning more accessible to them. Students draw relationships between emotional and cognitive development and performance. Kleinman notes the anxiety raised by failure, and the frequent example of a child who opts to become bad rather than stupid.

Ready to engage the article now, students can discuss from first-hand experience as well as their reading the ways in which difficulties in writing and remembering—the basis for many learning difficulties that become apparent in late childhood and early adolescence—may translate into school failure and demoralization unless they are addressed by compensatory teaching and learning strategies. Kleinman emphasizes some of the key ideas from the dense and complex reading, especially the behavioral clues of learning disabilities that often emerge in the transition from elementary to middle school: restlessness and difficulty concentrating while sitting still for long periods of time; problems with organization and planning; difficulty in paying attention, recalling information, sequencing ideas, and synthesizing information from multiple sources.

Students then break up into groups of three or four to discuss a case study of a student. Joe reminds them that "we are not therapists," and that they should try to understand the case, look for strengths, and design interventions. After a half hour, Joe goes to the board to record the groups' ideas about how to help Ramona, the case study student. He uses three focusing ideas that are similar to those heard at the start of discussions in many other Bank Street classes:

- What's going on here and why?
- What is the source of the school failure?
- How can we intervene?

In the discussion that follows, we learn that Ramona's strengths include her physical and musical abilities, as well as her social skills. Her difficulties include organizing things, synthesizing information, and memorizing certain kinds of material. Her move into middle school has been accompanied by attitude changes, growing rebelliousness, and severe test anxiety. The discussion of interventions includes, at Joe's gentle insistence, as much emphasis on strengths as needs as a basis for instruction. When students begin to debate whether to allow Ramona to draw cartoons or paint a mural rather than write an essay, he intervenes to remind them to ask the question, "What is the goal? There are several goals, including mastery of material and the development of writing skills. How would you be able to move Ramona into developing her skills in writing?" The discussion focuses in on how to use Ramona's strengths to help her develop these skills. At the end of class Joe urges the students to "take this question to your conference groups" in order to explore it further. The learning continues.

Observing in this same class several weeks later, we see him moderating a panel of young adolescents who have been invited to join in a dialogue with the graduate students about their educational experiences. The class has been reading a collection of articles on adolescent development from Shirley Feldman and Glen Elliott's *At the Threshold: The Developing Adolescent* and Lois Weis and Michelle Fine's *Beyond Silenced Voices: Class, Race, and Gender in United States Schools*. In the discussion, the young guests, who represent different racial and cultural backgrounds and who come from different schools, field questions such as: "What do good teachers in your schools do?" "What frustrates you about school?" "When do you tend to do your best work?" "What gets in the way of doing your best?" and "What kinds of supports do you feel you need in school to succeed?"

The young adolescents share their interests and fears. They speak of peer pressure and of teachers who are helpful, encouraging, and "fair." One notes that, "Good teachers are always fair and don't play favorites or humiliate us." When asked what motivates them to do well in school, most of the children indicate that they want to make their parents proud and go to college. Joe's manner that evening and that of his students reflect their genuine interest and concern for the issues that are important to young adolescents. Later on, we learn that these students come from a variety of urban schools to attend tutoring classes that are offered through the Liberty Program housed at Bank Street. The program is funded by New York state to help "at risk" students through a variety of academic activities such as tutoring, mentoring, and field trips to colleges and universities.

At the end of the evening, several graduate students tell Joe how listening to these students has helped them understand the social and developmental needs of young adolescents. Two graduate students compare the notes they have taken on the students' responses and try to look for differences between the responses given by girls and boys, as if responding to the gender issues embedded in developmental issues of adolescents.

The same dance between theory and practice, between findings from research and observations of individual children, occurs in other courses as well. Nancy Nager, instructor for one of the Child Development sections that addresses both younger and older children, describes the course goals as follows:

> Child Development is one of the foundations for working with children. Teachers have to know children. The course examines broad questions about development such as the relationship between nature and nurture, the role of developmental theory, and the tension between the search for developmental universals and the reality of individual difference. Developmental theory serves as a frame of reference. The course deals with the tension between the theoretical child and the child in the classroom. Students in this course develop general expectations for different ages, how children think at different stages, and how context shapes the child. We look at Bank Street's developmental inter-

action approach as made up of a family of theories including Erikson, Piaget, and Vygotsky to help students develop an understanding of using a selected theoretical framework for teaching. Individual research projects cover topics such as friendships in middle childhood, conservation in children seven to ten years of age, cooperation and competition in early childhood.

Readings for the course are primary materials that present classic and contemporary viewpoints about aspects of child development ranging from the emergence of mind to the intellectual revolution of middle childhood, developing a moral orientation, and the problem of identity. Texts, such as *The Development of Children* by Cole and Cole (1993), are used as background resources. The courses directly link theoretical study with continuous observation of children in classrooms, on videotapes, and in the course itself, where instructors invite parents or students to discuss issues of development that have implications for learning and schooling. Assignments encourage students to learn and demonstrate their knowledge in various forms that include individual and group reports, interviews with children of different ages, observations of children at work and play, and child studies during transitions between elementary and middle school. Together, the readings and assignments integrate multicultural perspectives with research on development and offer guidelines for theory-based practice.

Jean Jahr, the first-year teacher we encountered at P. S. 234, noted that:

> Child Development was helpful (to my practice) because we read Piaget and started thinking about what is appropriate for a child and what isn't. What can you reasonably expect at different ages. And that is really the issue teaching a combined second and third grade classroom.

Her colleague Risa Lasher also discussed Child Development and how it helped her become the kind of teacher she hoped to be.

> Child Development has probably been the most relevant course in my practice. I got to know where kids are in terms of their social interactions and stages of sociability. I'd say that's been real-

ly helpful. In fact, it's the kind of thing I want to revisit, to keep up with it and reread all those books. I knew that I wanted to work with older kids. I wanted to work with kids where I could share their excitement instead of feeling excited for them. I was also committed to making my kids feel respected, being very, very aware of things that humiliate children and making sure I would never do that. And I think 95 percent of the time I've succeeded. I suspect and I hope that my students feel that I respect them and take what they feel and think seriously. That's important to me.

A critical outcome of the courses on child development is a comprehensive understanding of research in the fields of development and an understanding of children from an experiential as well as theoretical perspective. The framework developed by the child development courses, taken at the start of the program, is further deepened in courses and fieldwork that follow.

The Observation and Recording Course, popularly known as "O and R" is constantly identified by students, graduates, and faculty as a trademark of a Bank Street education and a critical means for prospective teachers to learn how to look closely at children, to see them as growing individuals, and to find ways to foster their learning. The course stresses the interactions between knowledge of children, knowledge of one's own beliefs, and use of evidence and theory to make informed teaching decisions. It brings a base of knowledge and a disciplined understanding to what is often otherwise thought of as a "touchy-feely" domain. The instructor of the course describes how it seeks to foster rigor in the use of evidence and theory to understanding children:

> Observation and Recording or TE 502 is one of the courses specifically designed to help people get evidence from kids. That is one of the ways we help students to be rigorous. They have to see child behaviors in relation to context. They learn about learning styles, about temperament, about special needs, and subjects kids like. The learn about how kids think and how they make friends. The task of serious child study is to help students look for real evidence and to use theories that help them interpret what they see.

Students read texts on the observation and study of children while applying what they learn to their own child study. The main assignment for the course is an Individual Child Study for the purpose of "developing an increased awareness of the child's uniqueness, the relation of specific behavior to overall functioning, and the implications for learning." This document is developed over several months from a number of different assignments, including short weekly written observations of the child at school; a paper that examines the child in the context of his peers or group; an age-level study designed to see the child in light of developmental theory, and observations and interpretations of the child as a learner and member of a learning community.

Each session is framed by essential questions designed to sharpen the "why" and "how" required for documentation and assessment. For example, questions that frame the first sessions are geared to learning and reflecting on issues, ethics, and evidence, objectively and subjectivity. What is the meaning of objectivity? How should I select a child? And why did I select this child? What is needed in a record and how might the child experience my observing and recording what he or she is doing? Class discussions usually center on these issues and on the evolving nature of children as learners. The course outline describes how it is designed to sharpen the teacher's knowledge of her personal biases and her skills for seeking evidence:

> Almost everyone 'observes' children informally, but what we 'see' and remember is influenced by what we are looking for, what we expect to see and what we think about the nature and capabilities of children. Our observations of children are also influenced by our own values and feelings. In this course we will work toward sharpening awareness of our own cultural and personal assumptions when observing children. In this process we will work to develop greater sensitivity to ourselves as observers, to the language we use, and to the data we are choosing to attend to. The aim is to develop a personal style of observing and recording that is precise, vivid and non-judgmental, one that will serve us well in our work with children and families. Class time will be used to present, discuss and practice observational techniques. At times we will use films and videotapes in class in order to have common experiences for observation and discussion. (TE 502, fall 1995)

Instructors review weekly observation and provide feedback. For example, on early assignments instructors' comments might include questions related to the language the graduate students uses to describe a child, or the clarity of contextual descriptions, and the eternal "why do you think that?, how do you know?, and what is the evidence for this interpretation?" that often fill the margins of observation logs. Later on in the semester, the questions are more specific to the child as a learner and call for the use of a variety of recording techniques such as a running record of a child using expressive materials; observations of the child's use of language in different contexts; a collection of the student's work; recordings of children's responses to on-demand performance of specific tasks, and children at play or in unstructured interaction with other children. Final requirements ask that students review all documentation, create categories of evidence, triangulate evidence to support their assumptions, make recommendations for teaching or further study, and use theoretical understandings to back up their recommendations.

Child Studies are extensive documents on a particular child. Students often comment on the responsibility they feel after this experience to get to know their students well. Recent graduates sometimes mention feeling guilty about not being able to keep such extensive records during their first years of teaching; as they struggle with the logistics, however, all have nonetheless adopted the habit of looking closely at children. As Jean Jahr put it:

> O and R was very helpful in terms of a stance toward children. There was a huge amount of work, but it was worth it. One of the best things you can do is watch a child closely and try to understand why they're doing what they're doing.

Experienced graduates who are now cooperating teachers describe a variety of methods that they have invented and adapted to keep track of children and of themselves. In fact, much of the observation, recording, and documentation processes examined in this course can be found is recent processes for authentic assessments such as the Primary Language Record, Descriptive Reviews, and portfolios that are widely used by Bank Street teachers (see e.g., Darling-Hammond, Ancess, and Falk, 1995; Freidus, 1995). Lara*, another first-year teacher at Midtown West Elementary School, agreed that the course affected not only her practice but, because of the Bank Street influence schoolwide, that of her colleagues as well:

> "O and R" was very important because it showed me how to look at the children in my class and make nonjudgmental assessments of what's going on with them. We do portfolio assessment as a whole school. Individually, teachers have different methods of taking notes on children. Some teachers have separate little notebooks for each kid. A new method that one of the teachers brought in this year is doing it on stickers on a clipboard that you carry around to jot things down. Then you have a book with dividers with each kid's name and at the end, you pull of the stickers and put them next to the kids' names. When we send progress reports, they're all narratives describing what children can do.

In similar fashion, the course on Family, Child, and Teacher Interaction in Diverse and Multicultural Settings draws on the careful collection of information as the basis for professional decision making and partnerships with parents. As Virginia Miller, one of the course instructors, explains:

> Probably one of the most important parts of this course is learning to be informative and to probe for information without being judgmental—respecting families and their differences and making commitments to know and teach their kids. In small group projects and discussions, I try to mix students of different ages, experiences and interests. Those who come with previous teaching experience, are older, or have children of their own share perspectives with the ones who are less experienced. The issues between teachers and parents often call for empathy, for careful listening, and for providing real evidence of their children's performance in school. Sometimes we videotape these simulations and ask students to switch roles in order to get them to reflect on being a parent of a child with learning difficulties, or a parent of a brilliant but unmotivated student, a single parent with a busy work schedule, or a parent who is ill. (personal communication, December, 1995)

In this course, we observed students conducting simulations of teacher/family conferences, preparing progress reports of children, researching and reporting to one another about stressful social conditions—poverty, homelessness, parental work stress, substance abuse, violence—and their effects on children and families, and learning about different services available to children and families in the metropolitan area.

Understanding the lives and perspectives of others in order to work more effectively with them is one of the recurrent themes of Bank Street courses including this one. Course instructors help students take different perspectives by role playing teacher-family conferences and seeking to understand parent views in order to create constructive rather than adversarial relationships on behalf of the students. A first-year teacher notes that she learned from the Family, Child, and Teacher Interaction course that:

> . . . parents and teachers have different jobs, and that that's okay. The parents' job is to look out for their kids. Your job as a teacher is to have in mind the whole group. There are going to be conflicts at times, but you shouldn't resent the parents for looking out for their own child. So that gave me an important perspective because I am not a parent and that was very important.

Another noted that cultural perspectives are also emphasized:

> In the Family, Child, Teacher courses we talked about students who come from a different culture than the teacher or a different culture than the school. Since I'm working with a primarily Dominican population, which is different from my own culture, this is very important.

Assignments are carefully constructed to enable students to gain information about specific problems and services as well as to develop skills in working with families and children with particular needs. An educational autobiography provides the occasion for students to reflect on their own family's attitudes toward and involvement with school and to raise questions and issues they would like to work on throughout the term. An analysis of the school setting engages students in a critical examination of the patterns of interaction at their own school site between different kinds of families and parts of the school organization. This analysis includes a special focus on families who are in the minority in that school community and on students with special needs. Students develop a case study that tracks their own advocacy efforts on behalf of a child with special needs in their classroom, and create a year-long plan for involving families in their work—including initial introductions, home visits, curriculum meetings, parent/family conferences, individual reports, plans for general communication with families, and involvement of families in the classroom. The work students do in this course extends their ability to support students in their development and learning by understanding them in context and marshalling the resources of families and communities on their behalf.

## Principles and Foundations

Students' experiences in courses like Family, Child, and Teacher Interaction are extended in courses on the social contexts of education. Four courses focus particularly on social foundations issues: Foundations of Modern Education; Principles and Problems of Elementary and Early Childhood Education; Issues in Adolescence; and Anthropology in Education. Students must take one or two of these courses, depending on their area of concentration. Each course helps students develop a personal philosophical perspective informed by knowledge of the events, theories, and practices that have shaped educational experiences and decisions in this country and by their personal and professional responsibilities to educate for democracy.

Harriett Cuffaro, a long-time faculty member and Dewey scholar (1995) who teaches Principles and Problems in Elementary and Early Childhood Education, describes the aims of the course as those common to many courses in foundations:

> To develop an awareness of the history of early childhood and elementary Education in the United States; to deepen students' understanding of the social, political, and economic forces which influence their work and the lives of children; to deepen their understanding of the relations among educational theory, developmental theory and educational practice in a variety of settings; to strengthen their competence in achieving an informed and critical approach to teaching.

Rather than merely discussing what influences shape schools and education, however, students connect their readings directly to practice. Their own biographies and school experiences are augmented by visits they make to schools founded on particular philosophies; these school visits are the basis for research about educational policies and practices and presentations to their peers.

The course focuses on historical trends in views of education; equity issues, including racism, classism, and sexism; and multiculturalism defined broadly to include not only racial and ethnic cultures, but also defining factors such as geographic locale, family norms and roles, and one's identification as a member of a teaching culture. Questions are always raised from a personal and philosophical perspective with a view toward influences on practice. So, for example, when students read George Counts' *Dare the Schools Build a New Social Order?* (1932), they work through questions of: "What's the dare?" "What's the challenge?" "How do you feel about accepting it?" and "Why do you feel that way?" Throughout, a set of recurring questions arise: "Who determines the aims of education?" "Who defines and articulates the problems of education?" "Who is responsible for the 'solution' of these problems?" and "What principles may guide action?"

During our observations, students reported on small, democratically-organized public schools in New York City, a Montessori program, a program with a behavioral approach, a Waldorf School founded on the teachings of Rudolph Steiner, and a private school with a social justice and equity agenda. The school visits and the subsequent group presentations give students the opportunity to question assumptions, identify what is distinctive about each of the approaches, see how philosophies translate into very different practices, think about why parents may send their children to those schools and what students learn in them, and reflect on how they would feel working at those schools.

These discussions help students appreciate the range of potential practice, the different outcomes of teaching decisions, and their own goals as teachers. The dialogue is thoughtful and serious. Heads turn and shake every time a new comment seems to rattle someone else's assumptions, claims, or goals. Students discuss the type of setting where they would like to work and why, and how they would prepare to work in a place that might not be their first choice. In Harriet's words, "Everything we do is like a dress rehearsal for a time when we may have to defend something.

It's always getting people to think and to take the time to reflect, not just have snap judgments about things."

In addition to introducing issues that force students to develop and analyze their beliefs, foundations courses introduce questions that students will need to struggle with. There is a willingness to confront uncomfortable social issues, even when answers are not readily available. Cuffaro illustrated this with a case from a recent class discussion of issues of inclusion and multiculturalism:

> Last week one of the things we were talking about was heterosexism. I raised the question, 'In early childhood a lot of people are dealing with family, since we are talking about inclusion, what do you do about gay and lesbian headed families?' We talked about the fact that it is a difficult topic, more than any other topic we had discussed. There is a strong religious foundation for the critics, and I made the statement that this was one of the "isms," in contrast to sexism and racism, that doesn't necessarily have an economic base, other than people getting fired in some situations. As I said to the students in the class, 'We raise more questions than we have answers for, but the questions are important. I don't have the answers for a lot of questions, but to me its imperative to ask the questions.'

Students frequently cite these courses as having helped them to develop a broad understanding of schooling, to shape a personal philosophy, and to use analytic skills. One current student explained:

> I took a foundations course that really taught me about being a critical thinker. That had not been part of my educational experience before. I was very traditional. Even college was about, "let me figure out what this or that teacher wants and what I will need to give back to them at exam time and get a good grade." I was good at that. So this whole thing about having strong opinions, about reflecting in a deeper way about the philosophical questions, about what I want to teach and why and how will it be meaningful for me is new, and I learned it through Social Foundations.

Although foundations courses are not generally thought of as practical, many Bank Street teachers found that these classes directly influenced their practice and helped them succeed in New York City schools. As Lara*, a beginning public school teacher, explained:

> The Foundations class was very helpful to me for the kind of children that I'm encountering in this school. There are a lot of children in this school from homeless shelters who have a lot of emotional and behavioral needs. In this class, we studied a lot about children from these types of environments and the effect that it has on them, the types of education they respond best to, what they need, and what helps them. And the class made me come to a whole new understanding of how to deal with them.

In this teacher's kindergarten and first-grade classroom, 26 children from some of the most economically disadvantaged parts of New York were involved in mathematical problem solving using multistep word problems often considered suitable for much older children, continuous reading of children's literature (some reading and others being read to), and studies about the authors of their favorite books. Lara's ability to construct this environment was, she believed, a function of her understanding of the children, her commitment to an equitable, high-quality education for them, and the knowledge of curriculum she had acquired at Bank Street. She commented:

> I do a lot of word problems with them in math—the kind of stuff I learned in Hal's math class—using math manipulatives and problem solving. I see the kids can do it, so I know it's developmentally appropriate. I think a lot of people underestimate what five and six year olds can do. I think that a lot of people have buried in their mind that when a child is in kindergarten they're just learning in, under, on, in front of, behind, numbers 1 to 10, letters A to Z. I've had a lot of parents who have switched their kids in from other schools who have said to me, 'He wasn't doing this in his last class. You're doing addition with kindergartners? I can't believe that.' But they really get it, and with the word problems it's amazing to see the strategies they come up with to solve. They're really learning to use the

math materials to solve the problems and to show their think-ing. Now I'm trying to get them to understand why and how they they know it, so that they can start examining themselves as problem solvers.

Lara's enthusiasm and commitment to democratic practice were made effective because they were supported by her well developed knowledge and skill.

### Curriculum Design and Teaching Strategies

Whereas some schools of education have reserved courses in curriculum design for advanced masters or doctoral students who plan to become specialists at textbook companies or in central offices, Bank Street sees the development of curriculum as central to teaching. Because what is taught must connect to student readiness and interests as well as community contexts, even topics that are routinely taught or presented in texts require curricular thinking and development. Subject matter teaching is always infused with a developmental perspective and a sensitivity to social context. John Dewey's concepts of "experience," "child and curriculum," and "school and society" are central to the way Bank Street's curriculum courses are conceptualized and taught. In Deweyan fashion, the social studies are generally seen as the focal lens for viewing students and teachers as participants in a learning process that raises motivating questions and constructs learning experiences responsive to development, democratic education, and the disciplines. In using their knowledge of children, families, and learning to construct these experiences, teachers are curriculum builders rather than mere implementers of texts or programs.

In Madeline Ray's social studies curriculum course for prospective teachers of adolescents, students create their own elaborate, highly detailed interdisciplinary curriculum units that help them learn to enact this kind of knowledge building. Ray describes the program as seeking to conduct a "dialogue between the disciplines." For example, a social studies unit on the Harlem Renaissance weaves together study of historical, economic, political, and geographic conditions to understand what influenced the lives and artistic expressions of individuals in that time period. Field trips to research such a unit might include the Shomburg Center for Research in Black Culture and The Studio Museum in Harlem. While reviewing these units in small and large groups, instructors and peers invariably raise questions such as "Why is this an important study?" "Why and what would children of a particular age would learn through these experiences?" "What resources do my students and families bring to this study?" "Who in the school's community can contribute?" "How can we integrate other subjects in this study?" "What will students be able to learn about getting around the city to visit historical sites of this period?" "Are there walking tours we can include?" "What bus lines and subways take one to the Studio Museum?" "Are there special rates for students and families?" "Are there resources and opportunities to carry out this study?" and "How does it relate to the present and do we have a role to play?" This type of probing helps students realize that their curriculum decisions should attend to these issues. Field trips and other opportunities for building community through common experiences are required components of such a course. Sample curriculum studies are kept for reference so that students learn from each others' work. Independent studies that are done as one of the graduation options are also catalogued in the library and serve as resources and as samples of curriculum design.

For teachers of younger students there is always an effort to place the learners at the center of studies. Younger children study their communities in "the here and now," and as they get older they focus on "the long ago" to grasp historical, geographical, economic, political, environmental, and literary influences over time. For teachers of younger children, Early Childhood Curriculum offers strong integrative possibilities.

> This course assists students in setting a framework for planning and developing curriculum based on the principles of growth and development, areas of knowledge, and one's values. Emphasis is given to the opportunities offered by curriculum areas and materials, with the area of social studies being viewed as the core of an integrated curriculum. The course interweaves theory and practice as students plan, develop, and reflect on curriculum experiences from nursery through third grade. (course description)

Instructors in this course include coordinators from the Bank Street School for Children as well as faculty from graduate programs.

Cooperating teachers from the Bank Street School for Children and from various progressive public and private schools are frequently invited to discuss their curriculum development strategies. Assignments ask students to evaluate educational ideas from the perspectives of freedom, purpose, subject matter, and experience and always include the development of curriculum units and presentations. These must take into account a developmental perspective, an understanding of concepts, and the identification of resources to carry out the study. Class discussions, small group work, and videotapes treat such topics as the study of families, playgrounds, the neighborhood, markets, the city, immigration, the school, the Hudson River, Old Manhattan and New York today. Helping children understand the communities in which they live has been part of Bank Street curriculum thinking since its founder wrote the first edition of *Young Geographers* (Mitchell) in 1931, which was updated by current faculty in 1991.

Studies tend to take a humanities perspective that incorporates the role of people in events. Anne Marie Mott, coordinator of the Lower School of the School for Children, feels that one of the biggest challenges in teaching this course is broadening the narrow, event-bound conception of social studies that graduate students often bring with them from their own childhood experiences in school. Few have previously experienced social studies as a process that prepares individuals to live in groups and to develop systems that support democratic living.

The experience is an epiphany for many students. One current student, who is in the midst of a transition from a management career, noted of the curriculum course:

> Curriculum was very worthwhile, because I'd never seen this holistic way where you integrate math and everything else into social studies, and you can teach everything in a connected way. I'd never known that. This was an eye-opening experience for me. Having to devise a curriculum really helped me think out every little process. I liked this course a lot, and then I did a new curriculum for my directed essay. Now I can think in terms of the big picture.

A first-year teacher who came into teaching from a career in public relations noted of the same course:

The curriculum class I took was very important to me because it really showed me how to integrate curriculum. A lot of what I brought into my classroom came directly from that class. It came from being shown slides and videos and being talked to about curriculum and being able to do it yourself, including going out into the community, observing, and figuring out how to recreate experiences in the block area, in the dramatic play area, through art, through writing. That really all came together for me in the curriculum class.

Virtually all of the courses connect theoretical ideas and demonstrations with students' ongoing fieldwork, dealing with concrete problems of practice. Almost all courses are taught in a workshop manner. Each features plenty of curriculum resources, opportunities for working individually and in groups, opportunities for enacting methods—painting, counting, reading and writing books, feeding snails, growing butterflies, harvesting beans—and opportunities to see curriculum and teaching methods in action in classrooms or videos where children are working on different tasks or where teachers are sharing their craft. In conversations and interviews, we heard reference to almost every required course as being helpful in one way or another.

Math for Teachers is one of the most often cited courses, for a variety of reasons. Some students and graduates mentioned the course as a way of learning about different perspectives by experiencing how everyone solved problems differently. As one student observed:

I thought the Math for Teachers course was great because it's so hands-on. I really couldn't believe it when they talked about how does everyone add 20 plus 22, and everyone had a different way of figuring it out. It was just amazing to me. I mean you hear a lot about learning styles and you hear a lot about everybody has their own method and there's no one right way, but you kind of think to add two numbers there's one right way. But really everyone has a different way, and that was pretty amazing.

Others saw the math course as an opportunity to understand deeply the logic behind mathematical concepts, equations, and formulas they had not really understood deeply in their own schooling. Some experienced it as a key course for understanding patterns in music, science, and the world at large. For still others, the workshop format allowed them to try all kinds of materials in a playful and experimental manner. Students often stayed after class in the math resource room rolling dice to get a better grasp of probability before going out to teach it. Paul Gugliemella, a 42-year-old student completing his training at the College after changing careers, explained the learning process he and his classmates experienced in the course:

> What happens here—it certainly happened in math—is that we did the math in math class, we didn't just talk about it. Every week when we came in, we did problems like the kids would do problems, and we tried to make sense of it. We worked on some number stations activities and pattern stations activities, and that was important for me because there was this real piece of work. We had to do an activity and write about it mathematically, and that's what we're asking the kinds to do. I like math, but for the people who were math phobic, this was an especially wonderful experience for them. They went through this process of understanding. For me, the course was about beginning to understand and learn about learning styles. It sets my wheels turning about how in my nine- and 10-year-old classroom I can provide this variety of experience.

In discussing assignments, students and graduates mentioned how they had learned to be responsive to learning styles and developmental capabilities of students, to create or secure resources that would help students understand concepts, and to work with the new national standards in mathematics.

The utility of courses to students' practice is clear. We traced this in the cluster of courses on literacy development. For example, an evening session in Madeleine Ray's course, The Uses of Language, began with an introductory segment asking students for reports from the field. Students reported on humanities teaching issues that had arisen in their classrooms during the past week. One student discussed a writing assignment that bombed. He had had good success with the reading of *Greek Myths* with his eighth grade students. But he had had a difficult time getting students to write their personal reactions to characters they had played or read about. Another student suggested that it might have been hard for students that age to be so personal. Maybe if he asked them to write as reporters it would have been easier. "Yes," notes Madeline, "writing in the third person creates a little distance. Why don't you try that?" "I think I will," the student replies. "My advisor was there when it happened, and she also suggested that I not hit them so head-on with the personal reflection."

Ray engaged the group in discussion of the importance of practice in sharpening one's craft, and the importance of being sensitive to different approaches and interpretations of any material. To illustrate, the group was asked to develop portrayals of a scene from *Cinderella*. The groups commented on the different ways each individual has developed the scene. Madeline suggested that the same thing would happen with their teaching. They might all be teaching *Of Mice and Men,* but each would differ, based on their own style as teachers, on what they had experienced in their own schooling, and what they took from this class. These comments in turn elicited the issue of different entry points into a piece of literature. Students cited examples, such as how some fifth graders would rather perform plays while others would rather write them, direct them or design sets.

Opportunities to raise and discuss pedagogical questions are also frequent. An evening in Sal Vascellaro's class Language, Literature, and Emergent Literacy illustrated how a diverse group of students educates one another. The 23 graduate students included novices and experienced teachers. Among them were parents, career changers, and two teachers who worked in bilingual schools, one religious and the other public. The assignment for that night asked that each student bring to the class at least two books connected to their own personal experience that they would use to address some issue of diversity in their own classroom. Some students had originally expressed discomfort with the assignment. Sal reassured them that he had no hidden agenda, just a genuine interest in understanding how their previous experiences influence their own use of literature. He wanted them to experience the very personal experiences implied in the concept of diversity and the importance of the personal— race, gender, class, language, religion, age, culture, family style, geographical location, immigration, war, divorce—to children's literature.

During the first half-hour, students discussed their selections and reasons in small groups. When students mentioned why they had selected their particular books, there was always a personal anecdote. A Korean-American student reviewed books with the theme of belonging. In her discussion, she revisited some of her memories about learning a new language and a new culture as an adolescent. This led to a group discussion of development issues, the new literature on girls and middle schools, and issues of feeling different and lonely in an alien environment.

Students at another table were focusing on young children and what to do when sad things happen to children. How do you deal with sadness? Do sad books really help? Two of them cited sad stories of children in their classrooms. Sal led the discussion by bringing out the combined knowledge of the group and then incorporating theoretical perspectives that expanded the personal solutions. He asks the parents and more experienced teachers in the group to give suggestions about books that they had found successful with their own children in such situations. Students also mentioned developmental issues they learned about in readings they had been assigned. Ultimately, they decided it would be useful to have books about sad occasions available and to observe the children to see if they gravitated toward them or not and to report their observations to the class.

By the end of the evening, everyone had added their selections to a combined list. Sal collected the lists so that he could develop a master list for the group by the next week. In a short time, this group had reviewed about 100 books and bridged their personal knowledge with the theoretical understandings to help them develop knowledge for teaching. Students' appreciation for the course was widespread. One beginning teacher noted:

> I took the emergent literacy course and that was great. I'm very happy I did, even though I knew I wanted to work with older kids. I wanted to know how literacy began for kids. And you know what, I have so many kids who still haven't fully developed. I'm so glad I took the course so I know how to encourage them. And I can give book recommendations to the kids who are fluent readers.

Teaching this course has also been an intellectual exploration for Sal (Vascellaro and Genishi, 1994). One of the assignments is to write a children's book and to share it with the group on the last night of classes. After teaching the course for various semesters and experiencing these presentations as powerful cognitive and affective demonstrations, Sal examined the participants' own views on the course. He posed these two questions: (1) What about the course has led students to the unique ways in which they formulated and shaped their stories? and (2) What had these windows into each other's realities, these personal meanings, molded by the conventions of children's stories and directed outward to children and adults, to do with teaching or becoming a teacher? In describing his findings in Vascellaro and Genishi (1994) he writes:

> The process of writing a story for children seemed inextricably bound to the teachers' evolving professional selves. Many spoke of how their views of writing changed: they would teach in the future with a greater understanding and appreciation of the child's writing process. (p. 195)

In other related courses, such as The Teaching of Reading, Writing and Language Arts and Teaching Reading and Writing in the Content Areas, students keep reading logs, examine different methodologies, and learn about assessment. A first-year teacher told us how the elective course, Reading and Writing in the Content Areas, included English as a Second Language strategies that help her in her multilingual classroom. She found she must constantly assess whether children's difficulties arise from not knowing concepts in math or other subject areas or from not comprehending the English language in the texts. Using strategies from the class, she discovered that her children do better academically when they read the math problems or the science directions in the group rather than alone, because she can assess if they need more help in the subject or in understanding the language of the problem or its related instructions.

After a series of courses, a current student ready to enter the job market told us how confident he felt about teaching children how to read, an area that many beginning teachers find especially anxiety provoking:

> Teaching of reading was about working with kids. I have all my stuff here. The logs and everything. I know that if someone said to me, 'Can you tutor my six-year old in reading?' I could really teach that child. I know how to do the early assessment for read-

ing and see their interests and how to do reading with them and to them. I reviewed all my stuff in cueing and decoding from one course. Since I worked with one child extensively, the cooperating teacher told the child that she would help me become a reading teacher. So, Anna, the child took it upon herself to tell me how she had figured out things. I learned so much from her. Sometimes she would tell me that she remembered what a word looked like, while other times she sounded words out, and other times she had memorized the pictures. It was great.

Another fourth- and fifth-grade teacher expressed how important it had been to her to take a course in Learning Disabilities and Reading Problems as her final elective after she began her first year of teaching:

The course was really helpful. I took it with a few of my students in mind. I have three kids who can't comprehend beyond the most literal meaning and I have one kid who is reading at first or second grade reading level. And I have another students with expressive language problems. I have all these kids with very distinct and very important needs that I didn't feel well equipped to handle, so I wanted to get smarter. The course helped me realize that there are different factors for a problem: If someone is having trouble with expressive language, what could it be? and, How can you help? So it was helpful to me in my practice.

Other curriculum courses include three choices of Science for Teachers courses, taught either at the college or at a science center at Harriman State Park about 25 miles outside New York City, also cited as useful for their hands-on quality and support for curriculum building. Graduates and current students described Music and Movement as a course that made them aware of the public nature of teaching and of the need to help children bring their rhythms, histories, and traditions into the classroom. Art Workshop for Teachers and Music and Movement courses are often cited by graduates as places where they learned to teach for multiple intelligences and developed a larger teaching and assessment repertoire. Some graduates mentioned that in the Art course they had learned to talk to children seriously about their work and about their ideas for representing the world. The recurrence of strategies across courses is often seen as especially powerful. For example, one beginning teacher noted of the many courses she profited from:

> What's nice about Bank Street is that their philosophy is so consistent. And so you really can cull things from each course. For example, in Art I really learned how to talk to kids about their work. You don't just give a statement like 'I like it,' and you don't jump to conclusions about what the child can do, but you comment on what is actually there. And that helped me talk to kids.

## Advisement and Field Placements

The consistency of views and methods highlighted by students is in part a function of the College's very special advisement process. In many ways, it is the glue that holds together the many learning experiences students undergo and the linchpin for Bank Street's enactment of caring, community, continuity of learning, and attention to student development. Advisors are full-time senior faculty members who have had extensive classroom teaching experience and who, in addition to teaching courses and/or doing administrative work, supervise a group of student teachers in their field placements. The advisor works intensely with five to seven students for at least a year, identifying field placements and visiting frequently for long blocks of time, meeting weekly in a "conference group" for two-hour support sessions, and meeting with each student individually at least every other week.

This structure for advisement and supervision differs in significant ways from the norm in many universities where supervisors are often short-term graduate students, adjuncts, or retired teachers rather than faculty members, where there is little continuity in the function and sometimes little warrant for the expertise of the supervisor, and where faculty members who teach courses rarely see their students (or the results of their work as teacher educators) in the field. This normally fragmented structure contributes to the traditional disconnect among courses, between course work and fieldwork, and ultimately between theory and practice.

Bank Street's approach to the advisement process is quite deliberate and grounded in a sophisticated theory of teacher learning. In 1967, Barbara

Biber and Charlotte Windsor authored a Handbook chapter and monograph titled, *An Analysis of the Guidance Function in a Graduate Teacher Education Program* to explain the rationale for this unique approach. The rationale for an integrated approach to teaching and advisement which combines cognitive instruction and support for the teacher's individual development derives from a view of the teacher's role as personally and cognitively complex. This is particularly true when teachers are trying to develop children's learning that is active, inquiry-based, and focused on personal development (e.g. independence, perseverance, social awareness, etc.) as well as academic development. "It is self-evident," they argue, "that if the school is to offer children opportunities to develop personally as well as academically, then the education of teachers must, in turn, offer them more than pedagogic theory and a repertoire of approved methods" (p. 4). Offering the example of a prospective teacher who learned primarily through memorization in her own education and now needs to understand the process of productive inquiry, Biber and Winsor stress the complexity of a process in which teachers-in-training must acquire new knowledge and learn new skills and ways of looking at the world while unlearning old ones. They continue:

> Of critical importance is the assumption that teaching competence and style is tied not only to the information a teacher gets in training, but also very crucially to the mode in which that teacher experiences and internalizes the information and through which he transmutes it into continuous professional growth. This assumption leads to a model of learning which engages the student teacher in concurrent mastery of theory and responsible apprentice training; activates feeling as well as thinking; and regards personal maturity as relevant to professional competence.

> Teacher education (is) the task of moving the student from having learned deeply to readiness (and skill) to teach wisely. This means, in essence, that a program of teacher education must provide a situation in which the student can experience a change in his own psychological stance, a shift in position from the role of the student, partly dependent and not fully respon-

sible, to the role of the teacher in which he is the one to nurture, demand, judge, and appreciate. (A)ny teacher's capacity for teaching excellence at the classroom level depends upon the degree to which he has internalized a coherent rationale which regards teaching as an ever-changing process, involving not only a thorough grounding in substantive content and the psychology of learning and growth, but also a constant dynamic of actions, observation, analysis, and new hypotheses for further action. The theoretical basis for this dynamic rests upon a recognition of learning intimately related to the total process of development in child and adult, and the conviction that intellectual mastery cannot be divorced from affective experience if the goal is to facilitate personal and professional competence. (pp. 4-6)

The process of becoming a teacher—particularly one who is committed to developing high levels of competence, social awareness, and autonomy in children—is one that arouses deep feelings, ranging from passionate commitment to acute uncertainty born of internal insecurities and conflicts, while also posing major intellectual challenges. Putting ideas into action is also a nontrivial problem requiring the synthesis of new intellectual, practical, and logistical learnings with long-standing habits of mind, views of the world, and aspects of personality. In order to "facilitate individual integration of the totality of the training experience" (p. 7), the advisor as teacher/counsellor/supervisor is carefully selected for each student based on the match between student's needs and advisor's skills and stays with the student throughout his or her entire program, coming to know him/her equally as a student within courses, a practicing teacher-in-training, and an advisee.

The guidance program, as it is called, aims to connect the "third-person" analytic work of understanding learning and teaching with the "first-person" subjective, intuitive insights teachers more frequently act upon—and must actively develop in order to acquire greater sensitivity to children and their learning. The guidance function is also:

A means for helping the student coordinate and cross-reference potentially disparate aspects of the training program. The ideas and ideals about children and teaching that are presented systematically and theoretically in instructional courses appear and reappear in the work with the advisor as questions which originate in the student's work with children in the classroom are discussed and examined. Similarly, in the analysis of concrete elements of student-teaching experiences and the consideration of alternate ways of carrying out the teaching functions, the student is engaged, on a down-to-earth problem-solving level, in thinking through the implications of what otherwise might remain a remote and amorphous philosophy of education.

When Bank Street faculty found themselves dissatisfied with their psychological knowledge and skill for this task, they engaged a clinical professor of psychiatry from Columbia University to lead them in biweekly seminars that would strengthen their theoretical understanding and skills for the advisory role. These sessions helped them to formulate common principles for their guidance work, which include the following:

The primary material for the guidance work should be the educational experience of the student; the purpose is to focus on analysis of observation and participation with children in the classroom, but to encompass, also, the student's position and performance as a student in a professional preparation program.

a. The review and analysis should serve to concretize the role of the teacher, to bridge theory and application.
b. The work should contribute to increasingly differentiated observation by the student of children, of teaching practices, and of the student's own response to the teaching responsibilities and opportunities presented.
c. The advisor should help the student become increasingly clear about the multiple criteria for evaluating all teaching performance by which, ultimately, his own competence to begin to teach will be judged.
d. The advisor should have had considerable experience in teaching children and thus be a resource to the student for searching out teaching materials, as well as bringing a prac-

ticed eye to the analysis of observation of children and teaching practice.

e. The opportunity for active participation in classroom life should be paralleled to inviting and expecting the student's participation in all the lines of inquiry, explored in the advising sessions; evaluation, for example, should become a process of continuous, mutual thinking

f. The supervisory function of the advisor should be as pure an example as possible of non-didactic teaching. (p. 13-14)

Nearly 25 years later, an issue of *Thought and Practice: The Journal of the Graduate School of Bank Street College of Education* published in commemoration of the college's 75th anniversary in 1991 included 12 faculty and student perspectives on the individual, group, and field components of advisement. The accounts range from theoretical analyses of the process of becoming a teacher and the development of shared values and knowledge for teaching to narratives and stories of children and their teachers as these have evolved over the course of a year's intensive effort. Gail Hirsh (1991), a Bank Street advisor who studied the conference group process, describes this dimension of advisement as key to developing reflective teachers who build personal and practical knowledge for teaching (Clandinin, 1985) through this informal and collaborative, yet transactional and highly focused process. Hirsh writes:

> . . . the stories teachers share with each other (are) "fundamental particles" out of which, in group interaction, the significant "matter" of the teacher's practical knowledge is constructed and by means of which it is conveyed. In this perspective the dynamic small-group process becomes a powerful opportunity for the spontaneous telling and responding to the told that, in turn, functions to further catalyze the integration of the thinking, feeling, and knowing. (p. 129)

Bill Ayers, once a student at Bank Street, then a teacher of young children, and now a professor at the University of Illinois at Chicago, confirmed this view:

Here is some of what my advisor taught me in the year I attended weekly advisement seminars at Bank Street: People actively create and construct knowledge. Learning is characterized by discovery and surprise. Human development is complex and interactive. Cognition is entwined with affect, and intellect is inseparable from spirit, culture, physical, and psychological being. Teachers nurture and challenge people, and invite them to be more skilled, more knowing, more able, more powerful; teaching is, than at its heart an intellectual and ethical project. Advisement was like no other experience I have ever had as a learner. The curriculum was emergent; the experiences we ourselves had were the material for reflection and critique. I was a student but I was also a teacher. Now that I try to teach teachers in this way, I see the other side: I am a student of my students, a learner first, and I understand the essential paradox of teaching—they want to know what I cannot teach them, and only they know what they don't yet know yet. This is part of the challenge of teaching. (Ayers, 1991, pp. 25, 28)

Current students and graduates were also eloquent about their advisement experiences, often mentioning advisement as the place where their learning came together. These three noted themes that recurred with frequency:

I thought the strongest thing at Bank Street was the advisement. My conference group was really the place where we talked about what was going on. Generally I was talking about what was going on right then in my student teaching placement. Every week it would be some big thing that happened in class that week, and I could ask "How would you deal with this? What would you do?"

The fieldwork experiences coupled with having my advisor come and be an objective observer was valuable. It was such a support. It was really helpful to be able to sit down with her after a day or after a lesson and hear her comments and be able to hear about things that she had picked up that I just didn't.

In individual sessions my advisor and I talked a lot about what she had observed in the classroom. She watched me teach Math lessons with Pre-K kids that were going over their heads. She gave me feedback, but she also helped me figure out how to do it better. In the group she was more open ended; a lot of times it was like, "So what's going on?" And people would bring up stuff. I think I brought up my experience about teaching in a way that kids couldn't understand—and the people in the group discussed how hard it was to figure out what kids could and couldn't do. In the individual sessions that advice was more specific to me and my kids. Also in the field placement she communicated with my cooperating teacher to talk about what I was doing and what I was expecting to learn.

We observed how the dynamic of each conference group meeting was influenced by the particulars of the week or of the day. For a conference group of students in the early adolescence program in the fall, two issues were the focus for the entire two hour period. One was how to console children who were obviously in distress due to some "social" encounter situation, and the other was how to get respect from students who are taller and bigger than you are. Everyone in the group described examples of how these situations came up in their schools and classrooms and how their cooperating teachers handled them. Others discussed how they would address them if they were the teachers. Some sided with the children in their examples and others with the teachers. Some recounted experiences from their own adolescence and tried to develop better solutions than the ones that had been offered to them.

The advisor took the role of an active listener. She posed questions to the group as they brought up their observations and solutions: "Why do you think the teacher said that?" "Why do you suppose children seem to come back so upset after lunch everyday?" "Where do they have lunch?" "Who supervises them?" "Do they play outdoors or do they have equipment to play with?" "Would you say it is usually the same children who come back upset?" "How do you think the child feels when you ask one of their friends to go with them to help them feel better?" "How did you feel when the guard did not let you go on the elevator because he thought you looked young enough to be one of the students?" "How did you respond to the guard?" "How do others handle situations like this one?" "Do the men in this group find the same issues?" and "Take note of these issues this week and try out some of your own solutions." In this two-hour conference group session, the students discussed issues of development for children and for themselves, discipline and management, guidance, and gender issues. At the end of the session, the group viewed a video of one of them teaching mathematics and discussed what he had been teaching, why he had asked his advisor to videotape this lesson, and what his students had said about having their teacher videotaped.

Program directors and advisors try to form groups that include individuals with a range of different experiences. As much as possible, groups tend to include some career changers and some younger students who are going for their masters degrees shortly after their undergraduate schooling. Students and graduates spoke of the consistency and support they felt knowing that they would have a weekly opportunity to discuss privately issues they encountered in their practice. Others experienced the group as practice for developing ways of working as a staff member in a school. Others spoke about having learned about themselves:

> I realized how little experience I had speaking up in groups; the advisor helped me find my place, and eventually I learned to expressed my views and offer my solutions.

> I thought the group would always be this supportive place for me—but I realized that at times they expected me to be strong and very supportive to others, and they let me know it.

> I learned that in the group we all were in a position to teach each other. My advisor was like another member, but then in the individual sessions he would follow-up on things I had discussed in group.

The conference group experience provides a reference point with other students that is affirming, as well as educative. It also provides a support group that often continues long after the advisement year:

> In terms of group dynamics the group and the individual advisement are very different. In the group sometimes we were

going together through hard times. You try a lesson and you fall flat on your face and the chart falls down too. Just having people there to say, 'I know exactly what you mean, and that happened to me,' was important.

In a group of five beginning teachers from the early adolescence program who had continued to meet at one another's apartments into their first year of teaching, we heard discussions of boundary setting with students, the developmental meaning of various student behaviors, pedagogy, and classroom management. Two of these new teachers decided to ask their former advisor to come visit their classrooms to give them advice about particular situations they were facing. They were confident she would come and equally confident she could help.

The third dimension of advisement is supervised fieldwork. Candidates spend the full academic year in schools, usually in two or three separate placements of between nine and 15 weeks each. In all cases, at least one of the placements must be in a public school. New York state requires both a lower and an upper grades placement for elementary school candidates. These contrasting experiences offer students the opportunity to experience and reflect upon different educational philosophies, teaching styles, school cultures, and economic and social conditions that influence schooling. The diverse set of experiences helps students develop a repertoire rather than a one-modality approach to teaching and schooling. The rotating placements also allow candidates to test their interest in and comfort with different age groups of children.

Bank Street advisors and program directors know a lot about schools, effective cooperating teachers, and about teaching, and they work closely together discussing students' needs and identifying the best school or teachers for particular students.

Advisors tend to select the first placement according to interests expressed by students during the admissions interview process or in the summer before advisement. Later placements are informed by the advisor's and student's combined perspectives on what was accomplished in the first placement, what is now needed or desired, and by the state requirements. Advisors travel to the schools of their advisees frequently; whenever possible and appropriate, they place two or three students in the same school at the same time so that support groups form and discussions of individual experiences can be analyzed within the particular school context in which they occur.

In contrast with some teacher education programs for which cooperating teachers volunteer or are selected by their principals based on criteria ranging from competence to politics and patronage, Bank Street selects cooperating schools and teachers with great care. Advisors visit schools and make observations of potential cooperating teachers in their classrooms, as well as observing student teachers. They revise, update, and maintain a roster of current "good" spots for learning to teach particular age children. During College, faculty meetings, advisors discuss the field experiences they feel their students need, evaluate fieldwork possibilities, make contacts, and ultimately arrive at desirable spots. In these meetings, advisors also might raise issues with a particular setting and ask others about their own experiences.

The range of choices for field placements for preservice students in the early childhood and elementary preservice programs is very broad, including dozens of well-known progressive public and private schools like Central Park East I and II, River East, P. S. 87, and P. S. 234 (all public) as well as Manhattan Country School, Little Red School House, and the Bank Street School for Children (private). For teachers of young adolescents, the choices are more limited due to the need to find settings that are responsive to the social and developmental strengths and needs of adolescents and not bound by bureaucratic traditions of the old junior high school model. Bank Street looks for middle schools that feature interdisciplinary curriculum aimed at critical thinking and performance in settings where students are heterogeneously grouped. In the last few years several districts have opened new small public schools where Bank Street graduates work and serve as cooperating teachers. These include the Manhattan New School, Brooklyn New School, Muscota New School, Hostos Academy, and many more.

Although the selection of a school is very important, selecting a good cooperating teacher appears to be the highest priority. Many of those selected as cooperating teachers are themselves Bank Street graduates, and all teach in ways that reflect Bank Street's goals for education. Dick Feldman, one of the advisors in the preservice program, spoke of the broad range of these relationships:

> There is not just one way by which we either influence, support, change, or assess what we see in classrooms. Working with

cooperating teachers and schools is a very dynamic. It is about relationships that are professional and personal. It has to do with a lot of personal, trusting, and professional connections that take a long time to develop. But in the end, we are in schools to help the student teacher work well with the particular group of students and the cooperating teacher. In that sense, while we are there for the student teacher, the children, and the teacher, our first responsibility is the development of the student teacher and her or his responsibilities vis-à-vis the children in the school.

During a focus group where advisors shared their views about selecting placements, they were very clear that their main concern was to get the best possible experience for their student teachers: " One year is a very short period and field experiences are lasting influences,"and "I have to make sure they get a full understanding of everything that children experience in the school. I have to make sure they don't just stay with children during Math and Science periods but that they are there to greet children, to say good-bye at the end of the day, and to help them find their coats and bus passes." While some spoke of themselves as guests in cooperating teachers' classrooms, others described how cooperating teachers with whom they had long relationships ask them about practices and how they feel like participants in the work of these classrooms. Advisors who are also course instructors explained that their courses are informed by what they see in classrooms where they spend long periods of time observing their students.

Many principals appreciate this commitment as it ultimately translates into better-prepared teachers. Arthur Forresta, principal of P. S. 261 in Brooklyn, observed:

I find that the advisors treat placements with a lot of care. Here at the school we are in constant communication trying to find placements that offer students particular kinds of experiences they need. When I hire them I know that they have had good placements. I trust that their experiences in other places have been as carefully managed as the ones in my school. I also feel that their philosophy is compatible with my school.

For this study, we observed advisors, student teachers, and cooperating teachers at work during school visits and in advisory sessions after the school visits. The settings were several urban public elementary schools, a number of classrooms at the Bank Street School for Children, and new alternative schools such as the Museum School in Manhattan. In all of these cases, advisors seemed very comfortable, welcomed, and involved. Their visits generally lasted almost half a day. Some of this time, they observed and took notes of the setting and of their students' activities. Some of the time, they worked directly with children, side by side with the student teacher. Some of the time they sat with the cooperating teacher, either observing the student teacher lead certain teaching activities or trying to understand more intimately the cooperating teacher's approaches.

At these schools we also observed "three-way conferences," meetings between the advisor, student teacher, and cooperating teacher that occur at the beginning and end of each student teaching placement. The first "three-way" is designed to set up learning goals for the student teacher. The final "three-way" is designed to have each of the three stakeholders share perceptions on what was accomplished, suggest future directions, and assess teaching abilities and dispositions.

"Three-ways" in the Fall placements focused on the student teacher's experiences in setting up the environment at the beginning of the year, his or her opportunities to get to know and connect with individual children, and her performance in leading meetings, transitions, and developing lessons that are appropriate for the developmental level of the students. At one of these conferences at the end of the first placement in a combined kindergarten/first-grade classroom, everyone involved agreed that the student teacher had been able to meet most of her goals but that there was a question about the level of instructions she tended to give for the age of these particular students. They agreed that this would be an area to clarify when she moved on to work with older students in another public school setting. We visited the same advisor and student at the end of the year in the student teacher's last placement with third graders. The advisor commented on how effective the student teacher seemed with older children. The student remembered us from the earlier part of the year and mentioned that although she loved the younger children she really enjoyed thinking and problem solving with older children. Over the course of the year, she had gained both skills and clarification about her career path with the help of her advisor and cooperating teachers.

In most cases, it appeared that advisors had deep knowledge of the particular setting and that that their presence there was understood to be on behalf of their own students and, somewhat less directly, on behalf of the children in these classrooms. Some advisors clearly had a long, close relationship with the school, the director or principal, or with the particular cooperating teacher. Ana Switzer, principal of P. S. 234, noted:

> I like having the advisors around. I even feel that I can call on them, not just to talk about placements and their students, but about our school programs. I have called people up at the College when we are developing summer institutes. I also hope that if they notice something that I am not aware of that they will be able to talk to me about it. Also, many of my teachers who came from Bank Street enjoy having additional contact with their advisors when they return with new student teachers.

Although the term professional development school (PDS) is not attached to any of the school relationships, the partnership structures and reciprocal arrangements between Bank Street and several of these schools reflect aspects of a PDS model for educating children and teachers simultaneously. Most obvious is the close relationship between the graduate programs and the Bank Street School for Children, where about 80 of the College's student teachers are placed at some point in the year, in addition to others who visit to observe particular classrooms or children. The School for Children is described as an independent, progressive demonstration school, and most of its staff is composed of graduates from the various programs at the college. Many College courses are taught in the children's classrooms and both divisions share the library. Faculty at the College have often been advisors or instructors to the School for Children teachers, just as these teachers now mentor student teachers. Some cooperating teachers are course assistants in graduate courses; some teach sections of curriculum courses; and many of them are guest speakers in courses.

Rudy Jordan is the dean of Children's Programs, which include both the School for Children and the Family Center, a day care center that is designed to include a substantial number of students who are physically or mentally challenged. Both of these are sites for practicum experiences for student at the College. Jordan sees the school and college as interdependent, with each able to offer a superior quality of program because of the reciprocal collaboration:

> A lot of the student teacher's work depends on the skills of the individual cooperating teacher, and where they are in their own development as a teacher. You also need many adults to work well with children, so the advantages are for both the children and for the teachers. I ask myself to what extent do we need the student teachers to run our program and to what extent are we providing a service? The fact is that we are teacher educators. Furthermore, the younger the children, the more we need additional adults to run good programs. We need each other.

In a classroom for three-year-olds, for example, there is a teacher, an assistant, two student teachers, and an intern (a Bank Street student with prior teaching experience who receives a stipend during training and takes on greater responsibility). Most classrooms have one assistant or intern plus at least one student teacher. School for Children teachers are hired with the expectation that they will teach children and novice teachers. The directors of the upper and lower schools help teachers new to the school learn how to work with student teachers. Cooperating teachers in the upper school often use their weekly meeting time to discuss how to support and mentor their student teachers. Upper school head Toby Weinburger sees the process of working with a student teachers as strengthening the practice of the cooperating teachers as well as that of the novice teachers:

> A benefit (of being a cooperating teacher) is that, as you are continually articulating what you do for the benefit of the student teacher, you are clarifying for yourself in a way that you can't do otherwise. You are evaluating their curriculum development and you are measuring your own and seeing how it can improve as well. So that is a big benefit for the cooperating teacher and for the children as well, and I think people see it.

Because of the unusual career paths of Bank Street teachers, most of whom are switching careers, student teachers bring a range of skills into the classroom as well: "I have had bank vice-presidents, a guy who was a lawyer, another who had been in theater," noted Weinburger. "The richness of talent and the variety offer incredible opportunities to find the strengths of that person and integrate what they did into the classroom."

Over the years, a greater degree of collaboration concerning teacher education and school curriculum issues has begun to emerge. Jordan described a two-way conversation in the formative stages about "what kinds of things the cooperating teachers see should be part of a teacher's preparation and, conversely, what the advisors see should be part of the children's education." Weinburger described recent efforts of the upper school faculty and faculty of the graduate school to work together on the teaching of reading to students having difficulty in the Children's School and on the teaching of teachers for reading. In reciprocal fashion, the teachers at the Children's school were working with student teachers on how to teach reading in the upper grades, and teachers from the graduate school offered sessions with the cooperating teachers on assessing and instructing students with reading difficulties. After one such workshop, Weinburger noted:

> It was just superb. Everybody felt really lifted. We now understand what (the graduate faculty) is teaching because we experienced it. Teachers had agreed to have another workshop in the spring, but after this they felt 'let's not wait until spring, because this is great.' It's a wonderful thing that is coming together like a harmonic conversion of forces.

In another example, Children's School teacher Stan Brimberg, who works closely with candidates in the young adolescent program, developed a systematic set of tasks and learning experiences for inducting student teachers into his classroom. This work was soon incorporated into other classrooms and into the thinking of advisors about how to support student teachers. A project was underway during the year of this study in which faculty from the school and the college were beginning to work together to co-construct a 'curriculum' for the student teaching experience, a measure of the importance placed on careful induction into teaching.

Of particular importance is the opportunity afforded by the Children's School for prospective teachers to spend significant time learning to teach in a highly developed learner-centered environment that models teaching for deep understanding coupled with intense consideration of the learning approaches of different children. This kind of sophisticated pedagogy is so unusual that it has rarely been experienced by many of the new teachers in their own lives as students, much less in the schools in which they may ultimately teach. Because it is virtually impossible to teach someone to practice in a manner they have not themselves ever experienced, these practicum opportunities are extremely valuable—and the teaching they require of cooperating teachers is itself quite challenging. As one cooperating teacher in an upper grades classroom explained:

> Some student teachers already have an inclination toward this philosophy and may be relatively well-educated themselves—and it's still challenging because you need to lead them to understanding it deeply and embrace it. But others may not have any notion of this philosophy and so everything in them—their intuition, their background, their inclinations, their own education—makes what they're seeing here counterintuitive. It's a real challenge to get them to appreciate the subtle frameworks that guide our practice. When they should question 'why?' they say, 'I want to bring in onomatopaeia,' or 'I'm very interested in Edith Hamilton's version of this,' and I have to say, 'I know you're interested in it, but that's not really what the lesson is about for the children.' It's not something you can explain only in words. They have to go in and start wrestling with it, teach a series of lessons, and for each painful bump they're more ready to admit that 'there's something going on here with the children that maybe I hadn't thought about. I guess what the lesson's really about is having them put together an idea for themselves.' We are trying to teach our children to synthesize, make generalizations, find patterns, and react to things. For those student teachers who have not themselves learned those things, it's very difficult. In the end, what rescues us is experiential learning. New teachers need to teach and observe until they can understand ideas they could not admit before.

Another cooperating teacher made similar points about the stretch that many prospective teachers, especially in the upper grades, must make to understand this complex form of practice:

We are trying to prepare teachers who are interested in children and their development, not just in the content of the particular specialization that the teachers have. One thing that surprises my student teachers (particularly those from outside of Bank Street) is that emphasis on who the kids are, where they're coming from, what their particular needs are, how best to address those needs, not just to talk about what's the curriculum, what are we going to cover, how far are we going to get in the curriculum. And the amount of coordination that happens between colleagues here is also surprising to them. For example, this afternoon we were having a team meeting at which we talked about particular students in terms of how they were doing, what had changed in their lives, any information we had about how well they were doing in certain areas or problems that they were having—and that could be emotional as well as academic. With student teachers, I do a lot of explaining about what issues certain kids are trying to deal with, and I model for them. I let them see me and hear me talking to students when I'm having one of these conversations with students. I share with them the way I think about students and their needs. If they have an issue with a student that they need to talk about, we have a discussion ahead of time about what might be the best way to approach the problem. I'm there with them to support them in that process so that they also get a chance to put that into practice.

The power of this experience was noted by many of the prospective and beginning teachers we interviewed. This statement by a graduate who had done an internship placement at the School for Children expressed the widely held view:

My first placement was at the School for Children with the six- and seven-year olds. I found it an incredibly exciting place to be—the way the children were valued and the way education was approached. It's not just making sure that the children meet the city or state guidelines, it's about really preparing them for life and having them be workers within a community—a community of learners. It's really looking at attitudes and values: acceptance of others, both their culture and their thinking. Simple things that people might take for granted, for example, in math—sharing all the different ways kids can approach a problem and how each is valid. It's exciting to see the kids say, 'Gee, I didn't think of it that way, oh wow!' Or someone might say, 'I really don't understand how you did it your way, but I see, okay, you worked it out.' To see that exchange of ideas and the acceptance that you can be different and still have so much to share and bring to the group.

In many ways, the School for Children fills the role that the lab school at some schools of education was once meant to fulfill. In addition, Bank Street has strong, multifaceted connections with a growing number of public schools in New York City. The College's relationship with P. S. 234 is so organically close that principal Ana Switzer remarks, "We're helping to define what is a Bank Street education as much as Bank Street shapes that." With most teachers having graduated from Bank Street and 10 to 12 of its student teachers in classrooms at all times, it is not surprising that many of the trademark features of a Bank Street education are present and, Switzer argues, extended and strengthened in some ways, creating reciprocal influences:

Here there is a very rich curriculum where kids can enter in reading, writing, mathematics regardless of their initial level. That's supported by multi-age grouping. And thematic learning through social studies is both a community builder and a curriculum driver. The influence is two-way. When you've taken a course with somebody like Dorothy Cohen (one of Bank Street's seminal thinkers and teachers), she continues to live in your school through the other students you continue to work with, and you see her influence still impacting the school. At the same time, I actually think the work we've done here in mathematics has in some ways influenced the work at Bank Street. We were the people who brought Marilyn Burns (a widely known mathematics teaching expert) into the city, and she worked with our teachers and with my assistant principal, Lucy Mahon, who also teaches a course at Bank Street College. Laura Kates, another one of our faculty members, teaches reading at Bank Street, and carries with her the work we've done with people like Diane Snowball (an Australian literacy expert). Then another Bank Street faculty member came and did some videos here with kids that he then used in his work, and that influenced his teaching. A number of our teachers do guest lectures in courses and I think that influences our practice. We also work with the Principals' Institute. There's so much back and forth.

The P. S. 234 experience exemplifies many of the notions about synergistic practice and mutual renewal that undergird the concept of a professional development school. Similarly, at Midtown West, an intense professional development relationship between the school district and the college has existed since the school was founded about a decade ago. A district and college partnership was forged around the education of interns and student teachers, the creation of a part-time position for a college faculty member who serves as professional development liaison at the school, two days a week, and a graduate programs representative on the advisory board. Roberta Altman, Midtown West's professional development coordinator, is a College employee paid for by School District #2. Altman describes the same kind of synergy P. S. 234 experiences:

> When the school was started with the College, the original vision was that part of the connection with the College would be that the College would support the school in helping to develop teachers and work with parents, and in return, the College would be learning about how the methods that the teachers are being taught in their courses are playing out in this very diverse kind of setting. The connections play out in many ways. I have a foot in both worlds. I try to meet with the head teachers individually and in small groups, and we talk about what it is like to be a cooperating teacher, and what is working and what isn't. I teach graduate courses at the College and then I see some of the same students here during their supervision. Some of those students go on to become head teachers here, so there is a continuum that you can see of people in different

stages of development. Many of the teachers continue to take courses at Bank Street after they have finished their degree, because they then become cooperating teachers and go back to the college. We have one teacher who got her degree at Bank Street who is now in the Reading Program and another in the Computer Leadership Program.

Mary Timson, principal at Midtown West, is a graduate from the Principal's institute at Bank Street and would like to have Bank Street student teachers in every one of the school's 13 classrooms—a goal that has nearly been achieved. She sees the preparation of future teachers as a benefit to practice in the school as well as part of the school's mission. Timson, like Ana Switzer at P. S. 234, seems to have reinvented the concept of the conference group in the way in which she brings novice teachers together to discuss their practice. Mary explains:

When I was an intern in the Principal's institute, I initiated a practice of meeting with all of the student teachers twice a month. I was placed in a large school and I wanted the student teachers to feel that they were all part of the school. I wanted to discuss with them what was happening in their classrooms, to share those experiences with each other and to rely on each other as a support system. When I came here, it is also something I wanted to establish. At our first meeting many of the student teachers had not spoken to each other. We meet at eight o'clock. One day when I was very busy they ran the meeting themselves. One time I asked them to focus on classroom management techniques because that is really important. We have lots of children and very small classrooms. So we have to pay a lot of attention to that if we want to get creative work done.

In myriad ways, large and small, the schools and classrooms that are part of a Bank Street education model cooperation, collaboration, and continual learning.

## PULLING IT ALL TOGETHER: CURRICULUM PLANNING AND CAPSTONE PROJECTS

The coherence of the Bank Street experience rests in part on the means by which faculty organize curriculum together, in part on the relationship between teaching, supervising, and fieldwork, and in part on the ways in which students are encouraged to integrate their learning in capstone projects.

Two organizational structures support curriculum development at the faculty level: the curriculum committee and program curriculum reviews. The curriculum committee includes faculty members from the different programs. This group comes together to propose and help design needed courses. Criteria for courses include the infusion of developmental perspectives, grounding in relevant research, and balance of theory and practice. In curriculum reviews, instructors are encouraged to present their courses to colleagues at monthly faculty meetings. This process allows instructors to share their craft, connect their work to what is happening in other courses, and guard against redundancy or exclusion of important information. It also helps faculty to be updated on courses so that they can advise their students with a knowledge of the standards for the course and the nature of the assignments. Most courses include extensive assignments that are developed, reviewed with extensive feedback and revised over the whole semester period. It is not uncommon for students to have a 200-page Child Study evolve from the combined assignments in the Observation and Recording course or an 80-page curriculum design for a social studies unit expand over one semester.

Course assignments are often the starting point for a student's work on one of the three graduation options available to Bank Street students. These include a portfolio, a directed essay, or an independent study. All three options require evidence of knowledge of human development and curriculum, expression of a personal-professional philosophy, and reflection on the implications of the social context for teaching and learning. All are intended to give students an opportunity to engage in inquiry, to consolidate and extend their learning, and to make an important statement about their own personal contribution to the field.

Directed essays and independent studies have a long history at Bank Street. The directed essay resembles an extensive take-home examination, in which students have a 60 day period to answer a set of questions posed by the faculty in their program which treat major concepts in their field. Their lengthy responses draw together knowledge of the field and knowledge of practice in scholarly and personal treatments of these topics. The comments of a recent graduate who had completed the directed essay illustrated how the process of reflection required by the essay encourages synthesis of knowledge and internalization of ideas:

> The questions encompassed a lot of my course work, and I thought that was really good. It made me think about what is my purpose in the teaching field, what's my role? What I liked about the directed essay was the fact that not only could I pull together what I had learned, but it was like a reflection of me. I thought about myself and what did I stand for in the field of education and how were my past experiences relevant to what I'm doing today and to what I will be doing tomorrow.

Independent studies, which may take a year to complete, can take several forms, ranging from a classic research study to the development of original professional materials for classroom use to an analysis of an educational setting to an educational policy study. Independent studies are collected in the library for future use by Bank Street teachers. Among those we saw on display were, "The Art of Homeless Children: A Lens for Understanding the Implications of Environment and Experience," "Chester, the Cantaloupe: A Study in Writing a Children's Picture Book," "The Development, Implementation, and Evaluation of a Whole Language Kindergarten," and "A Learner's Guide: A Text on Logo for Graduate Students."

Portfolio development has been included more recently in response to new assessments for teachers that have emerged from the teacher education reform agenda. Like other institutions that are studying and shaping new assessment processes for teachers, Bank Street is examining how these processes capture the multiple approaches to learning and teaching that are desirable in a profession that seeks to support reflection and make its knowledge public. At the national meetings of the American Educational Research Association (AERA) that were held in New York in 1996, Bank Street faculty and graduates joined colleagues from Teachers College, Columbia University and New York University in a symposium to present their work in portfolio assessment. A group of advisors is continuing to study this process and its outcomes for students (Freidus, 1995). They posit that portfolios are among the tools that may help to address some of the fundamental dilemmas of teacher education, including the creation of a pedagogy for teacher education that enables learners to wrestle deeply with ideas that are foreign to their life experience and to connect the ideas they cognitively value with the sometimes dissonant notions they viscerally "know." The Bank Street portfolio process seeks explicitly to connect personal knowledge, classroom knowledge, and academic knowledge. As one student wrote in her portfolio reflection:

> My current beliefs and practices concerning reading instruction are grounded in [my early learning]. However my [university] experiences have shaped and refocused these original ideas. As my classes, readings, and child work experiences each built upon themselves, and connected to each other, I learned a great deal about teaching and learning. I saw how the ideas and passions and beliefs that I had brought with me could be applied within the specific context of reading instruction.

The capstone projects are major pieces of work—original curriculum documents, research studies, or compilations of work and recursive reflection over time on a topic—that are frequently of publishable quality. Sometimes these documents reflect an educational innovation or program created by the student him or herself. One independent study we reviewed, titled "Adaptive Learners, Adaptive Workers: Career Education for At-Risk Early Adolescents," evaluates a program that had been developed by the author for at-risk youth in New York City. The 158-page document reviews research on early adolescent development and "at-risk" youth and describes the program design and rationale in detail, including its curriculum, scope and sequence of program activities, characteristics of participants, and—in learner-centered fashion—evaluations of the program by its own students and samples of their work. The study includes focus groups and interviews of students as well as questionnaires. The analysis treats differences between older and younger students, examines the evolution of students' metacognitive abilities, assesses the relation between students' understandings of their career potential and the needs of a democratic society, and develops recommendations for future program development. Like others of these studies, it is an extraordinary example of practice-based scholarship that stimulates understanding and reflection while making a direct contribution to practice itself.

A recent graduate's portfolio, described as an educational philosophy portfolio, was titled "The Teacher as Self-Esteem Builder." This graduate, also now working in a program for at-risk adolescents, described how her interest in the topic began years earlier when she was an adult education tutor "when I realized that my tutoring these people to read also involved helping them boost their self-esteem. Then, I discovered that this theme ran throughout my life, since early adolescence." As an African-American teacher, the interrelationships between teaching, learning, and self-concept echoed in her life as a student and as a teacher in myriad ways. Through reflections and commentaries about her work as represented in a series of artifacts—discussions of teaching events, student responses, analyses of multicultural literature and identity development, critiques of teaching materials, and descriptions of curriculum she had created and evaluated—this teacher connected research to practice in wide-ranging ways. "The process (of assembling the portfolio)," she noted, "helped me to realize that I can do research; I can write a book; I can run a program. It required me to thinking holistically."

Connections between personal and professional experiences, between research and practice, and between general goals and individual children come up over and over in the portfolios. In one entitled, "The Importance of Creating a Caring Community in the Classroom," these perspectives are woven throughout a set of six studies: "Sam's Story" treats the story of the author's own handicapped son as a means for examining differences and universality of the human spirit; "The Classroom as a Community" explores the role of values in the classroom from a philosophical perspective; "Caribbean Day" reflects on a curriculum event used in the author's classroom as a means for celebrating different cultures while maintaining a spirit of inclusivity; "The Power of Books" examines how books can enable students to gain voice; "Building Community through the Arts" looks at how two art projects enabled students to learn about other cultures while developing self-expression; and "A Social Studies Curriculum" reflects on how to use a curriculum created by the author to achieve these goals. The portfolio lists as key theoretical influences Charney's *Teaching Children to*

*Care,* Cuffaro's *Experimenting with the World,* Dewey's *Democracy and Education,* and Etzioni's *The Spirit of Community.*

Among the portfolio presentations occurring during on a conference day in May of 1996 were: "How Children Construct Meaning and Understanding of their Experiences," "Remembrance and Reconstruction: Memory as a Source of Radical Renewal," and "Mathematical Transformation: A Professional Renaissance." In each case, students revealed how their own thinking and teaching had been transformed by the process of studying scholars, studying children, enacting their ideas in practice, and studying themselves and the outcomes of their work.

## MANAGING THE DILEMMAS OF PROGRESSIVE TEACHER EDUCATION

One major dilemma for teacher educators, especially those who are committed to a developmental view of human life and learning, is how and when to counsel a candidate out of teaching—to deny them certification—because their learning about teaching is inadequate to the needs of their future students. At Bank Street, the concern for and faith in prospective teachers that produces such concentrated work on their behalf is matched by an even greater commitment to the children they are preparing to serve. This means that some candidates, despite the best efforts of all concerned, are not allowed to proceed into teaching. As one advisor explained in the company of colleagues who nodded their agreement:

> There are times, and they are hard, that an advisor must say, "I don't think this is going to work. I don't think this is the right field for you. I think there are things that are getting in the way—most often they are psychological issues—and I would advise you to take time and rethink. There are some cases where it is very clear that this person could be destructive, not because he/she is a destructive human being, but because of the way the person enacts himself in the classroom, which gets in the way of the children's learning rather than enhancing the children's learning. Sometimes we help them to identify nonteaching areas where they could use their skills, such as writing books for children or working in an advocacy agency for children. We do have a strong sense of responsibility that we want to do every-

thing we can to help them get through it. We get so involved with the students and their development that even a millimeter of movement is seen as a victory. At the same time, we feel very deeply our responsibility to the children and to the field, just as we would if we were preparing doctors or any other kind of professional, and that's where our final responsibility lies.

Perhaps the most difficult issue for schools of education that seek to prepare teachers for a complex form of practice that attends simultaneously to the needs of children and the demands of deep learning is the relative scarcity of schools in which such practice is represented. The age-old dilemma of whether to prepare teachers for schools as they are or for schools as they might become is particularly acute for those who work at the most sophisticated end of the pedagogical continuum. Can teachers who are prepared to treat children with care and to treat curriculum as an opportunity for genuine exploration transform schools that are organized for impersonal, superficial teaching? Can they even survive in such schools? Can their carefully developed ideals and practice survive and take root outside the hothouses of progressive teaching and learning that are so diligently cultivated by the descendents of Dewey, Ella Flagg Young, Grace Dodge, Lucy Sprague Mitchell, and others who fought for these ideas?

When we launched discussions about whether Bank Street teachers were being prepared to meet the challenges of teaching all children in all settings, faculty were thoughtful and reflective. They reiterated the founder's credo that, although Bank Street practice is difficult to enact in many schools, as long as one is learning (and teaching), there is hope. Linda Levine, chair of teacher education at the time of the study, spoke of the constant effort to infuse cultural understandings throughout the whole program and of the importance of doing detailed observations of classroom and school cultures in order to understand the social and cultural context of teaching and learning in urban settings. Other program administrators spoke about expectations for continuous growth and about the need not only to look at what teachers can do, but at what schools ask teachers to do. Acting dean Katherine O'Donnell noted:

Public schools are not monolithic. There are many public schools that have a social mission. Our graduates do well there right from the beginning. Others work for a couple of years in more protective independent settings and then move into public education. Others stay in independent schools that are progressive. I think it's important to look at teachers as well as students in a developmental way and to look at schools in light of what they expect teachers to do with the children.

Lisa Gelb, associate dean for academics, stressed the need for continuous growth and the importance of the extensive field experiences as a place for practice to take root:

One thing we can depend on is that our graduates are going to have to continue learning and struggling. They will always have to think about what they are going to give and what they will need to sacrifice. Hopefully the practicum will give them experiences to question and the ability to continue to struggle.

We observed the close fit between a Bank Street education and the work of the growing number of progressive public schools in New York City. But what happens to new teachers prepared with these ideals who work in less supportive environments? Do the outcomes of a Bank Street preparation hold up when ideals meet the more predominant reality? Research indicates that many new teachers leave the profession within their first three years in part because they feel unsupported in developing their practice. Bank Street graduates also face the difficulties and doubts of the first years. However, it seems that, for many, their preparation encourages them to find or continue relationships with colleagues to discuss teaching and learning in both isolated settings and those where there is a culture of collaboration and shared educational values. They also seem to seek additional learning experiences, like the teacher we met who was planning to spend the summer in Costa Rica to improve her Spanish because of the influx of Spanish-speaking children in her school.

For Sara Beyers*, the conditions of first year teaching are not easy. Sara teaches as part of a Math-Science team in an urban middle school that is attempting to meet the needs of students who come with many different and often deficient elementary school experiences. The organizational structures aim to support learner-centered teaching: Children are organized by houses; teachers team teach and plan together. There is time for advisories and for after school help. However, there few resources. There are not enough books, paper, or materials for the students. The well worn phrase, "Less is more," is used sarcastically at meetings to describe budget cuts rather than curriculum decisions. And many teachers were not prepared for the kind of practice the new structures might hope to encourage.

Sara's teaching partner openly rejects her Bank Street ways and discourages her from using manipulative materials. Sometimes, Sara gives in for the sake of collegiality, but in general her teaching prevails. Her knowledge of the subject she teaches and the pedagogy that accompanies it is evident in her work. The walls of the classroom are covered with clues to her teaching and her students' learning. Every surface features charts with directions, definitions, examples, pictures, graphs, and clues for solving problems. Each child privately knows his or her grades, and Sara chats with them about what they need to do if they want to improve. She is keenly aware of her responsibility to bring every resource to bear to help them learn to succeed. Even at this early and difficult juncture, her practice is ambitious in its goals and centered on student's learning. Because many of her students don't bring paper to school and don't have books at home, for example, Sara creates references for them:

> When I prepare the classwork I model for them. Like in the book it says 'This is how you do the percent problem,' and I walk them through it so that they can take it home as a reference. I also try to put things up so they can use the walls as reference.

Students have her phone number to call if they have homework questions, or their parents may call. She started a tutorial program during open office hours at 7:30 a.m. every day. She looks for ways to create success that will breed more success. Sara's orientation to look closely at her students and try to understand the world through their eyes produces the various small victories that bring satisfaction:

> One of the kids sitting up in the front went to tutorial and saw how other kids were doing their work and he all of a sudden got it. And now he is into making sure he's ready and his grades are on the rise. It lets them see what a good student is. Some had

never seen what a good student was, or didn't have a quiet place to study at home, or didn't have resources, whether it was crayons or tape.

The other thing is to empower the kids through the content—which sort of sounds crazy and impossible—but Math is something you can get and then you can feel good about yourself. I also think that knowing them and being in contact with the families helps me to understand what they do and why they do what they do.

For support, reflection, and a place to vent, Sara meets regularly with six other Bank Street beginning teachers from the early adolescence program. They share conversations they have had with their advisors, with whom they tend to stay in touch, strategies they have developed for their students, and approaches that have worked or failed as they learn to respond to the expectations of their supervisors or the families of their students. A contract that Sara tried with students has been discussed with peers in this group. They reviewed it with her, gave suggestions and eventually put it to the test. At these meetings they also raise their insecurities about teaching in unsupportive settings, without materials or recognition. At one meeting in the Fall each member of the group talked of changing to another type of work or to a different school or age level—in ways that lead an observer to belief that without each other's support they might leave the profession or lose their focus on learner-centered practice. Two months later, they proudly discussed the small victories of first-year teachers: the child who discovered what a good student looks like, a new management tip, or the call from a satisfied parent. At the end of that year all had signed contracts for the following year and were confident in their abilities.

This support group during the beginning year of teaching is an unintentional byproduct of the fact that Bank Street's postbaccalaureate program, which includes an extensive set of courses and a year of supervised fieldwork and advisement, is rarely finished in one year. Most of the group members who meet with Sara have completed their core courses and a year of advisement and fieldwork, but are still finishing off their last courses and final products: a portfolio, independent study or directed essay prior to graduation. Many, especially in the early adolescence program, are offered jobs after the intensive year of preparation and many accept, completing their final courses under greater stress but gaining a support group and continued connection to their advisors during the crucial first year of teaching.

The fact that students call one another and their advisors for years after they have graduated, return to Bank Street for study groups, courses, and conferences, and continue always to seek new knowledge for their work reflects the view at Bank Street that learning to teach is a neverending developmental process. That process, patiently and carefully nurtured, builds strength in teaching and success in learning. The words of Lucy Sprague Mitchell (1931) come often to mind as this process is observed:

> We believe that the purpose of education is to help students develop a scientific attitude of eager, alert observation; a constant questioning of old procedures in the light of new observations; and a use of the world as well as books and source material . . . Thus, the most fundamental clause of my personal and institutional credo is: While we are learning, there is hope.

# REFERENCES

Ayers, William (1991, Summer). Spreading out its roots: Bank Street advisement and the education of a teacher. *Thought and Practice: The Journal of the Graduate School of Bank Street College of Education, 3*(1), 25-28.

Bank Street College of Education. (1995, fall). *TE502: Observational Recording of Young Children Course Syllabus.* New York: Author.

Bank Street College of Education. (1992). *Curriculum guide for the early childhood education program.* New York: Author.

Bank Street College of Education. (n.d.). *Bank Street viewbook.* New York: Author.

Biber, B. (1973). *What is Bank Street? A talk to educators.* New York: Bank Street College.

Biber, B., & Winsor, C. B. (1967). An analysis of the guidance function in a graduate teacher education program. New York: Bank Street College. Also published in *Mental Health and Teacher Education,* 46th Yearbook.

Cole, M., & Cole, S. R. (1993). *The development of children.* New York: W. H. Freeman & Co.

Counts, G. S. (1932). *Dare the school build a new social order?* Carbondale, IL: University of Southern Illinois Press.

Clandinin, D. J. (1985). Personal practical knowledge: A study of teachers' classroom images. *Curriculum Inquiry, 15*(4), 361-385.

Crow, G. M., Levine, L., & Nager, N. (1990, May). No more business as usual: Career changers who become teachers. *American Journal of Education,* 197-223.

Cuffaro, H. (1995). *Experimenting with the world: John Dewey and the early childhood classroom.* New York: Teachers College Press.

Darling-Hammond, L., Ancess, J., & Falk, B. (1995). *Authentic assessment in action: Studies of schools and students at work.* New York: Teachers College Press.

Dewey, J. (1956 [1900]). *The school and society.* Chicago: University of Chicago Press.

Feldman, S., & Elliott, G. (1990). *At the threshold: The developing adolescent.* Cambridge, MA: Harvard University Press.

Freidus, H. (1995). *Contextual learning: Portfolios as connecting teaching and learning.* Paper presented at the annual meeting of the American Educational Research Association, San Francisco, CA.

Goodlad, J. (1990). *Teachers for our nation's schools.* San Francisco: Jossey Bass.

Hirsch, G. (1991). The social construction of teachers' practical knowledge in the advisement conference group: Report of a case study. *Thought and Practice: The Journal of the Graduate School of Bank Street College of Education, 3*(1), 94-134.

The Holmes Group. (1986). *Tomorrow's Teachers.* East Lansing, MI: Author.

Macdonald, M. (1991). Advisement: The journey for preservice teachers. *Thought and Practice: The Journal of the Graduate School of Bank Street College of Education, 3*(1), 32-39.

Mitchell, L. S. (1930). *A credo for the Bureau of Educational Experiments.* New York: Bank Street School.

Mitchell, L. S. (1931). *Young Geographers.* New York: Bank Street School.

Shapiro, E. (1991). Teacher: Being and becoming. *Thought and Practice: The Journal of the Graduate School of Bank Street College of Education, 3*(1), 5-24.

Sizer, T. (1992). *Horace's school.* Boston: Houghton Mifflin Co.

Toppin, R., & Levine, L. (1992, April). "Stronger in their presence:" Being and becoming a teacher of color. Paper presented at the annual meeting of the American Educational Research Association, San Francisco.

S., & Genishi, C. (1994). "All the things that mattered:" Stories written by teachers for children. In A. Haas-Dyson and C. Genishi (Eds.), *The Need for Story* (pp. 172-199). Urbana, IL: National Council of Teachers of English.

Weis, L., & Fine, M. (1993). *Beyond silenced voices: Class, race, and gender in United States Schools.* Albany, NY: SUNY Press.

# APPENDIX A: METHODS OF DATA COLLECTION

The research for this case study was conducted from Fall 1995 to Spring 1996. Data collection included:

- **Interviews** with College administrators, principals and directors of schools where graduates teach, a random selection of current students and graduates (drawn systematically according to student ID number from a complete list of students and recent graduates), and selected students and graduates whose characteristics represented aspects of the program we were seeking to understand.

- **Focus groups** with faculty and college administrators, with advisors in the program, and with cooperating teachers at three schools with a large percentage of Bank Street graduates in the teaching staff (Bank Street School for Children, PS 234,and Midtown West).

- **Observations of teaching and advising** with pre- and post-interviews of those observed. We observed 8 College instructors who taught core courses, each on multiple occasions; 6 randomly selected first- and second-year teachers (in elementary and middle schools) who had graduated from the program, plus more than 10 beginning and veteran teachers in schools where many student teachers are placed and 5 student teachers in their classroom placements; 7 advisors working with their students in conference groups, elementary and middle school classrooms, and in three-way conferences; 2 portfolio presenters and their mentors.

- **Shadowing of current students** in classes, the cafeteria, the library, and other settings.

- **Review of documents,** including college registration and application materials, catalogues, course syllabi, seminal writings by current and past faculty derived from an ERIC search, graduate theses from 1990-95, published curriculum documents, and self assessment documents.

- **Survey Data** from 62 former students who had graduated within the last three years.

- **Survey data** from 11 school administrators who had hired Bank Street graduates within the last year.

# APPENDIX B: RATINGS OF THE QUALITY OF PREPARATION BY BANK STREET GRADUATES AND EMPLOYERS

| **Graduates were asked:** *How well do you think your teacher preparation prepared you to do this?*<br><br>**Principals were asked:** *Compared to graduates of other teacher education programs, how do you rank Bank Street graduates on their ability to do the following?* | Comparison Group (% responding "well" or "very well" prepared) | Bank Street Graduates (% responding "well" or "very well" prepared) | Principals (% responding "well" or "very well" prepared) |
|---|---|---|---|
| Teach the concepts, knowledge, and skills of your discipline(s) in ways that enable students to learn. | 67 | 82* | 91 |
| Understand how different students in your classroom are learning. | 63 | 82** | 100 |
| Set challenging and appropriate expectations of learning and performance for all students | 69 | 79* | 63 |
| Develop curriculum that builds on students' experiences, interests, and abilities | 68 | 97*** | 91 |
| Evaluate curriculum materials for their usefulness and appropriateness for your students | 58 | 87*** | 91 |
| Create interdisciplinary curriculum | 56 | 93*** | 91 |
| Use instructional strategies that promote active student learning | 78 | 88* | 91 |
| Relate classroom learning to the real world | 68 | 84** | 91 |
| Understand how students' social, emotional, physical, and cognitive development influences learning | 74 | 88* | 100 |
| Provide a rationale for your teaching decisions to students, parents, and colleagues | 62 | 82** | 82 |
| Help students become self-motivated and self-directed | 57 | 73* | 100 |
| Use technology in the classroom | 40** | 20 | 64 |

| | Comparison Group (% responding "well" or "very well" prepared) | Bank Street Graduates (% responding "well" or "very well" prepared) | Principals (% responding "well" or "very well" prepared) |
|---|---|---|---|
| Develop a classroom environment that promotes social development and group responsibility | 70 | 90*** | 82 |
| Develop students' questioning and discussion skills | 64 | 90*** | 91 |
| Engage students in cooperative group work as well as independent learning | 80 | 95** | 91 |
| Teach students from a multicultural vantage point | 57 | 87*** | 82 |
| Use questions to stimulate different kinds of student learning | 69 | 82* | 82 |
| Help students learn to think critically and to solve problems | 62 | 90*** | 91 |
| Encourage students to see, questions, and interpret ideas from diverse perspectives | 54 | 80*** | 100 |
| Use knowledge of learning, subject matter, curriculum, and student development to plan instruction | 70 | 80 | 100 |
| Work with parents and families to better understand students and to support their learning | 45 | 66** | 91 |
| Conduct inquiry or research to inform your decisions | 47 | 69*** | 82 |
| Resolve interpersonal conflict | 43 | 56* | 91 |
| Plan and solve problems with colleagues | 45 | 69*** | 91 |
| Overall, how well do you feel your program (Bank Street) prepared you (these graduates) for teaching? | 65 | 83** | 91 |

Significance of Z-test of proportions, p<.05*, p<.01**, p<.001***

# APPENDIX C: COURSE REQUIREMENTS IN THE EARLY CHILDHOOD, ELEMENTARY AND EARLY ADOLESCENCE PROGRAMS

| Early Childhood and Elementary Program | Early Adolescence Program |
|---|---|
| Child Development | Child Development with a Focus on the Upper Elementary and Middle School Years |
| Family, Child, and Teacher Interaction in Diverse and Inclusive Educational Settings | Group Processes in Adolescence AND Issues in the Physical Development of the Early Adolescent |
| The Study of Normal and Exceptional Children through Observation and Recording | The Study of Normal and Exceptional Children through Observation and Recording |
| Curriculum in Early Childhood Education OR Curriculum Development through Social Studies | Curriculum Development through Social Studies |
| Principles and Problems of Elementary and Early Childhood Education OR Foundations of Modern Education | Assembly: Issues in Early Adolescence AND Foundations of Modern Education |
| The Teaching of Reading, Writing, and Language Arts | Teaching Reading and Writing in the Content Areas for Elementary and Middle School Classrooms |
| Language, Literature, and Emergent Literacy OR The Uses of Language: A Perspective on Whole-Language Curriculum for Reading Programs | Children's Literature in a Balanced Reading Program OR The Uses of Language: A Perspective on Whole-Language Curriculum for Reading Programs |
| Mathematics for Teachers in Diverse and Inclusive Educational Settings | Mathematics for Teachers in Diverse and Inclusive Educational Settings: Focus on the Upper-Elementary and Middle-School Years |
| Science for Teachers OR Integrative Learning for Children in the Natural Environment | Special Study: Integrated Environment of the Hudson River |
| Arts Workshop for Teachers OR Music and Movement: Multicultural and Developmental Approaches | Thinking and Learning in the Arts and Sciences: Physics for Kids |
| Supervised Fieldwork/Advisement (Minimum 2 semesters) | Supervised Fieldwork/Advisement (Minimum 2 semesters) |

# Knowing Children–
# Understanding Teaching:
# The Developmental Teacher
# Education Program at the
# University of California, Berkley

## BY JON SNYDER

*There is a long, if not honorable, tradition that regards teacher education programs as fragmented, a theoretical and intellectually flimsy. The most striking aspect of the Developmental Teacher Education Program is that it is none of the above. DTE is a conceptually cohesive, theoretically grounded, carefully wrought, self-reflective program.*

**–Amarel, 1989, p. 31**

# INTRODUCTION

The Developmental Teacher Education (DTE) Program at the University of California at Berkeley recommends credentials for approximately 20 elementary school teachers each year. UC-Berkeley houses two other graduate education programs—a single subject secondary program in English and one in math. Like DTE these programs are small (20-25 students per year) and are centered within a coherent conceptual orientation to teaching and learning. Unlike DTE, the other two programs are in their programmatic infancy. We chose to highlight DTE primarily because of its nearly two decades of exemplary practice.

Cut to its essence, the goal of DTE for its students (the program's "vision" of good teaching) is that they become teachers who bring to their classes an ability to mesh the developmental needs of children with the cognitive demands of the curriculum. As its state-approved program document explains,

> Children are inherently active, self-motivated learners, who bring to the classroom a wealth of prior understandings that are relevant to schooling. They also bring a desire to become competent and to have that competence acknowledged by others. In this regard it is important for prospective teachers to understand that many seemingly unproductive behaviors engaged in by children reflect that striving, and when understood in that light can be used as starting points for supporting more productive behavior.
>
> More generally, the teacher's task is to channel children's inherent interests, motivation, and developing competencies to the goals of the classroom, recognizing that part of that task is to establish conditions for the child to accept the goals of schooling as personally valuable—to see them as a means for acquiring competence and self-esteem. (Amarel, 1989)

A DTE faculty member, with a heartfelt humility not normally attached to the Berkeley stereotype, commented of DTE students' abilities to weave these types of classroom environments, "I am grateful to work with people who achieve what they achieve."

The graduates feel DTE prepares them well for teaching. In a survey conducted for this study, 96.4 percent of program graduates reported feeling "well" or "very well" prepared for teaching. In addition, DTE graduates were nearly three times more likely to report that DTE prepared them "very well" for teaching than a randomly-selected comparison group of other early career teachers (60.7% to 21.8%).

What is it about those teachers, beyond their own perceptions and the admiration of their faculty, that would recommend studying DTE? At a broad, but not insignificant level, DTE graduates get teaching jobs. Ninety-one percent of the graduates from 1993-1995 sought K-12 teaching positions and all of them were teaching in the year they graduated. Eighty percent of the graduates taught in public schools—66 percent in urban settings, 32 percent in suburban settings, and two percent in rural settings. Eleven percent taught in private schools. Of the nine percent who chose not to pursue teaching positions, two percent decided to pursue further study leading to a Ph.D. and seven percent chose to enter a career endeavor outside of education. Ronni Gravitz, the career advisor for DTE students at Berkeley's Career Guidance and Placement Center, expresses little surprise at these numbers: "Whenever a district hires its first DTE graduate, they always come back for more. Once a student gets in, it is a flood. And this, despite the fact that DTE graduates, because they have a master's, are more expensive for the district." Rather than locating jobs for DTE graduates, Gravitz's biggest challenge is helping them decide which offer to accept: "Most of my conversations with them are personal counseling sessions helping them choose between their multiple options."

Jim Bolar, principal of Wilson Elementary School in San Leandro, Calif., has hired eight DTE grads in the past several years. He says, "I take all the DTE grads I can get." Wilson Elementary, with over 850 students, is the largest elementary school in the district with the largest population of students of color and the largest population of Title I-eligible students. Jim does not just want good beginning teachers, he needs people who can hit the ground running. DTE graduates, he adamantly maintains, come in as experienced teachers. "They are the best teachers—outstanding, dedicated. It is a program that stands out. It is current, research-based, and really attuned to the California Curriculum Frameworks. Their graduates understand development. They have warmth, love, and craziness—the essentials of teaching."

These students also show their promise within their teacher education experiences. DTE students take several classes at the Lawrence Hall of Science, birthplace of numerous innovative materials for the teaching and learning of math and science and organizer of workshops for tens of thousands of experienced teachers. A Lawrence Hall presenter, when asked to compare the workshops he does with DTE students with the decades of workshops he has done with experienced teachers noted, "They (DTE students) are open. They latch onto the "I know that will work" just like experienced teachers, but they can step back into their students' heads better. When I work with them I am not just presenting activities, I am exploring pedagogy and content."

**Vignette: Student-Teaching Practice**

During the spring of 1996, the Oakland Unified School District experienced a teachers' strike that, perhaps least among its effects, interrupted the student teaching experiences of DTE candidates. Two student teachers assigned to a school in Oakland for the fifth and final field experience in their two-year program did not let labor conflict stand in the way of their learning or their work with students. In the midst of the strike, Jenifer Anderson and Samantha Miller joined with Melrose neighborhood children to design an 8 by 20 foot mural depicting an illustrated map of Oakland surrounded on all sides by self portraits of the children. Meeting at a community center after school hours during the five-week strike, they constructed a paper prototype of the mural design. Children chose what to include, and their mural map celebrates widely recognized Oakland spots (the zoo, downtown) as well as lesser known Melrose neighborhood landmarks including the local burrito truck and, of course, the school. With the restoration of labor peace, the work continued at the school site. Fortified with donations of materials from businesses in the local community, the 110 participating children completed their work. The mural map, a rainbow of colors, illustrates the area from the Bay to the hills and brightens the formerly monotone playground. At recess students crowd around the wall, pointing out their favorite spots and reveling in their own, and others', self portraits. After school and into the evening, the mural gathers a crowd of community spectators marveling at the talent of the neighborhood youth as well as discussing elements of their community and the school's place in it.

## Vignette: First-Year Practice

*Note: The names of schoolteachers are pseudonyms. Actual names of program faculty and staff as well as school and district administrators are used.*

Mary, one of Bolar's recent DTE hires at Wilson Elementary, teaches in a portable classroom a fair country hike from the office. She has 32 first-graders (14 girls and 18 boys). An eyeball ethnicity check indicates 25 children of color (a majority of whom are recent immigrants from southeast Asia with a smattering of African Americans and Latinos) and seven children who may be European Americans. While the school is predominantly Latino, it assigns a large majority of primary-age Latino students to classrooms with bilingual teachers in order for them to receive some content instruction in their native language. The purpose is to prevent them from falling behind academically while they learn English. Mary has no paraprofessional support and there are rarely any other adults in the classroom. The room, a smaller than usual portable with a low ceiling and very loud air fans, has one kidney-shaped teacher table and six rectangular student tables with six chairs for each. In one corner, a reading area is set up with books and a carpet.

Mary fosters an active learning environment with her active group of students. She has plastered the walls from floor to ceiling with student work—math graphs, group-experience stories, a student collage from *Bringing the Rain to Kapiti Plain.* The ceiling provides another layer of learning. Hanging down, so adults have to either duck or wend their way through the room, are student-constructed science mobiles and multitudes of "What We Know" and "What We Want To Know" charts. When she realized the classroom had no "cubbies" in which students could place school materials, coats, lunches, and miscellaneous treasures, she and her spouse built them on their own time and with materials paid for out of Mary's own pocket.

On a February noon, with the Bay Area fog beginning to lift, Mary eats lunch with two other first-grade teachers in a classroom within the main building. One of the people at lunch is a first-year bilingual teacher from another teacher-education program of some renown and the other an experienced teacher affectionately referred to as "Mother Hen." In order to alleviate the inadvertent segregation of students created by language-based placements, the three have presented plans to the principal for multi-grade classes with mixed-language student populations for the next year. Some of the faculty expressed concern about the plan, so the idea is on temporary hold. The DTE graduate speaks confidently of it happening: "Next year when we have multi-grade classes I'll be inside the building." Eating messy Subway sandwiches which goop out the sides, the three discuss regrouping their classes for the afternoon science activity in order to achieve some ethnic and language heterogeneity for this year's students.

The other two teachers, while not enamored with the assigned prepackaged activity, have decided to use the materials pretty much as directed. Mary agrees that the lesson is hardly first-rate and says she is not going to use the pre-packaged activity: "It doesn't make any sense to me. There is no active engagement, nothing particularly grabbing." She explains her own "sink or float" activity that touches on the same concepts as the pre-packaged lesson and uses the same materials. Unlike the pre-packaged lesson, Mary's redesign engages students in both the recording of data and in the generation and testing of hypotheses based on the data. The other teachers laugh and ask if she "woke up with this one." She responds, "No. It was in the shower this time."

On the way back to the classroom, she explains that the packaged curriculum, like many packaged curricula, dumbs down the content or "leaves out the kids entirely." When asked how often she comes up with her own use of school-provided curriculum and materials, she responds,

> I have totally thrown out the language arts program; totally tweaked Mathland, and more or less tossed out science. It isn't that I don't teach it or the kids don't learn it. I try to make sure that they do. That's why I use my own stuff. I am lucky to have a principal who doesn't come in here checking out all the time whether or not I am using the prescribed materials.

She carefully qualifies her next statement to avoid speaking ill of her colleagues with the caveat that she is speaking about the caliber of preparation programs, not of other first-year teachers:

> I'm miles ahead of other first-year teachers. There are five other first-year teachers here this year. I am more confident. I had a plan for where I was trying to go. I knew what I was doing and why—from the beginning. The others spent more time filling days. They are catching up now.

Earlier in the day she showed her diplomacy and political savvy when describing an interaction with the physical education teacher who threatened to return Mary's children to the classroom for rambunctious behavior, "Sometimes my kids have a difficult time with some of the specialists. I like my kids to talk with each other and with me. Not all the teachers like that. Sometimes my kids have a hard time making the adjustment." She gets along without compromising her integrity or the learning experiences of her children. Chances are she will see the multi-grade, multi-lingual plan through to fruition.

At 12:20 p.m., half of her class leaves the room to participate with a bilingual class for the science lesson while half of the bilingual class comes to her. She groups the students in mixed language and gender cohorts and introduces the science activity she has designed. The room is full of the required materials. There are cups in large tote trays, two trays filled with salt water; two with regular tap water; and small totes full of small plastic bears, different kinds of tiles, quarters, rocks, and paper clips. The activity is to experiment with how many objects it takes to sink the cup in the different types of water.

The 30 students conduct experiments, record on a yellow sticky note how many objects it takes to sink the cup, and then place the yellow sticky on a large piece of chart paper she has labeled in two columns, salt water and tap water. Before starting the activity, Mary reads the labels and asks students to read the labels. She has the students point out interesting language and spelling features. Two children excitedly point out, "That's the same weird spelling we saw this morning." While organizing the groups, Mary directs the children to go to their assigned table and sit on their hands. She points out that they will be unable to put their hands in the water if they are sitting on them. This is one of many "management techniques" she uses to assure students equal opportunity to engage in the work.

Another example of a management technique is a set of student-generated and signed rules, called a "Peace Treaty," which hangs from the ceiling:

PEACE TREATY
We, Room 31 first-graders, promise to be peaceful in Room 31.
To help make our room a place of learning and friendship, we promise these things:
We won't pick on anyone.

We won't fight at school.
We won't mess up the room.
We will be peaceful and good.
We will listen.
We won't say any bad words.
We will be quiet.
We won't fight with guns.
We won't touch anyone's plant.
We won't karate kick.
We won't push.

Others techniques include:
- praising (often) those who are behaving;
- stopping and waiting until she has everyone's attention;
- questioning whether all can hear;
- positive re-focusing of disruptive behavior. For example, "Lots of talking, which means lots of news out there, but I need you to share it with everyone." Or, "this is so exciting because no one's ever published a book at the publishing center before. If you are excited to hear about it, sit on your stars." (Stars are spots marked on the group rug in the shape of stars.);
- ending or extending an activity based on behavior: "I have time for one more. Do I have a class ready for one more?";
- stars on the board when the group is behaving and stars erased when they are not;
- understated table competition (e.g., activities for points);
- asking people to sit at their tables when not behaving in "on-the-floor" group time.

About the techniques, Mary says, "I do different things for different kids. I don't like all that I do, but it seems to make a difference for some kids." Of the Peace Treaty, she chuckles, "It worked for a day." Out of her hearing range, however, students praise and scold each other on their behavior, referring to "our treaty."

Once the class is into the science activity, management appears invisible. There is, of course, some splashing and throwing things into the water, ignoring the cup, but yellow stickies start to show up on the class chart. The adult observer sits down. The students are regulating themselves. As the lesson progresses, the teacher engages in on-the-spot management decisions. For instance, everyone is supposed to get a chance to go to the table holding the objects and choose. After naming the first person to go, Mary sets them to the task, but very quickly, the students do not know how to decide who should get the next turn. At first she says, "You choose," but then foreseeing an, "it's my turn; no it's my turn," problem, she redirects them to go around the table counterclockwise.

At the end of the activity, Mary brings the class together to discuss the recorded information. Students generate their own hypotheses and then, with teacher encouragement, match their hypotheses with the data. When the language turns abstract, she asks students to come to the front of the room and demonstrate their generated concepts with the materials all had used. In California, this is one component of what is called Specially Designed Academic Instruction in English (SDAIE), a core pedagogical reform focused on increasing the learning opportunities of English-language learners. Workshops educating teachers in these techniques take place all over the state. "I learned it," she says, encapsulating in three words the essence of DTE's program design, "from watching kids."

Other components of SDAIE, many of which are visible in this description of Mary's teaching, include: cooperative groups encouraging development of leadership and group-dynamic skills; alternative assessments such as performance tests, projects approaches, portfolios and journals; student-centered learning including such hands-on/minds-on activities as discrepant events, simulations, and research projects; extensive use of visuals such as slides, posters, tapes, realia (e.g. classroom aquariums, terrariums, field trips); inclusion of community members as conduits of language and culture; integration of first language and culture; scaffolding techniques utilized when multiple levels of language proficiency are present within a single classroom.

## DTE PROGRAM DESIGN

The Developmental Teacher Education Program at Berkeley is a recursive two-year postbaccalaureate program that includes a year focused substantially on course work and observation followed by a second year of intensive clinical experience with ongoing connected course work.

California eliminated all undergraduate teacher education programs over a decade ago, so, within the California context, DTE's difference is its two year time frame, not its postbaccalaureate students. According to program documents, DTE contains the following primary design features:

- Professional preparation is integrated with the pursuit of a master's degree that culminates in an individually chosen research project relating developmental theory to teaching practice.
- Courses are sequenced to provide the opportunity for repeated consideration of teaching-related issues at higher levels of understanding over the two years.
- Five student-teaching placements [the first two placements are each nine weeks in length and the last three are each 18 weeks in length] distributed over the two years make it possible to provide a gradual introduction to teaching, as well as multiple placements in diverse settings where teaching issues can be addressed from increasingly higher levels of competence.
- A small cohort of [20-25] students who attend courses designed especially for them promotes the establishment of collegial and cooperative relationships early in the teaching career.
- A weekly student-teaching seminar with a complex and flexible organization promotes integration of theory and practice, small-group problem solving, and interaction between first- and second-year students.
- Individual clinical supervision is provided by highly experienced staff. Although the introduction to teaching is gradual, the amount of supervision remains relatively constant over the five placements to support adequate reflection on teaching success and failure and to monitor the development of teaching competencies.
- Research faculty participate as instructors and there is an ongoing program of research and program evaluation.

It is difficult to capture DTE through a listing of a course sequence; the 1995-96 academic year listing is provided in Appendix B. It was different the year before and the year after. In some ways, DTE has not changed much in over a decade. The sequence of development seminars, the multiple placements over the two years, and the use of the Bay Area Writing Project and the Lawrence Hall of Science for some teaching methods courses have remained intact. Yet, in another way, because of its unshakable centering convictions about the nature of teacher education, DTE is constantly changing. When told that a colleague had called the 95-96 school year the "year of the schedule change," a long-time faculty member laughed, "Every year is the year of the schedule change." The changes, however, do not represent incoherence but rather a focused and consistent growth.

### Structural Description

Bearing in mind the caveat that DTE is a highly integrated program, the following thematic description of how the program is structured provides one entryway into understanding the program. A "walk-through" of the student experience within DTE follows the thematic description to provide another entryway to understanding the program.

### *Core Seminars*

Students participate in seminars in human development in each of the four semesters of the program. These four seminars create avenues to understanding human development in multiple domains and provide the frame upon which the program is structured. In its own words to the state accrediting body, DTE suggests that:

> One way to conceive of the goals of the core seminars is to provide teachers with sufficient background to understand, and hence to value, the activities of each child in the classroom and to promote development in each area. . . . Of particular importance is the effort to combine social and moral development with an understanding of psychological development to establish principles of classroom organization that promote social and psychological development while also promoting the acquisition of knowledge in the various subject areas.

The primary aim of the first-year core seminars is to provide participants with an understanding of how developmental theories address the learning process generally, rather than to apply theory to instructional methods and curriculum. Students observe children's behavior in classrooms, assess children's developmental levels, and propose explanations based on theory for children's behavior and thinking. Thus, students seek and identify manifestations of development in curriculum. In the second year, the core seminars focus on how the developmental process is realized in classrooms as students learn "traditional" school subjects.

### Courses on Teaching Methods

The teaching-methods courses are largely concerned with developing skills using methods that maintain interest through active engagement, such as "hands-on science," "manipulative-based" mathematics instruction, and communication of meaning in developing literacy. DTE takes advantage of several mature University of California subject matter networks to support its students, including the Lawrence Hall of Science and the Bay Area Writing Project. Both resources provide:

- a rich intellectual and experiential source of content-specific pedagogical knowledge;
- exemplary instructors with extensive classroom teaching experience;
- a coherent emphasis on the teacher as the constructor of curriculum; and,
- a consistent theme on the role of inquiry and reflection in teaching.

The content of the teaching methods courses, however, is only half the story. The concurrent experiences provided in the core seminars link the study of development with the developmental demands of schools and school subjects. Introducing an activity that holds the interest of the student is only one half of the task. The other half is to identify the knowledge that is the target of the activity, and how this knowledge relates to previous and future understandings. To do this well requires an understanding of developing cognitive abilities within a particular content area, the kinds of activities that promote their development, and how the same abilities are manifested in other areas of the curriculum. DTE believes that lack of success in school often can be traced to a lack of understanding on the part of the teacher of the current level of understanding attained by a student within a particular subject area, of what subsequent levels look like, and of the kinds of activities that facilitate transition from one level to the next.

### Field Experiences

Students have field experiences throughout the DTE Program. Students and faculty agree that the consistent concurrence of placements and classes is a key program design feature. Said one graduate of the program, "We were always in classes and classrooms simultaneously. That's the key." When asked where the program addressed issues of balance between theory and practice, a faculty member responded, "Everywhere. And it has to, because the students are always in classrooms."

The program designs and sequences field experiences based on a professional model of teaching that require the conscious cognitive effort of differentiating and integrating multiple perspectives in the service of one's clients, rather than an apprenticeship model requiring the copying of a "master's" advanced skills. That is why students have five placements with five teachers with five differing pedagogical styles: the goal is understanding rather than mere mimicry. In addition, DTE bases field experiences on developmental principles of learning to teach by creating multiple placements in diverse settings and at multiple grade levels. The design builds in increasingly complex teaching responsibilities over the course of the five placements. One professor provided another rationale for the design and sequence of the program's field experience. Paraphrasing Kant, he noted, "Percept without concept is blind. Concept without percept is empty." Extending the notion, the classes offer access to the concepts that provide students the opportunities to "see" children and classrooms. Continuous and long-term placements in multiple and diverse classroom environments provide access to the substance that makes their vision elegant, full, and rich.

### Master's Project

Work on the culminating master's projects begins in the first year of the program. Midway into the first semester, students receive a copy of the previous year's topics and respond to such prompts as: Which are interesting? What themes emerge from the topics? Every other week through their first year, students submit thoughts about possible topics on e-mail. The program coordinator reads and responds, usually with I wonder's . . ., How would you find out's, or How can you ask that's. In addition, Berkeley professor and researcher Judith Warren-Little gives workshops on practical inquiry-related issues. Students complete their M.A. projects in the fourth and final semester of the program on a wide range of teaching-relevant topics of interest to individual students. Some illustrative titles of recent projects include: A Case Study of How the Use of Cantonese in a First-Grade Bilingual Classroom Serves Two Newcomers in Adapting to Academic

Settings; Integrating Social Studies: A Comparison of Traditional and Constructivist Methodologies; A Study of How Different Discussion Structures Affect the Rate of Student Engagement in Diverse Language Arts Classes; and Math Recovery: Toward a Program for Individualized Math Intervention and Remediation.

## THE STUDENT EXPERIENCE

A second way to understand the program, its deep structure, and how that structure enhances the students' work in developing their knowledge, skills, and dispositions is to let the reader "walk through" the two years of the program. This excursion into the student experience is by no means a thorough rendering, but rather an overview with an occasional stop for an in-depth look at representative and illuminating assignments.

### Year One: September Through December
*Field Experiences*

DTE students spend two mornings a week for the first eight weeks in an elementary school classroom. These placements, referred to as "participant observation," acclimate the student teacher to the world of the classroom. For the first placement, the program attempts to put students in "something different from your previous student or teaching experience, to broaden you." At the end of the first eight-week period, the student switches to a classroom at a different grade level with a different socio-economic student population. For instance, the first eight weeks might be in an upper socio-economic K-3 setting and the second eight weeks in a grade 4-8 classroom with a lower socio-economic population. In addition, the placements provide students with differing ethnic and language populations (e.g., opportunities to observe and participate in bilingual and specially designed instruction for English-language learners), as well as diverse teaching styles.

In the afternoons and into the early evenings, a student takes courses either on campus or at the Lawrence Hall of Science. In each of the four semesters, students meet weekly in a student-teaching seminar. This seminar has multiple purposes and is split evenly between small-group and whole-group sessions. In the small groups, students meet with their supervisory cohort groups to reflect upon their ongoing classroom experiences. The whole group work consists of workshops on teaching related issues

(e.g., technology, management, lesson planning, cross-cultural communication, etc.)

### Teaching Methods Courses

The "pedagogical" courses this term include a full semester of a reading methods course, 10 weeks of math methods and five weeks of science methods. These methods courses provide state of the art "inservice education" for these preservice students. They relate directly to the work the students are doing in the classrooms in that students can actually teach using the methods presented with the support of their cooperating teacher, the instructors, and their student colleagues. With this support, they can be successful in the classroom, building their confidence while they acquire a background that will ready them for the integration of content, pedagogy, and development the program will ultimately demand.

The math course students take during this semester serves as an example. Meeting three hours a week for 10 weeks in the Lawrence Hall of Science, the course requires participation in hands-on approaches to the learning of mathematics. Each class session includes modeling of learning and teaching strategies proposed by the California Mathematics Framework and the National Council for Teachers of Mathematics Standards. The course emphasizes a discovery learning approach and includes opportunities to learn and practice such processes as the use of manipulatives, cooperative learning, integration of language and writing, use of technology, and alternative means of assessment. As with the other teaching methods courses, the math course emphasizes and provides access to networks of teachers—in this instance, teachers of mathematics.

Assignments for the course include:
- reading and discussing state and national frameworks;
- analysis of the "math environment" of the student teacher's classroom;
- a finely honed documentation of all math-related activities undertaken by students in one's placement classrooms;
- implementation of, and reflection upon, an exemplary math lesson learned in class or taken from the class text (Marilyn Burns);
- design, implementation of, and reflection upon math lessons that incorporate reading and writing into math instruction;

- collection, selection of, and reflection upon student work in mathematics—especially comparing products generated by traditional and alternative forms of assessment; and
- implementation of and reflection upon a family math activity that begins in the classroom but that students must complete in the home.

The assignments, all requiring classroom-based observation and practice, carefully pace the introduction of teaching responsibilities. The program can afford such luxury because students will, throughout the next three semesters, have other, deeper opportunities for teaching mathematics as well as for learning about how children learn in the cognitive domains of mathematics. The students do not have to "learn it all" in 10 weeks. Program faculty do not have to feel as if they have to "teach it all" in ten weeks. The students have two full academic years to visit and revisit the practice of teaching as well as ways to think about and integrate their growing knowledge of children, content, and pedagogy.

### Human Development Courses

Students enroll in the first of the four-seminar human development sequence this term. They learn theories of human development, including cognitive development and language acquisition. The assignments use a clinical method for assessing levels of cognitive development and use samples of children's spoken and written language for assessing their language development. Like the entire four-course sequence, the first human development seminar melds with the teaching methods courses and student teaching through overlapping assignments and experiences. As an example of how this works, the sequence of assignments for the first seminar in human development is detailed below.

**Assignment One:** Using the Piagetian "clinical method," assess the cognitive-developmental level in different domains of knowledge of two or more of the children in your field placement. Write a report clearly describing what you did, why you did it, and what hypotheses you have formed about the cognitive-developmental level of children and about this type of cognitive assessment. The focus in this assignment is on assessing the cognitive level of the child related to schooling. The use of different domains of knowledge is crucial in that it helps the prospective teacher to understand that one cannot assume a "general stage of development" across domains or subject matter and thus, cannot use general labels to describe a child.

**Assignment Two:** Select two learning tasks from the curriculum in your classroom (e.g., school learning, not simply copies of Piagetian tasks) which your students will understand at different levels. Administer interviews based on these two tasks to three children in order to investigate the different levels at which tasks might be understood using Piaget's method and his theory of development as a basis for interpretation. The focus in this assignment is on assessing the difficulty of the tasks in terms of the level of operational reasoning required for mastery. Write a report including a clear description of the tasks, a summary of the interview procedures and each child's responses, and conclusions about each child's level of understanding and about the level of reasoning required for mastery.

**Assignment Three:** Collect and interpret at least 5 examples of developmentally interesting language data from children. In your write-up, include the "raw" data and address the following: (a) Could the child's use of English reflect some underlying hypothesis or qualitatively different knowledge that the child has about language? How so? (b) Could the child's use of language in this example be constrained in some way by cognitive and/or social factors? How so? (c) Could a teacher do anything to foster the child's development toward greater maturity regarding the aspect of language in question? How so?

### Year One: January Through May
#### Field Experience
During the second semester, students spend either three mornings or two full days a week for 16 weeks in an elementary school classroom, nearly always at a different grade level than either of the two fall placements. In this third placement, student teachers usually plan instruction for at least one

subject area (i.e., science) for the duration of their placement that culminates in a "mini-takeover" of two days with full teaching responsibilities.

### College Course Work

Course work continues in the late afternoon and early evenings. Along with the student-teaching seminar, students enroll in "Education in Inner Cities." This course alerts students to the challenges of urban settings, particularly those challenges related to race and class. In addition, the course allows students to begin to access and understand their own stereotypes and prejudices in a non-threatening environment. Students also take either an educational law course (e.g., legal rights and responsibilities of teachers) or a comprehensive health-education course (e.g., common human health issues with a multicultural twist to address differing conceptions of health and healing). These courses are offered in alternate years so that all students take them together: one during their first year and the other in the second. In this way, first- and second-year students have opportunities to interact and learn from and with each other. These opportunities serve to socialize second-year students into the professional responsibility of supporting the education of those just beginning the journey of becoming a teacher. First-year students also benefit from working with people who, in the recent past, have experienced what they are currently experiencing and have emerged competent and confident.

The second seminar on human development begins with a study of moral and social development. From there, the course moves into psychosocial perspectives on classroom contexts and the implications of those perspectives on classroom organization. Students learn the deep structure of differing "classroom management" techniques as well as the profound social and emotional benefits and detriments of those structures. They study, for instance, the aversive stimulus principles of assertive discipline and its long term psycho-social effects as well as the social psychological principles of "tribes" and their long-term psycho-social effects. In this way, as the students' classroom-based experience grows, they build a background for conceptualizing that experience. The assignments help students understand how and why one structures a classroom for social development purposes.

In this course, students add the social construction piece to their classroom learning puzzle. As the instructor explained the course to her students:

The intent is that social and ethical development become part of your core curriculum, not just an add-on. . . . When the content of school is related to children's experiences it becomes a tool to raise issues that are important to young people as they try to understand themselves and others. In this way, content raises important social and ethical issues such as building empathy and understanding for diverse others, and it provides examples of good people trying to be better in the context of human interactions.

**Summer**

Students are free to pursue a variety of non-academic activities during their "time off." Some work with children in summer school or summer camps; some find other gainful employment; some (a fortunate few) live the Italian phrase "dolce far niente" (how sweet it is to do nothing). Increasingly, students study a foreign language, especially Spanish. Regardless of how the time is spent, students and faculty alike are convinced that incubation time for the ideas students have begun to develop during the first year is crucial. As one faculty member stated, "Something happens over the summer. They come back different people, more committed and more confident."

**Year Two: September Through December**
*Field Experiences*

Students spend five mornings or three full days a week in a classroom for the entire 16 weeks of the fall semester. In this, the "take-over" placement, students take on greater lesson and unit planning, culminating in a two-week full assumption of all teaching responsibilities. Because of the increased teaching responsibilities, students have only two courses plus the supervision seminar on campus this semester.

*College Course Work*

One class is a teaching methods course in language arts and social science. Here students spend 10 weeks studying with the "mother of all writing projects," the Bay Area Writing Project. The writing project approach engages teachers as full participants in the writing process. The series of writing activities in which the project engages teachers introduces methods they can use to engage their students as writers. Like the earlier math course, the writing project includes a healthy dose of "by teachers for teachers" (e.g., a network of teachers) with a grounded theoretical base on the nature of writing and of learning to write.

The second college class is the third course in the human development sequence, Advanced Development and Education: Mathematics and Science. Here, students focus on a developmental analysis of elementary school math and science curricula. The assignments emphasize identifying and remediating common problems in math and adopting a hands-on, minds-on science curriculum. At this point, the program explicitly revisits and builds upon the math and science teaching methods course the students took during their first semester in DTE. Once again, the assignment sequence provides insight into the students' increasing ability to integrate understandings of content, pedagogy, and development:

> **Assignment One:** (a) Using clinical interviewing skills, interview your cooperating teacher about mathematical concepts that children have difficulty learning each year and what children learn easily each year. Include what the teacher does that seems to work. b) Review the mathematics curriculum for three grades, with the grade you are teaching in the middle. Then, for the number knowledge strand, do your own ordering of topics by picking a concept to be taught in your grade and breaking it into subtopics that can be ordered from least to most difficult. To begin with, include at least six steps in your hierarchy. Give a brief, concrete example of what you mean for each step.

> **Assignment Two:** Pick a second mathematics topic (e.g., a domain other than number) for the same grade. Do the same type of learning hierarchy for this topic with an example for each step. Link the concepts between the two domains in content and/or cognitive developmental requirements. We will call this a horizontal linkage between knowledge domains. Indicate milestones in cognitive development for the identified strand(s).

> **Assignment Three:** Use one or both of the ordering of topics produced in assignment two to construct a mini-math curriculum complete with teaching methods. Choose two Piagetian-type tasks you feel will tap the key cognitive concepts required

to master the material. (Students are encouraged to invent their own Piagetian-type tasks so that they construct the connections between development and content. Again, the purpose is not to label the child, but rather to understand the child's reasoning about key conceptual issues.)

**Assignment Four:** Use the mini-math curriculum from assignment three with a small group or a whole class. Target three or four children for closer study, including at least one child experiencing difficulty. For the entire group taught, collect the results of your lessons to obtain initial and final math performance levels. In addition, for the in-depth students: (a) administer Piagetian-type tasks to assess the extent of their understanding of the targeted concepts; and (b) attempt to remediate with one or more of the children by finding a level within the curriculum where they are truly proficient and then move them forward. Give careful thought to the factors limiting the success of your teaching program.

### Year Two: January Through May
#### Field Experiences

Students spend two full days a week for 12 weeks in classrooms during this time period. In the first four placements students are assigned on the basis of the individual cooperating teacher and often are singleton student teachers in a school site. In this fifth placement, the program clusters student placements in a small number of urban schools with a high density of students whose first language is not English. This is another luxury of a two year five placement program. The program can use an individualistic, cooperating-teacher-based approach to placements as well as a social, school-based, clustering approach. It can "pick and choose" isolated exceptional cooperating teachers as well as select schools for placement sites.

The fifth placement has several foci, including:
- a "school project" requirement (such as the Melrose Mural, described above) as a vehicle for structured study of the school as an organization;
- a focus on individual children, especially English language learning children, to complement the course Teaching Linguistic and Cultural Minority Students also taken this semester; and,

- a focus on the school's role within the community and the teacher's role within the school.

Sometimes an additional function of the fifth placement is as a location to complete the required master's project. Also, on occasion, students with common needs (i.e., constructing a classroom environment) are placed in a cluster and receive additional support through structured peer coaching.

### College Course Work

In the afternoons and early evenings students again have a heavy course load, including the following courses:
- Assessment and Education of Exceptional Pupils in Regular Classes (e.g., characteristics of special-needs children and strategies to work effectively with those children);
- Whichever of the law or health courses they did not take in the spring of the first year;
- Teaching Linguistic and Cultural Minority Students; and,
- The fourth human development seminar, Advanced Development and Education: Language Arts.

Teaching Linguistic and Cultural Minority Students, in coordination with the fifth placement, provides integrated and experience-based opportunities for students to construct practical answers to the questions they began asking over a year previously in the Education in Inner Cities course—specifically, what can a teacher do about the gnarly issues of race, class, and first- and second-language development in classrooms, schools, communities, and the educational "system?"

The fourth seminar in the human development sequence focuses on a developmental analysis of reading and language arts curricula. The assignment, as described below, demands that students outline and explicate a complete curriculum for teaching reading and writing through a developmental approach from Pre-K through sixth grade, including provisions for students who are culturally and linguistically diverse and those who are learning-disabled or handicapped. Students produce a document describing and explaining the curriculum for an audience of teachers. The "capstone" term project requires students to collaborate with one another on integrating information gained from their previous study of reading and language arts and multicultural education with developmental perspectives on literacy. The starting point for this assignment is the previous cohort's curriculum. Thus, the product of this assignment actually becomes the initial text for the following year's class.

## PROGRAM SUPPORTS

It requires the whole village to raise a DTE graduate. Essential components of the DTE village include the graduate school of education as an administrative structure, university faculty members, supervisors, cooperating teachers, and perhaps most importantly, students.

### The Institution

When people think of teacher education, Berkeley is not usually the first place that comes to mind. Yet, the first thing one sees upon entering the Education Building is a large bulletin board outside the Dean's office showcasing the work of DTE teacher education students through the work of the students in their classrooms. The same holds true outside the Educational Psychology Office.

Berkeley pays DTE supervisors nearly double what other campuses of the University of California pay for the same role. Program faculty express a profound fear that the program is losing its institutional standing (and intellectual rigor) when, despite retirements and changing professional interests, senior level ladder faculty still teach over 50 percent of the required courses. The institution also provides a three-quarter time secretary to the program, and a credential analyst to show students the way through the state credentialing maze, as well as the support of the placement and career counseling center and the alumnae association, who prepare students for resume writing, letters of application, and interviewing.

In addition, in the words of a non-ladder faculty member at Berkeley, "has an embarrassment of resources . . . . There is the media center, the computer center, the Lawrence Hall of Science. I am dying to form relationships with ethnic studies departments we have here. We have incredible people."

### The Faculty

One of the unique qualities of the DTE program is the direct involvement of research faculty as course instructors for the core seminar sequence of the program. These faculty were hired for their research expertise as measured in the traditional manner (e.g., publications in refereed research journals), which is not always an indication of one's knowledge, skills, or dispositions as a teacher educator. Yet, of their own accord, the faculty chose to take on the often unrewarded and always time- and labor-intensive teacher education courses. It is not always, however, their research reputations to which students refer when recollecting them. One graduate, in the most meaningful, if back-handed, compliment an elementary teacher can give to a university-based researcher, said of two key research faculty, "Because they have exceptional understanding of kids, I don't think of them as ivory tower." In a tautological statement that may lose some of its meaning on the page, one faculty member described core seminar faculty as "People with authority and depth of knowledge. . . . When we give theory it is from people who know the theory. . . . When they talk about what they know, they know what they are talking about."

Teaching methods courses tend to be taught by non-ladder faculty with conceptual and pragmatic ties to the graduate school of education. Increasingly, a key criterion for instructors in these courses is recent classroom experience. In addition, math and science courses tap into the rich resources of the Lawrence Hall of Science. For instance, the math-methods course, taught in coordination with the core seminars, is taught by the director of mathematics education at the hall, who is also the coordinator of the nationally recognized Equals Project.

### The Supervisors

Supervisors observe, coach, counsel, and cajole student teachers on an individual basis as well as sharing responsibility for the student-teaching seminar—a weekly session combining "planned instruction" and "small group debriefing of the week's traumas and successes." There were eight part-time supervisors in DTE during 1995-96. All were women with elementary-school teaching experience. One was African American, one Asian American and the rest European American. Two of the supervisors also held teaching roles in the program. Five of the eight were graduate students in the Ph.D. Program at the Graduate School of Education and one was a recent graduate. One was a long-term employee of the Lawrence Hall of Science and the other was a DTE graduate on leave of absence from her position as an elementary school teacher in Oakland.

Five of the eight were serving their first year as supervisors in DTE.

Della Peretti, DTE coordinator, leads the supervisory team. In that role, she coordinates the student teaching seminar and the work of the supervisors. Peretti taught for 19 years in urban elementary and middle schools in Oakland, serving children of diverse linguistic and cultural backgrounds. Throughout that time, she also served as a "teacher-center person." Her doctorate, from Berkeley, is in policy studies as they relate to the teaching profession. Before being appointed as program coordinator, she served five years as a supervisor for DTE.

DTE selects and nurtures supervisors with care. The basic criteria for selection are teaching experience, flexibility in schedule, the ability to work within a team, the willingness to engage in the time- and labor-intensive work required of the role, and a "match with program philosophy and issues." Internally, DTE recruits most heavily from the Graduate School of Education's Language, Literacy, and Culture Program. This has helped keep the DTE program fresh because, according to a program founder, the Language, Literacy, and Culture Program offers a different, yet complementary, theoretical grounding. For instance, DTE founders tended to reside in the "development" world of research while students of the Language, Literacy, and Culture Program tend to be engaged in the conversations of the "socio-cultural" world of research. Students and faculty benefit from the cross-fertilization of these different ways of understanding, teaching, and learning.

Weekly two-hour meetings among supervisors serve as information-dissemination-and-processing opportunities as well as times of emotional and educational support. Students, selected by their peers, attend the sessions every other week. Grounded by discussion of individual student teachers, the sessions are rich sources of supervisory professional development and program improvement. In addition, the coordinator "asks to be invited in to observe the other supervisors' observations of their student teachers." In this way, she can support the supervisors as well as get to know cooperating teachers better.

Supervisors of student teachers play at least two key roles in DTE. The first is the obvious support function as they help the students make the connections between program strands. One program faculty member went so far as to state that "The key link in the program is the relationship between the supervisor and the college. Supervisors are the cohesive thread." A second function is to keep the program fresh. An original program faculty member perceptively commented, "The supervisors are a key source of change." The coordinator of the student teaching placements echoed the theme, noting that supervisory "turnover is a real strength—as long as it doesn't happen all at once."

Graduates in particular sing the praises of their supervisors. One graduate likened working with her supervisors to "a series of personal counseling conversations. They listened." Another graduate, repeating the "listening" theme, recollected, "The supervisors were great coaches—listening and responding and thinking about what you wrote in the journals. Letting you make mistakes. They really cared about me."

### The Cooperating Teachers

The importance of the ability of a cooperating teacher to be a teacher's teacher is well documented, but in DTE, with its intense cognitive demands to combine learner- and learning-centered understandings, it is even more important. As one graduate recollected, "The placement can put it all together for you or be totally demoralizing."

Supervisory issues that DTE takes into account when choosing cooperating teachers include: (a) the ability to provide useful feedback; (b) where they fit on the non-threatening vs. aggressive continuum in the nature of their feedback (not because DTE values one type of feedback over another but as needed information to optimize the match between student and cooperating teacher); and (c) expertise in a particular aspect of working with children (e.g., curriculum, classroom environment, etc.). In order to gain information on these issues, the program relies on recommendations from principals, graduates, and current students as well as observation by a supervisor.

The program requires approximately 100 placements per year, so Peretti is always on the lookout for potential cooperating teachers and information about existing cooperating teachers. Here, the joint supervising she does with supervisors is exceedingly valuable. In addition, during team meetings as supervisors report on their observations and conversations with student teachers, her notes often focus on cooperating teacher behaviors, classrooms, comments, and role much as on student teacher behaviors. While the program uses a relatively stable pool of cooperating teachers, each year DTE "tries out" new cooperating teachers. New cooperating teachers usually receive their first DTE student teacher during the initial eight week participant-observer placement to establish relationships and grow a "good fit" with the program.

Another important variable in the cooperating-teacher equation is that the program aims to have each student teacher work at least one semester in a DTE graduate's classroom. Across the board, current students and graduates rate this variable as essential. One graduate put it this way, "Always there is at least one placement with a DTE grad. That was my favorite placement. I guess that was harder to do at first but now that there are more grads out teaching it must be easier." Mary, whose work as a first-year teacher is described in this report, is now in her third year of teaching and has her first DTE student teacher. Another graduate recollected, "My first cooperating teacher was like having [a core seminar instructor]. He taught me how to be a student teacher."

Whether graduates of the program or not, all cooperating teachers receive a folder of information that the supervisor reviews with them individually. The folder includes:
- a student-teacher goal-setting form;
- a narrative description of the role of the cooperating teacher, which also includes expectations for student teachers as well as college course work assignments;
- a narrative description of the process and indicators for rating the development of student teachers; and,
- a listing of the benefits the Graduate School of Education provides for cooperating teachers, e.g., library card, access to recreational facilities, summer-session stipends, reduced fee for concurrent enrollment through UC Extension, and newsletters/informational packets from the Bay Area math, writing, and science projects.

Cooperating teachers also participate in a three-way goal-setting meeting at the beginning of each placement and a three-way exit meeting. These serve as feedback to the student as well as support for the cooperating teacher. In addition, some cooperating teachers have taken advantage of meetings at the coordinator's home where new and experienced cooperating teachers developed and analyzed case scenarios of work with developing teachers.

## The Students

Though some may see DTE as more Piagetian than Vygotskian, the program is structured using precepts from both perspectives. That is, the program understands children (and DTE students) as individuals who follow some consistent patterns of growth as well as members of social groups that shape in significant ways the nature and direction of individual growth. For instance, the supervisory role is consistent with Vygotskian scaffolding by a more knowledgeable other, while the intense peer interaction is quite Piagetian. As one graduate said with a recollected smile, "In some ways in DTE you are more dependent on the cohort than the program. . . . You see, you are in the same classes doing the same thing with the same people. You have to stay together or you die." Because of this, selection of students is a key program process.

Each year, the program receives approximately 120 applicants. Application files contain college transcripts, a statement of purpose, documentation of experience with children, an academic letter of recommendation and a letter of recommendation regarding the applicants' work with kids, plus a third letter. An initial paper screening reduces the total by about 50. The remaining 70 students participate in a three-hour screening-interview process. Held on Monday or Friday mornings during the spring semester, each session includes eight applicants who have 20 minute individual conversations with the Director of the Program (a ladder-faculty member), the program coordinator, a DTE supervisor, and another person (usually an elementary school principal). In addition, three to four current students host a hospitality room where interviewees have breaks and snacks and can ask questions. Interviewers are told:

> You may ask any questions you want in your quest to determine which candidates are the most suited to the teaching profession and, more specifically, to the DTE program. Each interviewer will do the same and we will come together to compare notes after interviews are completed.

Some guiding thoughts include: "What would it be like to work with them? For them to work with us? For them to work in schools?" At the end of the interviews, interviewers independently rank the candidates and rate them on a 1 to 5 scale.

Lunch and discussion follow each morning interview. "The purpose of the discussion," according to the program director, "is pooling our intuitions." Though no explicit criteria are outlined, the lunch discussion sheds light on at least two generally accepted implicit criteria: the candidate's disposition not to seek only one right answer and the candidate's ability to move between levels of abstraction. Undergraduate grade point average and GRE scores are considered but are rarely a deciding factor. As the discussion unfolds, there is usually little disagreement about the top candidates. By the end of the interview process there are more top candidates than available openings.

Like only a few other institutions in the country, the University of California at Berkeley has reached the status of institutional icon. With that status come stereotypes. The stereotypical Berkeley student may come from the movies (e.g., Elaine Robinson in The Graduate) or from the projection of high school nerds—awkwardly dressed folks walking around with pen stains in their pockets and calculators hanging from their belts like six-shooters from a holster or the 60s image of long-haired social activists chanting freedom slogans. If these stereotypes are true, or were ever true, they do not apply to DTE students. All are socially adept, and, though one might spy an occasional tie-dyed T-shirt, they are their parents' children—not their parents.

In earlier years, there was a distinctly white cast to the cohort. One graduate lamented, "My classmates were all very similar—all white women. Diversity is one of the things that is left out of the program." In recent years, however, reputation, recruitment, programmatic changes, and financial resources have led to an increasingly diverse student population. The 1995-97 cohort was 50 percent students of color. Still, DTE continues to expand its outreach efforts. Its efforts became significantly more complex and politicized following the UC Regents' decision to abolish affirmative action considerations in admissions decisions and the passage of Proposition 209 (a voter sponsored law abolishing affirmative action throughout all state agencies). Higher education is no longer inexpensive anywhere, so cost is another factor for lower socio-economic students. Still, Berkeley, at the in-state tuition/fee rate of $4,394 per academic year is certainly not in the high-rent district of prestige universities. In addition, not only are DTE students eligible for basic university and federal aid, there are also a number of "credential only" awards (e.g., Retired Teachers Association) and a 1989 graduate of DTE recently gave a $250,000 gift to the campus to be used solely to support DTE students.

Whether "nerds" or not, Berkeley students also have an image of being the best and the brightest. This raises the question of whether:

- DTE is good because the program recruits good students (but does not really have to do much with them); or
- DTE may add value to its students, but it only works because the students are so bright and thus the program would not work in most other contexts; or
- DTE adds value to students, and one does not have to be a potential Nobel Prize winner in order to reap the benefits of DTE.

The program does demand a cognitive complexity that matches the cognitive complexity of teaching. In this regard, DTE may be difficult and not for everyone, but no more so than teaching. One third-year teacher put it this way,

> People should not be teachers if they can't understand the theory. Every teacher needs to understand children and development. If they can't, they shouldn't teach. Teaching is not a management program. Not everyone can do it, but not everyone should.

In general, however, program graduates did not rate themselves as particularly academically gifted. Graduates rated the key common feature of DTE students as commitment rather than intellect. Their level of adamant intensity rose when they were asked if DTE only worked because they were smart.

> I'm not that intelligent. I performed at that level because they told me I would . . . . Anyone with the desire, the commitment to two years, could succeed at DTE. [third-year teacher]

> You don't have to be brilliant to learn what DTE does—to learn developmental psychology, curriculum design, etc. With commitment, most everyone could do it. [first-year teacher]

Faculty members were pleased when they read these comments. They interpreted them as indicating a lack of "elitism" on the part of their graduates as well as validation that how DTE educates teachers corresponds to what teaching is about. While program faculty understand that their applicant pool may not be "typical," they, like their students, believe the challenges of the program correspond to the challenges of teaching.

## CONTENT THEMES
### The Center

DTE's inviolable orientation is a deep, consistent, profound, and sustaining centering on children and how they develop. The same professor who complimented his colleagues by saying "When they talk about what they know, they know what they are talking about," continued the conversation with, "I want our graduates to know what they are talking about when they talk about children and learning." In official language from the DTE program review document,

> The study of human development and education provides the unifying framework for DTE. The core-program seminars are devoted to understanding direct implications of levels of cognitive, social, and personal development for educational practice, including the sequencing of curriculum and the structuring of social interactions.

Students recognize this as well. In a data-collection activity completed as part of this study, students were given a card for each program course or experience and asked to identify those most significant for their learning. Every student clustered the seminars on human development together and began an explanation of the program with that cluster of cards. One student's typical comment, was, "The 211 (human development) sequence is the most important, the core for me." Graduate surveys completed for this study reinforce these perspectives, with over 93 percent of graduates reporting feeling "well" or "very well" prepared to "understand how students' social, emotional, physical, and cognitive development influences learning."

For DTE, the more important contributions of developmental psychology are "the analyses of how knowledge is acquired (constructed) in all domains, along with the specific steps in knowledge acquisition within those domains of knowledge encountered in schools" (Kroll and Black,

1989). This approach to the use of developmental psychology in teacher education does two things. First, it recognizes "that development is a function of the interaction between an individual and the environment and that schools exist to establish environments where individual children are not faced with reinventing all knowledge on their own" (Kroll and Black, 1993). In this way, development and pedagogy are linked.

Secondly, DTE links development and content. One of the core faculty members commented, "Traditional disciplines do correspond to children's construction of knowledge. But good teachers do not analyze content and impose it on the child. They analyze the child and fit the subject to the child's developing understanding." One DTE graduate in her third year of teaching gave these relatively abstract notions a concrete, complementary twist:

> The focus was on how students learn and I really appreciated it. It is not so much a specific developmental-level kind of thing I learned in the program, but how kids learn and how I'm learning as a teacher. That frustration and struggling are good. It is what you can create on your own and what kids can create on their own. Kids can do so much. It is not you giving it to them.

In the core seminars especially, DTE moves students towards both the abstract and the day-to-day understandings that the linking of development, pedagogy, and content require. One core seminar instructor put his challenge this way: "The purpose is to help students expand their inherently behaviorist notions—in fact, students almost always enter either Rousseauian or Skinnerian—or both." That is, some students begin the program believing children enter the world "trailing clouds of glory" and if left alone will bloom. Others enter the program believing in the need to control children's behavior through rewards and punishments—and some simultaneously hold both beliefs. The challenge is to help students put ideologies aside and seek to understand children.

In the core seminar in the Spring of her first year, one student, positing a Piagetian ideology, demandingly stated, "Eternal questions are not developmentally appropriate." The instructor took a moment to respond,

> The issue is not to get kids to think about them the way you do, but you need to remember they are thinking about them . . . .

What may be helpful is: 1. Kids are not lumps of clay but come with ways of thinking and motivation and theories about the world. 2. There is an order to how those theories of the world develop. Knowing the characteristics and directions helps you understand and support children. What doesn't work is trying to supplant their thinking with your own.

A second challenge in linking content, pedagogy, and development is to flesh out what different stages look like in different knowledge domains, because stages of development do not tell one much without reference to a particular domain of knowledge. Here the issue is acquiring an understanding of and respect for the uniqueness of domains of knowledge, and how students can be at different developmental levels within different domains. In a quote that could only come from a DTE graduate, one first-year teacher lamented, "Horizontal decalage (the differing levels of her students in different developmental domains) is driving me crazy."

### Vignette of Teacher Education Practice

In the third core seminar, during the fall semester of the second year of the program, the instructor is leading students in a series of activities to complete their assignment to develop a task capturing an essential understanding in a non-number mathematical domain and then to assess students' understanding of that domain. The final piece of the assignment is to go back and re-work the domain with a child who "failed" the task. The instructor's unspoken goal is to force assessment of knowledge rather than an assessment based on "The students were all involved," or "They all liked me." He first provides a handout from a third-grade activity sheet from a typically used text series requesting that students determine area by multiplying the length times the width.

| | |
|---|---|
| Instructor: | How many students do you think could do this? |
| Students (together): | Not many. |
| Instructor: | Why? Who is going to be able to do what? |
| Student One: | Filling things up will be easy. And they will conserve. |

| Student Two: | They will be in trouble, even when the directions tell them to multiply the perimeter to determine the area. |
| --- | --- |
| Student Three: | You could give them tiles and ask them to make different shapes to get at their readiness levels. |

The discussion continues and students provide several more examples establishing their understanding of the domains combined in the worksheet as well as tasks they could use to assess the child's understanding of those domains. The instructor moves on, telling a story:

I had a student teacher who had three students for whom the third grade teacher had serious concerns about their math ability and their ability to progress in school. She was trying to teach two column addition and subtraction and the students just could not get it. The teacher asked the student teacher to give the students a cognitive assessment. The student, daunted by the challenge, asked for my help. Here is what I did.

He hands out a sheet of paper listing five principles:

| Principle 1: | Errors are knowledge and frequently represent over-generalization of partial knowledge or a lack of integration with other knowledge. |
| --- | --- |
| Principle 2: | The child's misunderstanding extends further back in the hierarchy of subject knowledge than it first appears. Therefore, do not immediately confront the child with the error and teach the correct algorithm. Rather, probe to reveal what the child did that represents misapplied knowledge. |
| Principle 3: | Discover and maintain a balance between computational procedures and conceptual knowledge. |
| Principle 4: | Disequilibrium that leads to a progressive understanding of the material is between conflicting understandings held by the learner and |

not the disequilibrium engendered by getting a wrong answer.

Principle 5: A facility or virtuosity at one level of understanding is necessary for achieving a higher level understanding.

He then shared excerpts from the actual worksheets the children had completed, incorrectly, of two place addition and subtraction requiring regrouping. At that point, he led them through the seven tasks he decided to use to assess the students' number knowledge. With each of the seven assessments, he demonstrated how each student approached each task. At the end, in typical DTE fashion, he asked, "So? What should be done next with each child?"

So? Do DTE graduates do anything with this profound knowledge of development and how to assess it? One third-year teacher, following a math lesson using manipulatives to develop an understanding of multiplication took the observer aside and whispered conspiratorially,

> I just got a real understanding of what's happening cognitively—so I can understand why I use the pedagogies I do. You don't use unifix cubes so they can do the worksheet. We ask so we can find out what the kid is really understanding. You also really have to know the content to know what's in between. It's not just that you got it right or you got it wrong.

Sometimes the learning take the shape of little actions. In a group activity in this same classroom, several third-grade students are sitting off to the side. The teacher asks if they can see. By this she means, in typical teacher talk, that they should move in with the rest of the group. The students respond they can see. The teacher, without fuss or delay, moves to where they are sitting, squats down, sees that they can see and lets the matter drop.

### Vignette of First-Year Practice

Wilson Elementary first graders in San Leandro, California enter the room at 8:15 in the morning. Mary, the first-year teacher, arrived at school at 7:15 to meet with the researcher and has had little time to gather herself or her room for the day. As the students enter, she gives hugs and greets each by name. The children know the routine. They are in the room, have placed coats and lunches in cubbies, and gone out to physical education (PE) in under four minutes. On the long walk across the asphalt playground to PE, Mary follows lines painted in the asphalt to keep them in line. She spreads out her arms as if balancing on a high wire. She pretends to lose her balance several times and each time, students immediately behind her rush to catch her. As she falls, she puts just enough pressure into it to give the children a sense of catching her.

Her class safely engaged in PE with an itinerant specialist, she meets with a student support team consisting of three support personnel, the principal, and herself. Mary is on top of the paperwork and lays it out on the rectangular table around which the team is sitting. Though the case history, begun in kindergarten, focuses on the child's tardiness and absences, she brings with her the child's work. She focuses the experienced team on the journal entries she has collected. The journals are indecipherable pictures. She shows other journals with scribbles, some with recognizable letters and some with readable, inventive spelling and appropriate capitalization, in order to give the team a sense of what the student may be missing by missing so many school hours.

She then takes out a notebook with yellow stickies attached to each page. Thumbing through the pages, she gets to the page for the child of focus. The final yellow sticky on the page (and there are not as many stickies as for the other children—another loss created by time out of school) reads "Uses pictures to decode." Later in the day she walks the researcher through the notebook:

> I keep notes about each child on these (yellow stickies) and then transfer the notes onto a page I have for each student (kept in the notebook she used to help the Student Support Team understand the student's performance). These were a life saver at report card time. . . . I try to say something positive on each of the notes.

Each note is labeled with the child's initial and dated. Sample notes she took on one day (for different students) looked like this: "Easily discouraged but is starting to coordinate strategies." "Uses pictures to decode."

"Using letter cues to unlock meaning. With practice he's going to be fluent." "Just beginning to pick up on repetition."

Another first-year teacher explained:

> The developmental psych background from DTE—moral, physical, cognitive, emotional, social—is incredibly valuable. Without it I would have no way to figure out what's going on— the multiple levels within each child. Without it, I would just give in and simplify the curriculum." She thought a while, looked around the room, and concluded, "I couldn't continue without those understandings.

### No "One Right Answer"

Humans possess a basic need for some certainty and structure. In times of stress, that need often overcomes the balancing need for ambiguity and freedom. The process of learning from teaching is definitely stressful— "nuts making," as one graduate put it. DTE is aware of the drive for certainty in the stress of its program, but refuses, despite repeated pleas, to provide students with the certain security of "the one right answer." Next to its focus on children, "no one right answer" may be its guiding content. DTE staff consider this principle so important a variable that it is taken into account in admissions decisions. Though program faculty do not go so far as to put students through an authentic assessment, they attribute some of their success to "attracting students willing to suspend their desire to learn the 'right way' to teach as quickly as possible while investing the time necessary to construct, for themselves, ways to put complex theory and research to work in their classrooms" (Black and Ammon, 1992). One of the ways DTE builds this "content" structurally into the program is through the consciously diverse set of field experiences provided. Again, the purpose is not to find the good teacher and copy the one right way he/she does it, but rather to seek out multiple approaches to meeting one's professional commitments to children and their families.

Within program courses, students are advised, often told, to think deeply about the different ways of teaching being presented and always to question. The health class taught to both first- and second-year students in the spring provides students with an understanding of the issue in both a pedagogical and cultural context. The guest lecturer, a Vietnamese immigrant, opens her session with the question, "What causes a cold?" She says to be creative with answers and have fun. Students generate a variety of less medically-correct causes for the common cold, such as kissed by a frog, lack of a sense of humor. She then asks the group to think about how they would cure a cold based upon what one thought was the cause. Following their responses, she says,

> This is not about specific cultural health practices but about ways to think about cultural health practices so that when you come across issues you will have a basis to know what is child abuse and what is not. . . . There are many ways to think about what causes colds and the way you think about causes determines how you think about prevention and cures. [In Vietnam we say] 'I am hit by the wind.' To cure, you scratch/rub the wind out of your body.

She then demonstrates the technique and where the scratching takes place to rub the wind out of one's body. She is careful to note, however, that if marks are elsewhere, "It is not medicine." From the back of the room, a first-year DTE student, a Vietnamese woman who arrived on U.S. shores at the age of eight, demurely, but with a smile, walks to the front of the room. Yesterday she had felt terrible. Several students had commented and worried about her health with her. Today she is standing straighter and there is luster in her hair and her eyes. She explains she rubbed the wind out of her body last night and shows what the resulting markings look like.

Just prior to that class session, a second-year student, stated at this nearly culminating moment in his teacher preparation program, "The most important thing I've learned is that there is no single right way or perfect philosophy."

## PROCESS THEMES
### Recursive Learning

Within the context of California, it is essential to understand just how significant and different a two-year program is. The state abolished the undergraduate major in education and required a fifth-year postbaccalaureate program for earning a teaching credential more than a decade ago. Berkeley was one of the first, although other campuses of the University of California have picked up on its lead, to require two years. To do so, however, required special dispensation from state regulations. As Ammon and Levin (1993) explain,

> Even with the more modest goals we have set for the DTE program, it still is important that the preservice period have sufficient duration to make them attainable. Two years may not seem like a very long time to prepare for elementary teaching, and it isn't. But it certainly compares favorably to the one-year postbaccalaureate programs that are typical in California. Having some additional time not only opens up the possibility of studying development much more intensively than usual, but it also means that basic issues regarding development and teaching can be addressed *recursively* as students progress through the program. (p. 322)

In some ways, DTE students experience a good traditional California teacher-education program in their first year. Like other teacher education students, they must establish proficiency in content knowledge prior to entry (thus the undergraduate degree). Once in the program, they learn to study children, pedagogy, and important social and philosophical issues impacting the education of children in schools. Like traditional programs, however, students study these elements in the education of teachers separately. In Piagetian terms, the students learn to differentiate. In the second year, DTE students have the luxury of taking their knowledge of the different domains of teaching and integrating them. One core seminar instructor put it this way, "In the first year we recapitulate a human development major and a traditional teacher-education program. . . . The second year is the recursive process. We go over the same thing and integrate it."

Teachers and students use the time to learn and make visible the linkages hidden in the time press of "covering the content" in a single year. For instance, in one 15-minute student presentation in a second-year core seminar, the presenting student referred four times to Piagetian tasks studied the year before, three times to presentations from other students this year—and the instructor topped this number. These types of reflective connections only happen because the program is organized recursively. If the students had not studied X or read Y in year one, they would not be able to recognize and build upon their knowledge in year two.

School administrators notice the difference, usually linking teacher development issues with commitment issues. One principal, who also tries to "get as many DTE grads as I can," said, "The two years makes a big difference. Its developmental, but its more than that. The two years is also an indicator of commitment." Graduates, and even students from other well-respected teacher education programs also credit the two years. At a lunch conversation with another first-year teacher, the DTE graduate commented, "The time is crucial. You can't do it and be successful in one year." Without being asked, the other first-year teacher agreed vehemently and added, "I wish every program was two years."

Aside from the second year of integrative study, a two-year program provides a summer. Faculty often comment that students "change over the summer." The basic theme is that the time to reflect, away from school and college classrooms, gives the first-year experience, especially the more "theoretical" components, power. The summer, according to a program faculty member, is "Time out from pressure. It is percolation time. The power of the second year comes from the students' recognition that they learned something the first year. It is a huge confidence builder."

Something does happen over the summer, as evidenced by the different way students talk in May and September. In a conversation with first-year students, graduating second-year students reassured them,

> The biggest gripes at the beginning are the journals, but at the beginning of the second year, I really valued them. That is when things really started coming together. I started being able to figure out and create in the classroom. In June I was asking myself, 'Why did I come here? I could be teaching now.' It comes together the second year. It has to sit for a little while.

A perhaps unexpected benefit of the recursive process of the second year is that it takes the student teacher's focus off him/herself (another product of time-induced stress) and shifts it to children. This, in turn, allows students to take up the program's centering focus on children as their own. As one observed:

In the second year, the theory became mine so I could tell if something was happening or not happening in the classroom. Also, by the second year I had enough experience in classrooms not to focus on me and to see individual kids and the group at the same time.

The first year I knew development, but it all flew out the window. I kept wondering, how do I connect it? I felt I wasn't using what I learned. I would hold back. What would Piaget think of this lesson? Then I decided to do it anyway and watch the kids and what they do. I am still not sure how theory fits the practice, but now I try stuff and watch the kids. I still don't know, but I allow the kids to do what they do and learn from that rather than have an agenda and make the kids do that. . . . I wish more teachers would think like that—focusing on the kids and learning.

### Reflective Processing—Collaboration

Reflection (and its derivatives such as reflective practitioner and reflective processing) has attained the status of silver-bullet buzz word in a remarkably short period of time. Beneath its flippant use as a phrase, however, lies its initial meaning—to think about and come to deeper understandings of what one does in order to avoid previous mistakes and improve future practice. To function, reflection requires that the individual value it and possess the skills needed to use it constructively. DTE students value reflection and credit the program with the development of that value. One first-year teacher noted,

I always want to be open minded. To see what's working and not working. I see some people don't do that anymore and I don't want to become like them. I don't want to get stuck in what I'm doing. I seek input from other sources, here at school, in workshops, and elsewhere. My program is not set 'cause I am a first-year teacher, but I hope it is never set. I don't want to open up the notebook in September and just go through the pages. . . . DTE fosters that by constant processing.

Conversely, simply valuing reflection does not guarantee constructive reflection. Going home each night and bashing the children in one's thoughts might constitute reflection, but it does not constitute constructive reflection. The program's focus on children is a key element in enhancing the constructive nature of the disposition to reflect. Time, and its inevitable lack, are major constraints to constructive reflection. Thus, a second key structural component enhancing constructive reflection is the two-year program. One third-year teacher remembered, "At the end of the second year, one of the assignments was to read my journals through from the beginning. I kind of knew I learned a lot, but I couldn't believe some of the things I thought and how much I had grown."

A third key program feature enhancing the constructive nature of reflection is DTE's emphasis on writing. One program faculty member commented, "We have always had students do much writing—but it is much more important now. We do weekly response journals; five papers in the Development course. People grow as writers in the program and this is a key because writing is a key to reflection." One graduate agreed, noting that journals, "served as an opportunity to bounce off my own thinking. I can really see it when I look back through my journals." A second-year student noted the value of the journals in helping him to understand the relationships between his field experiences and the core seminars: "I can make the connections in the classrooms to the 211's [the human development sequence]. The reflective journal helped me do that."

A fourth program component enhancing constructive reflection is the small cohort which enforces collaboration. In the intense two years they share, students, in the words of one graduate, "have to stay together or die." Several graduates likened their cohort bond to family. Over two years, students definitely come to know each other and become close. Hugs are regularly exchanged, celebrations for life events are common class experiences (e.g., an "auntie" party for a first time aunt). A graduate reflected, "The other thing that helps the constant processing is the small program and the shared experience. We could really share. We had the same classes, the same readings—but different classrooms and we were different people—so the sharing was opened."

DTE's use of journals to promote reflections illustrates how they use these four components supportively. Each week, students write up two events relating to their growth as teachers. In addition, they write a weekly summary examining their development over the course of the week. Students are informed that they should schedule four hours per week to complete their journal writings. Students make two copies of each journal entry—one for themselves and one for the program. On occasion, one of the two "critical incidents" from the week is replaced with a program-assigned topic (e.g., peer observation write-up, educational autobiography, classroom newsletter to parents, school-community observation, analysis of the role of holidays in the curriculum, etc.) The act of writing and receiving weekly feedback from supervisors and peers leading to sustained written dialogue enhances both writing and reflection. In addition, the program uses the time available by assigning students the task of re-reading their entries at different stages throughout the two years and asking students to write their reflections on their growth and goals. Finally, the program recently introduced "peer journalings" where one of the journal assignments each week is read by a student colleague and that colleague responds in writing rather than the supervisor. This approach both takes advantage of the cohort's collaboration and expands collaboration among students.

**Program Pedagogy**

Program courses follow the "student teacher as teacher" principle. As teachers, the students in the program share responsibility for the learning that takes place in the courses. Sometimes they take on the actual teaching in the form of student presentations of core curriculum during class sessions. For instance, students prepare and present handouts, lectures, and class activities to cover the readings in the third course of the human development seminar sequence. In the Teaching Linguistic and Cultural Minority Students course, students make presentations both on core curriculum content (e.g., different cultures and what "every teacher should know about that culture") as well as open each class with a review of the salient points from the previous class session.

Their shaping of the curriculum itself often takes place through written feedback provided at the end of a class, which becomes the curriculum for the next class session. The second core seminar, for instance, began one class session with the instructor announcing, "I am going to focus on the issues you e-mailed to me on using literature to foster social and ethical development." Another way the students shape the curriculum (e.g., take on the teaching role) is by completing charts in which the gaps become the content of the course. For instance, again from the Multicultural and Bilingual Education course, students complete a chart on the first day of class listing the pros and cons of the rationale for bilingual education on each of the following items: linguistic, economic, political, psychological, cultural, religious, and educational.

The answers the students provided, as well as the answers they did not provide, created the curriculum for the instructor. In the final class session, she used the chart as the closing review for the course.

Instructors also make their pedagogical decisions and processes visible to students. They often reflect actively and overtly on their own historical and in-the-moment practices, sharing their thoughts on how, why, and what they should be teaching. For instance, after an extensive class discussion arising from a student's question regarding when she should follow the children's interests and when she should bring them "back on task," the instructor summarized the discussion by saying,

> I face this in this class. It is a constant dilemma you face and will always face. My guideline, taken from my reading of Gardner, is that the most important goal is the need and ability to understand. Given that, then in-depth class time is doing that, developing your ability through careful inquiry that pushes for understanding. I keep that goal in mind when making my decisions whether to stay or to move on.

The combination of students' shared responsibility for pedagogy and the instructor's willingness to make it visible to students leads to more than a trickle-down effect with graduates. A common marker of DTE graduates' classrooms is the use of "What I Know and Want to Know" charts—the elementary school equivalent of the charts used in the Multicultural and Bilingual Education course. In one third-grade classroom, the DTE graduate opened the day reading the questions the students had written at the end of the previous day. She did not, however, answer them. The students did.

# PROGRAM THEMES

## Change

Given the institutional and personal constraints on change, the evolutionary changes in the DTE Program over time are nothing short of remarkable. These changes are not just "tinkering," but constitute both significant midcourse and year-to-year improvements. The notion of constant development does not, in Berkeley's case, mean flitting about from one notion of teaching and learning to another. Over the past decade, the program has focused its changes in several areas (generated from its own inquiry and experience, as well as from an advisory committee of K-12 and college-based educators):

- designing supports for cooperating teachers (see description of supports in this report);
- increasing the number of students of color and students coming from low socio-economic backgrounds;
- enhancing students' abilities to work effectively with learners and parents from increasingly diverse communities.

DTE's efforts in the latter two categories are continuing long-term efforts based on the assumption that the best recruitment strategy is to provide educational experiences that recommend the program to students of color. Over time, the DTE student population has become more representative of the student population in schools. In this way, DTE students, as a cohort, have become increasingly capable of working with program faculty to enact educational experiences that enhance their abilities to work effectively with learners and parents from diverse communities. For instance, in the year following this case study, four first-year DTE students led a series of supervisory group sessions "aimed at assumption-busting," using the literature on white privilege as their starting point. One program faculty member noted, "We have more and more students who are prepared to do anti-bias work and using a multi-ethnic cohort of students to facilitate this growth has been very effective."

Describing DTE is like shooting at a moving target, because the inquiry never stops. As Ammon and Hutcheson (1989) write,

> We are still learning . . . how best to use the additional time to support teacher development. Our learning in that regard—or, if you will, our own development as teacher educators—derives from

two kinds of activity: 1) our day-to-day work with student teachers, and 2) our efforts to engage in more formal investigations of teacher development. . . . All of us—both teachers and teacher educators alike—need help from research in order to arrive at more useful understandings of our students. The problem for us in DTE, though, is that we mainly have to help ourselves, because—despite the recent interest in teacher cognition and teacher development—there still is no well established body of research on adult cognitive development in the domain of principal interest to us, i.e., the domain of developmental pedagogy.

## History

One way to understand DTE's current changes is to look at its history of change. In the early 1970s, the Graduate School of Education at Berkeley had nearly three dozen long-term supervisors and instructors (adjunct faculty) who, over time, had become more and more separate and unequal from regular faculty. External reviews of the programs, (e.g., by state accreditation teams) consistently raised the issue of this separation. In addition, and perhaps equally tellingly, the need for new teachers declined and graduates were not getting hired.

In the mid-70s, several faculty members who had been teaching the required Ed Psych course shared their frustration with each other. "Two weeks for development is ridiculous," these developmental psychologists preached to themselves. If they were to put together a teacher-education program, their "first order of business would be to put some substance to teacher education." A subset of these faculty members, Paul Ammon, Nadine Lambert, and Elliot Turiel sat down and asked, "What would a program look like if it centered around a core of child development?" Their first answer was that it could not be done in a one-year program. "Now, remember," reminisced one of the three, "none of us had really been involved in teacher education before." As the 70s slipped into the 80s, the GSE recommended discontinuing teacher education entirely.

Following a protracted purging of programs, a sentiment arose that "the onus is on us to be in line with what Berkeley should be doing if it will be doing it at all." Turiel, Lambert, and Ammon stepped up and offered to teach the core courses. Black joined in the first year as the program's coordinator. He was hired because he was a good developmental psychologist. He had no background in teacher education and he had to work to become a teacher educator. His development was a key, however, because the general view of history is "Black made it work." According to Ammon, he (Ammon) backed into the leadership role because the GSE required someone in the academic senate (e.g., having a tenure-track position) to take on the role. He has never requested nor received release time for the role yet was quick to point out that the role certainly did count towards his advancement. Over time, he, like Black, grew to want to know more about what was going on in the program and together they initiated a line of research on teacher development. As Amarel (1989) notes, this core group's remarkable stability enhanced program change:

> The DTE was developed by a group of faculty who were interested in giving a developmental perspective more weight in teacher education and undertook to plan and implement such a program. This initial group remained remarkably stable, collaborating in the evolution of the program for the past eight [now 18] years.

Despite initial fears that two years and intellectual demands would scare away applicants, over time, DTE found its niche within the Berkeley environment. The reputation of the program grew, and the applicants came. If you build a quality teacher education program, the lesson seems to be, the students will come.

**Research and Inquiry**

As noted above, DTE changed and continues to change based upon research as well as inquiry into its day-to-day practices. The research not only probes into the program but also follows program graduates. One faculty member outlined his view of the key questions in these complementary lines of research:

> How do we narrow the gap between sufficient and necessary conditions? In other words, how do we understand not just developmental pathways but how to facilitate that development—especially in math, science, and language. Secondly, how do we develop an epistemology of teacher development? We are not at

a curriculum-stage theory yet. The question is, How do you structure the environment for teacher learning? We have a start here with some principles we have discovered though . . . recursion and the integration of different perspectives such as development, pedagogical studies, practice. We have been working, and will continue to work, assiduously on these questions.

The fact that research is conducted regarding the program and its graduates is an obvious factor supporting change in DTE. It is of equal importance, however, that the program is an open system. Some faculty argue that this is so because DTE students are always in field placements. Another key factor here is a basic disposition of excellent teachers at any level which DTE faculty share. A key disposition for an elementary teacher is to be intrigued by what intrigues a child. Key DTE faculty members, in strong enough numbers to be a critical mass, are equally intrigued by what intrigues developing teachers. This, too, drives change and the program's unquenchable thirst for excellence. A former supervisor and currently an elementary school principal, commented of the program, "It is changed so totally I hardly recognize it in some ways. All the changes are so totally driven by what the students need and want."

DTE students learn from this modeling of inquiry. Over 93 percent of the surveyed graduates reported feeling very well prepared to "engage in self-evaluation and improvement through reflection on successes and failures." Over 96 percent reported feeling "well" or "very well" prepared to "interpret and utilize research related to teaching."

### Vignette: Teacher-Education Practice

Like all educators who allow race, class, and ethnic issues to surface authentically, DTE faculty struggle personally and with their students with the charged tensions posed by these issues in this society as they surface in the classroom. In a supervisor's meeting, an African-American woman supervisor commented on a lesson she observed: "The student needed help on being firm and direct and not being afraid of her actions being racist." The coordinator responded,

It is as if our students need somebody of color to authorize them, give them their power of judgment. It bears a conversation, probably in supervisory group. We've almost ignored race, but now when we have vowed not to ignore it anymore, we're almost stepping back. . . . They seem to be scared of the kids, scared of their own racism, scared of cultural differences.

The timing of the supervisory meeting where the above comments were exchanged added to their intensity. Immediately following the meeting, the total cohort tried to raise a discussion of race and class issues phoenix-like from the ashes of the previous session's failed attempt. Following her own inquiry into the failed class discussion, the coordinator e-mailed her thoughts and plans to the students:

> Two weeks ago in 390 we tried, with little success, to discuss *Life On The Color Line.* Everyone left the room with a great deal of frustration and with many questions about what went wrong. It was a dramatic illustration of how overpoweringly difficult it is, even for articulate, well-intentioned people, to discuss race in a group setting.
>
> There are two issues here which we must address: 1) the content of the discussion; 2) the format of the discussion. Both are important.
>
> The first will be the focus of 390 this Tuesday. It is my impression that we have all given a lot of thought to the experience and that many substantive personal conversations have resulted. We would like to build on these to meaningfully address the very relevant pedagogical issues raised by Williams.
>
> At the beginning of class you will have a few minutes to note (in writing) a critical incident from the book which most affected you and to think of an event (or a silence) in your own background which you have thought about since reading the book. We will then have discussions in pairs, followed by foursomes. Supervisors and I will all participate.
>
> The second issue will be addressed by repeating the topic in a different format. You may use journals and/or your supervisory

groups for more detailed comparison of the two sessions. . . . I look forward to working together with you to keep developing our collective potential. Till Tuesday.

In the second attempt at discussing race in a group setting, the program coordinator led students through the process she had outlined in advance to help students relate their reading of *Life On The Color Line* to their own lives and to their chosen career. The weather was hot. The small room was windowless and close. Quickly, heat and intensity brought sweat. Following individual, small group, and whole group processing, several students, with more than a trace of annoyance, wondered why not everyone was participating. The group labored in response and the result, at times, seemed less a coherent conversation than a series of individuals speaking across each other from deep out of their own experiences with the issues of race:

> Coordinator: I don't agree with the notion that it is too early to raise these issues, that we have not bonded yet. It is always going to be hard. We cannot blame folks for their assumptions. We have to get them out. Many of us have grown up thinking the police are benevolent or at least benign. But many of us grew up knowing that was false in our experience.

> Student 1 (to her peers): Did you not read the same book? We are trying to be deep and multicultural and we can't even have a discussion. You guys have a choice to discuss. People of color don't have a choice. We live with it 24 hours a day.

> Student 2: It made me feel pity, anger, and guilt. The whole thing made me feel guilty and wonder if I can ever work with children of color. How do I find them? Where are they? How do I take them with me? It is scary, sad, and depressing.

> Student 1: When we feel discriminated against, how do we respond? When and why are we capable of responding? We have to take a look at our surroundings every time we enter a room. Think about how the kids feel.

Student 3: I feel like I cannot function in this society with the values I have. So, what do we tell our students? The world ain't safe for them and it ain't gonna change in my lifetime?

Student 4: Should we teach as we wish the world was or as the world is? It is every African-American's parents' dilemma. What's the ultimate goal? What are we preparing kids for?

Coordinator: Truth, and you will be chipping away at it all your life.

Student 1: Try not to intellectualize so much. Let it hit you in the heart, not in the head. Forget the theory for a while. Genuineness will always come across. Have a heart for the kids. Feel the pain.

In some ways, nothing happened as a result of the class meeting. The discussion did not resolve racism, did not construct "ism-free" pedagogy. Yet in other ways, the discussion in and of itself was a happening of significance. This type of discussion, conducted with an intensity written words cannot convey, is only possible because of the racial mix of the cohort, the extensive time together, and the commitments of all involved. Given enough of such racially heterogeneous conversations, perhaps there will be less talking across, and more talking with, each other from deep experiences with the issues of race. Still, it was visibly difficult for the two African Americans in the room who were put into a position of speaking for their race. It is, however, the only way knowledge will be recreated and it does take pain. There are insiders and outsiders and those groups (for a multitude of reasons) have become calcified, which exacerbates the natural tendency to feel comfortable with one's in-group and to fear one's out-groups. Teachers must learn to listen to their "out-group" students, and teacher educators must structure opportunities for prospective teachers to feel safe enough to open up those conversations and develop those skills. The episode also highlights the balance of socio-cultural and developmental components within DTE. Development, as DTE conceives it, is neither psychologistic nor culture-free.

Following the group meeting, a core-seminar instructor and program founder took the observer aside from the sharing of tears and hugs with which the class terminated and commented,

> It became clear 10 years ago that we would have two foci: development, which we had always had, and multicultural. Multiculturalism had to come because the students are in the schools all the time. The program initiated in theory, primarily Piaget, then multicultural-cultural issues arose from the constructivist/developmental practice we were asking of our students. The issue now is to integrate the two in a significant theoretical way.

### Student as Worker

DTE believes that "teachers must acquire expertise as curriculum developers, not merely as curriculum managers." This requires that its students "analyze how knowledge is acquired in all domains, along with the specific steps in knowledge acquisition within domains of knowledge encountered in schools" (Kroll and Black, 1993, p. 418). As noted earlier, this consists of linking content, pedagogy, and the child. Conceptually, structurally, and pedagogically, DTE is designed for its students to differentiate and integrate ideas within and between these three areas. As Kroll and Black (1993) note, curriculum developers historically "have attempted to introduce changes in educational practices by constructing developmentally appropriate curriculum for teachers rather than by providing teachers with the theoretical knowledge necessary to understand the inadequacies of existing curricula and to construct or implement viable alternatives for themselves" (p. 418).

As one of the founding faculty members explained,

> We broke out of the model of one half of a program being the classes and then one half of the program being the student teaching. We do it all at once and always will. For instance, we will always constantly vary placements. This is not a 'copy' theory but rather the romantic idea of developing one's own philosophy and style through seeing many philosophies in action. It is an individualist constructivist approach.

The work of that construction is the student's. One graduate put it this way:

The core seminar faculty don't claim to know how to teach—only how kids develop. It was our job to make that connection (especially in supervisory group). With the placement, we could always go out and see it and learn how to do it.

Another graduate seconded the notion that it was her work to put it together:

There is a large emphasis on theory. But they tell you , 'You're smart enough to figure out how to apply it.' You're constructing it. You're figuring it out. You have to be willing to let go of the need for answers and not to be confused.

A first-year student, with equal traces of annoyance and pride, put it quite simply: "They tell us to do it, but not how to do it."

Perhaps the best illustration of this student construction within the program is the program's pedagogy of choice. By conceiving of students as participating co-learners in classes, program faculty provide structured and supportive environments for students to construct the knowledge and skills necessary for the kinds of learner- and learning-centered environments DTE envisions for school children. For instance, after reading student questions from the previous week, the core seminar instructor asked how the students would answer their own questions. In another session, a student asked why the provided curriculum required grade school students to read the directions and the story twice and wondered if other student teachers followed the curriculum as written.

Student 1: Did you read the directions and the story twice?

Student 2: It was different directions so I read them several times.

Student 3: That's what I did, too.

Student 4: That didn't work with my 5 year olds. I paced and had discussions as we went along. I just didn't know if the students would sit still for it.

Student 5: Yeah, I was afraid to read it twice so I split it over two days. I set it up by asking if they had ever read a story twice. They said, 'Yes' and gave lots of examples. Then I said, 'Great, because we're going to do it.' (Laughter) It worked great because their interpretations were trivial after the first read and after the second read they were much deeper.

Student 6: I was scared, too, so what I did was use the same author with the same theme, but a different story.

Without the instructor saying a word, the students heard multiple and grounded perspectives on content, practice, and the developmental levels of children. Program classes especially put this pedagogy to work in "answering" pedagogical questions from students. In the more theoretical courses, the instructors do not wait for students to ask for a practical application. Instructors ask the students first. This happens in several ways. One has simply to ask: "You can think of hundreds of applications for this. You're the experts here. Tell me a couple," or, "How would you do this with younger kids? Response: Reduce the variables. Response: Increase the structure with slightly more explicit directions."

Another method consists of providing actual student worksheets and asking students to analyze their developmental appropriateness for different age groups (and also to compare and contrast those answers with the scope and sequence of the classes they are teaching). Still another method involves looking at math texts and tests and predicting the percentage of students who would answer the problems in them correctly following a specific type of (pedagogically appropriate) learning activity. Regardless of the approach, students do the linking of theory and practice. The effectiveness of this approach is enhanced when the instructors fire a pre-emptive strike—asking students for practical applications before students can ask the instructors.

This type of pedagogy requires a deep and abiding faith in one's students. That faith, though rewarded, demands difficult and sometimes frustrating labor of the students, just as teaching does for teachers. The increasing ability of DTE students to perform this intense labor is evident in how they talk about it over time.

First year student (May): I guess I had a hard time thinking on my feet. I didn't know what to do with their understandings and connections. . . . I am mired by developmental discipline and developmental theory. Developmentally, I hate even saying that word, I don't know. I am trying to work stages into everything but I may be too stuck—tacking myself to something that's not going to work. . . . I feel I am treating my students like guinea pigs and that the guinea-pig syndrome will go on for a long time. It is going to take forever to know kids and all the variables. . . . I am not going to be prepared. My stress level is intense in trying to put it all together.

Conversation between first- and second-year students (May):

First-year student: There is always so much responsibility on us. . . . DTE asks you to be so thoughtful. It is unrelenting. I need to collapse. That's a toughness I didn't expect.

Second-year student: In the beginning I felt I had to be perfect. I have moved out of that. I am going to make tons of mistakes. I am never going to be super perfect. That's OK.

First-year student: The program has systematically shown me . . . that it is hard.

Second-year student: I've gone through being overwhelmed— thinking I can't be a teacher. I've come to realize I have some strengths. I can do this.

First-year teacher (February): It is the getting everything flowing developmentally. Reading and writing I have done this year—sometimes. I just let Marilyn Burns do my work for me sometimes in math. She's done it already. I lean on a lot of people. I can't do everything at once.

Third-year teacher (June): DTE treated us as intellectually intelligent people. They expected us to understand. . . . Teachers should know what to be looking for in lessons, in kids—what they are learning and what they understand.

The program does, however, support students through this work. It is not a case of each individual student wandering in the desert until he/she chances upon an oasis of understanding. As one graduate said, "It is a pain in the [body part], but good. Yes, you have to put it together, but they help you." Program content and pedagogy provide support. In addition, the structural features of time, recursion, reflection, collaboration, and constant and varying field placements all play a role. One faculty member laid out several supports for a frustrated student:

The answer is usually, 'You have to figure it out.' But we cannot just let it go at that. We may not know how to do it but we will provide a space to work on it together. And some of our supervisors can help you integrate what faculty says and what teachers do and some of our graduates will show you how they do it.

Additionally, program faculty will provide an occasional answer or two—usually in response to first-year student requests such as, "Just give us some tools so we're not lost all the time." A program founder explained:

When they come and find out it is hard, we will give them an answer sometimes, but we never let it go at that. We engage in dialogue about why it is the right answer. That is especially what the journal writing is about: 'Why am I doing this? Why did that happen?'

Of course, idealistic teachers, prospective and experienced, put intense pressure on themselves. Sometimes, program faculty support students by helping them maintain their commitment, but remember the virtue of patience. One course instructor nearly demanded, "You need to give yourselves a break . . . lighten up. These are opportunities for controlled failure. Try things and see how they work. You are all keen observers. In this instance, you were adjustable and flexible. Your changes were not failures but appropriate decisions."

Students and graduates identify a common process that program faculty (school- and college-based) used to support them in their labors, "a real genuine willingness to let you flop and then [to] support you." They also distilled the following list of school- and college-based faculty personal traits from which students benefited: humanity, responsiveness, cheerleading, frank ability to tell you hard things, and willingness to seek you out, to be proactive, to say, "Let's talk about this."

To exhibit these personal traits, program faculty have to understand teacher development, the content of teacher education, and multiple pedagogical approaches—and they have to meld these understandings together in the service of their students. They have to be what they want their students to become. In addition, at Berkeley, a tier one research institution, they have to create and share their new understandings in the form of research.

Just as the program is demanding of students, it is also demanding of faculty. The coordinator's time for e-mail with students begins at 6:00 a.m. daily. In order to respond to student questions, one core-seminar instructor asked students to, "put them into the little box on top of the file cabinet in the DTE office; I'll read them over the weekend." When asked if this was a sustainable model, a program founder commented that to do anything well requires a consuming passion—a passion that does not know the meaning of a time clock. Here, the intrigue that drove program faculty to develop and constantly revise the program continues to drive their efforts. The coordinator commented of one core seminar instructor, "This is going to be her research agenda for life." In many ways, the program design reflects, and program faculty live, the Persian proverb, "Let the beauty in what you love, be what you do."

## DILEMMAS

### Teacher Education Within a Research University

DTE is a product of its residence within the context of the University of California at Berkeley. It began as an attempt to create an appropriate teacher-education program for a prestigious research institution. It has been sustained by spawning a viable and valuable line of research. It has influenced, as the university mission mandates, other teacher education programs through impact on state policy. For instance, the use of multiple placements and some background in human development are now state requirements. The program also influences other teacher education through the education its supervisors receive. An exemplary teacher-education program at nearby Wells College, whose core faculty received their graduate education and their introduction into teacher education at Berkeley, is referred to in the area as "daughter of DTE." An instructor/supervisor highlighted in this study was recently hired by Trinity University in San Antonio—another exemplary teacher education program included in this series of studies—and so it goes.

In addition, the very nature of the students' experience is perhaps uniquely Berkelerian. DTE enacts a professional curriculum within an academic tradition requiring empirical testing and a refined theoretical frame. It begins with, and flows through, an intellectual core rather than clusters of methods courses followed by practice. Nor is the program primarily "field based," as the term has come to be defined elsewhere— although students are in field placements throughout the program. It does not derive its content or pedagogy from the normative practices present in most schools or from practice divorced from research and theory. The program provides more time (e.g., courses, placements in schools, assignments spread out over two years) but greater abstract-conceptual demands. Given these differences, what from DTE is of value in the very different kinds of contexts in which a vast majority of teachers receive their preparation? Amarel (1989) posed the question eloquently,

> Is the DTE transportable, is it a plausible model for the planning of other programs? Transplanting educational programs has proven a chance undertaking. The confluence of factors that supported the development of DTE are unlikely to be duplicated elsewhere, but they may not be essential for realizing a program that has conceptual integrity and that evolves in response to the reflection and inquiry that are built into the program. (p. 34)

Graduates were adamant that the issue for students is not intelligence but commitment. Nevertheless, the graduates were also quick to point out institutional issues that impacted the program. One graduate from the early 90s focused on standards and finances:

> I was concerned about the young white middle-class cohort. Is that who we want in schools? But it comes with the "standards"

for academics at Berkeley, the admissions requirements and the expense. I have to pay $400 in student loans each month. The sacrifices required to become a teacher are just wrong.

This graduate also spoke of a dissonance she felt between DTE and the Berkeley environment in which it resides—the contrast between an egalitarian "all children will learn" program within an institution based upon a "best and the brightest only" elitism. Some of that dissonance can be heard in the comment of a founding member who recalled that in the beginning, "Working with the CTC (Commission on Teacher Credentialling, a state agency) was easier than working with the GSE at Berkeley." In most regards, state credentialing policies have been, at worst, a benign influence and at best, a support for the goals of DTE. For instance, when DTE designed a two-year program and state law limited teacher education programs to one academic year, they requested and received "experimental program" status from the CTC. Here, the state had a policy mechanism that allowed an accountably innovative program to "do its thing."

A final related issue has two components. First is the basic tension between the demands of a research orientation and the demands of a professional preparation orientation. For instance, discussing institutional support for the program, the coordinator noted, "We would get more resources if I wrote grants and published more about the program but it is so difficult to balance doing it and writing about it. . . . (It's) a career buster because of the time and labor involved."

The second component is that, for a period of time, DTE found "research faculty" with the ability, inclination, talent, and time to meld those two orientations—the "confluence of factors" to which Amarel referred. The program's success in this area is exemplified by the bibliography of research papers and presentations generated by DTE and written by those actively engaged in the program (see Appendix C). In the past several years, however, three of the four core-faculty members have left the program. A worry persists that DTE may end up a conceptually sound program with good students, but that eroding support from ladder faculty will signal its demise. Is a teacher-education program at a prestigious research institution a serendipitous "Camelot moment in time" that is ultimately not sustainable?

The remaining core member put a positive spin on the turnover in key personnel: "Retirements opened up possibilities." The GSE, he pointed out, is committed to hiring new professors who commit to professional education. The problem, so far, is that it has proved difficult to locate "stars in their academic field" with that interest and with the commitment to the time and labor-intensive work of professional preparation. A related problem, according to another faculty member, is that Berkeley looks for Nobel Prize winners and "There aren't too many Nobel Prize winners in teacher education." Still, the search continues.

The program also aims to involve well-established research faculty currently at Berkeley. The involvement of such faculty as Pedro Noguera (urban education), Judith Warren-Little (teacher inquiry and leadership), and Lilly Wong Fillmore (bilingual education) are promising signs in this regard. Interestingly, the "newcomers" have different (e.g., not development) research interests and therefore bring a different flavor to their work with DTE students. As faculty with other research interests assume programmatic leadership roles in the program in the years to come, it may very well be that DTE becomes something quite different.

A second outcome of teacher education in a research institution is that another group of research faculty may, following DTE's lead, create their own teacher-education program. For instance, Alan Schoenfeld and other math-education-oriented ladder faculty have created another teacher-education program focusing on their research interests. That teacher-education program, although possessing a different conceptual frame (mathematics thinking versus human development), a different area of preparation (secondary versus elementary school teachers), and different ladder faculty, can be considered an offspring of DTE. Or perhaps more appropriately, DTE could be considered the older sibling descended from a common institutional parent. Both created a niche for teacher education within a research institution.

### Graduates At Risk

The world students experience within DTE is very different from the world most encounter as they begin their teaching careers. The transition is often painful and traumatic. One founding faculty member worries,

> I want them to be teachers, strong teachers, and make it a good life for them. But our ethical dilemma is, are we setting them up for burn-out? The ones who keep going have colleagues who

think the same way, who are trying to do the same thing. The program teaches that teaching is not a solitary activity, that teachers learn from and support each other.

Because the work environment of many teachers does not subscribe to this notion of the teacher, many program faculty fear they are putting their graduates "at risk." For better or for worse, schools are often not developmentally appropriate environments for adult learning or teacher development. As one third-year graduate commented, "I do wish I had someone around who understood what I was trying to do." Another lamented, "I learned collaboration is necessary and how to do it. DTE pushes collaboration but I didn't take those 20 people with me into the school." Still, Susan, a first-year teacher working in a challenging urban setting [with glistening eyes and a slow, husky voice] when asked where she gets her support to continue, responded:

> A couple of teachers will recognize what I am trying to do and comment on it. . . . Friends pat me on the back and that drives me crazy. It overwhelms (my fiancee's and my) life. . . . I can't imagine being alive after five years of this. . . . I feel completely misunderstood.

In June, this first-year teacher was released because she was on a one-year contract. She phoned the researcher because he "was the only person who was in my classroom this year." However, following a protracted period of decision making, Susan chose to remain in teaching and located a position in a neighboring (urban and still "challenging") district.

Adding to the difficulty of the mismatch between the educational environment provided for teachers at DTE and that provided for teachers at most schools is the level of commitment DTE graduates bring to children. If graduates had a common complaint about the program it would be the need for more help in understanding and working through their own passions.

One graduate began to tell the story of one child and a violent day he had. "You know they are in pain and you want to help them." She told how she spoke with him and tried to draw out his anger and pain. Her eyes began to tear and she could not continue. When capable, she continued,

It is trying to meet the needs of children emotionally and being aware of what's going on in their lives and how that affects their work and their learning. . . . I am providing the best I can, the safest environment for learning. I am very happy and pleased with that. Still, it pains me. I can't even fathom what they go through. . . . They get nothing in this society.

The issue here is not that DTE does not prepare teachers for their first-year of teaching. The evidence is clear and irrefutable: it does. DTE has certainly not failed because it nurtures high expectations for the teaching profession. The graduates are certainly not failures because they continue to care so passionately. The issue is that teacher education does not end when one is very well prepared for one's first year of teaching or with one's first paid position as a teacher. This reality, and the need for constructive learning conditions for children and adults in schools, is not reflected in either policy or practice.

One program founder has made it his personal crusade to see this changed. He has been active at the state level in linking expectations for beginning teachers with the conditions of work and learning that make meeting those expectations possible. In addition, he has taken on the co-chair position in a legislative mandated commission to totally redesign the state's credentialing system—including induction support as an integral thread in a seamless web of professional licensing policy and practice. The payoff for his efforts is seen in the practice of DTE graduates and the successes of their students.

## SUMMARY
### Vignette of First-Year Practice

Susan is a first-year teacher in San Francisco. The neighborhood immediately surrounding the school is classic San Francisco three-story townhouses with, usually, separate households on each floor. Housing in the area is much more expensive than the school population can afford. "The kids in the school cannot afford to live in the neighborhood. They are bused in from the projects. The neighborhood kids go to private schools."

The school where Susan works was "reconstituted" this year by court order. She explains, "All the teachers are new to the school, and a teacher with three years experience is considered a senior teacher. The principal is new to the school and has only one year previous experience as a teacher." The school serves approximately 420 students with a staff of about 20 teachers. The student population is approximately 45 percent African American, 45 percent Latino, seven percent recent immigrant Asian American, and three percent European American. At the beginning of the year, standardized test scores indicated only two or three marginally independent readers among Susan's fifth graders. Her assessments indicated the same.

Susan always knew she wanted to teach in the inner city and tailored her DTE experience toward this goal, but is still tormented by the extremes of her environment.

> It isn't the practicalities, but the psychological impact on me. . . . You never know what happens the night before or on the bus ride. I often stop the entire curriculum to resolve conflicts. It is something that happens, usually, on the playground or in the cafeteria—racial slurs, play fights turning into real fights, somebody saying something bad about their family. Not teaching the curriculum is really teaching the curriculum.

> More and more I am able to step back—not feeling so driven to make everything OK in the moment. I don't want to control, but feel like I am learning when to step in, intervene, or when just to set an example. It is when I go home that I can't decide what's my fault and what's their fault. Then when I come in the next morning we reflect together.

Susan's class has the same feel as those of other DTE graduates reflecting the on-going work and learning of the students. The room contains five rectangular tables with cubbies sitting on them, a reading corner with pillows and carpet, and a carpeted area for class meetings. Like other DTE graduates' classrooms, Susan's possesses a different richness at different heights. What one sees at adult standing level is amplified by an entirely different set of visuals at desk level, and again at floor level, and yet again at a lying-on-the-floor level. It is as if each level uncovers another layer of the essential humanity that unfolds in the room.

Susan enters the building with her class following the mandatory whole-school assembly held on the asphalt postage-stamp playground each morning. There is order to their entry but it is not linear. Susan touches base with each student and defuses possibly stressful situations as they climb the stairs to their third-story classroom in the traditional egg-crate school building.

A girl complains about the behavior of the boy standing behind her. Susan asks, "Are you willing to give him another chance if he promises not to do it again?" The student responds "No." Susan speaks privately with the boy and he apologizes. The complainer smiles and all seems right with her world. She hears that the girl's basketball team won their game last night—a "grudge match" against a team that had beaten them the last time. The interactions are quiet, contained, and without a trace of public humiliation. Upon entering the room, each individual in the class is in control of his or her behavior.

On the board at the adult standing level, which is the same as student level for these fifth graders, are specific, immediate directions for how to begin the day and the daily schedule. As Susan puts on a tape of music, the class focuses on the immediate directions and sets to work without a word from the teacher. The directions are:

> FIRST THINGS
> Put Everything Away
> Take Out Your Diary and Your Math Homework
> By Time Music Stops—Reading Only
> Meet with your partner
> Read until 9:50
> Then Discuss or Write-in Response (your choice but partners must come to an agreement)

The students whisper to each other that when the music is turned off they should be in readers workshop. Within four minutes the homework is collected, corrected, and feedback provided to each student. All the partners are on task. First one student reads aloud while the other follows along and helps as needed. They rarely interrupt the reader and never leap in before reader had the opportunity to work through the stumbling block word/phrase. Then they switch roles. Some of the titles they are reading include: *The Magician's Nephew; Sweet Grass; Just a Few Words Mr. Lincoln;* and *Finding Buck McHenry.* Students brag to each other of their reading accomplishments; "I'm gonna read this whole page," or "I've almost read this whole book."

Students choose their own books. Susan provides "exploration time" each month in which students list the books they might like to read. She uses those lists for assessment purposes as well as for helping students select their next books. At least once every other week she uses a running-record-type reading analysis with each student using a rubric she has developed. Twenty minutes into class Susan gives them the five-minute warning. They read through the warning and the five minutes. Susan beams a comment of pride to the observer.

When she stops their reading 10 minutes after the appointed time, students move to the rug at the front of the room for "Tribe Circle" in less than 30 seconds, without fuss. Following a class meeting on the rug where they analyze how well reading went, and do a manipulation-based math lesson on multiplying fractions, Susan sits on a tall chair in front of the group to read from *The Air Down Here*. She waits for silence before speaking, a common classroom management strategy. Students pick up on it within seconds. Another common strategy is a "tone-of-voice" infraction—given with her best referee's voice when a student's tone, tenor, or volume exceeds classroom standards.

Susan stops reading after several paragraphs and asks a question about the topic of the section she had just read—peer pressure. From this topic, the class begins to touch upon the notion of intrinsic rewards—which is about all they can see of value that comes from not succumbing to peer pressure. She pushes the group to bring the concept to their own experience:

| | |
|---|---|
| Susan: | Let's talk about this classroom, right here. Why do you stop yourselves in here? |
| Student: | So I don't get in trouble. |
| Susan: | Do you get anything for doing the right thing? Something that you value? |
| Student: | Friendship. |
| Student: | More PE time. |
| Student: | Not getting beat up. |

Later in the day, two boys vying for leadership get into a verbal spat where each has to top the other. For the only time that day, Susan speaks with an edge in her voice:

Stop! Stop! Stop! I don't want to hear it. You're not interested in what you have to say. You're just trying to get into a fight and we're not interested in folks getting into fights. There is nothing so frustrating as watching people who know how to resolve conflicts and get along get into a capping match and not use their skills. You are just going back and forth with the snotiest comments you can think of. Somebody has to give in or it doesn't stop. Only time or kindness can break that cycle.

After lunch the class engages in silent reading. Again, music is playing. The class will be writing a skit with a civil rights theme based upon the song. The two boys who verbally sparred with each other earlier in the day are sitting together. They read silently but lean against each other as they do so.

Towards the end of the day, the class again gathers on the rug for singing. Each student uses a song book which, like everything else described about Susan's classroom, develops reading ability. Students ask questions directed to Susan but most are answered by another student. Susan jokes, "Here you are answering all your own questions. You don't need me." As she strums her guitar, she explains the acoustical science of it in response to further questions. The final song they sing is "The Circle Game."

Yesterday a child came out to wonder
Caught a dragon fly inside a jar
Fearful when the sky was full of thunder
And tearful at the falling of a star
(chorus)
And the seasons, they go round and round
Painted ponies go up and down
We're captive on a carousel of time
We can't return, we can only look
Behind from where we came
And go round and round and round in the circle game
(the song continues)

The day ends with "Congratulations." Susan asks students to:

> Put yourself in a quiet space and think about people who have
> really stretched themselves, who have taken risks to help them-
> selves and help the tribe. . . . Think about the people for whom
> it hasn't come easy. Think about the people who trusted the
> tribe to help them, to guide them.

More than a few of the students have grown up hard, living questions most of us are afraid to ask. Susan uses language-experience techniques to teach reading. The language experience stories she uses are not the class field trip but the lived questions of their lives. As Dewey proposed, Susan's class is not preparation for life, it is life itself—the carousel of time. In explanation for how these students have become readers in less than one year, six years into their formal schooling, Susan answers, "It is because everything is a lesson."

In "Congratulations," students congratulate another student on something she or he has accomplished in the past week. Susan writes the congratulations and then chooses a student to read aloud what she has written. These records of their accomplishments, collected over the year, grace an entire wall of the classroom.

The remarks this day are both individual oriented ("Risking going it alone." "Pushing through embarrassment to read aloud to the tribe") and group oriented ("Not giving up on each other"). Susan, and sometimes students, question each statement to analyze the nature of the stretch. "It is not the specific, it is the ongoing work. They keep trying. That's the amazing thing, don't you think?" The two sparring boys want to congratulate each other for learning that "getting along is harder, but more important, than winning a topping match." Throughout the lesson, the students lie in a circle on their stomachs, elbows on the ground, chins tucked into their hands, their heads centered inward facing the butcher paper upon which Susan is writing the words of their lives.

Susan says, just before the students leave the security of their circle, "You guys always make the mistake of proving that you are capable of extraordinary things."

# REFERENCES

Amarel, M. (1989). Some observations on a model of professional training: The developmental teacher education program. *The Genetic Epistemologist, 17* (4), 31-34.

Ammon, P. & Levin, B. (1993). Expertise in teaching from a developmental perspective: The developmental teacher education program at Berkeley. *Learning and individual differences, 5* (4), 319-326.

Ammon, P. & Hutcheson, B. P. (1989). Promoting the development of teachers' pedagogical conceptions. *The Genetic Epistemologist., 17* (4), 23-30.

Black, A., & Ammon, P. (1992). A developmental-constructivist approach to teacher education. *Journal of Teacher Education, 43* (5), 323-335.

Kroll, L., & Black, A. (1989). Developmental principles and organization of instruction for literacy: Observations of experienced teachers. *Genetic Epistemologist, 17* (4), 15-22.

Kroll, L., & Black, A. (1993). Developmental theory and teaching methods: A pilot study of a teacher education program. *The Elementary School Journal, 93* (4), 417-441.

# APPENDIX A: DATA COLLECTION

The bulk of the data was collected in three week-long site visits. The first site visit, in the fall of the 1995-96 academic year, focused on the structures and processes of the teacher-education program. Data collection techniques included:

- interviewing program faculty and support staff;
- becoming a student for the week (e.g., observing all the courses students attended);
- observing faculty/supervisor meetings;
- interviewing cooperating teachers and administrators;
- observing student teachers in their placements.

The second site visit, in the winter of the 1995-96 academic year, focused on program graduates. In this phase, the author corresponded with eight program graduates prior to observation to establish rapport, obtain general thoughts and feelings about their teacher preparation, and obtain baseline information regarding their teaching assignments and school context. The author then spent an entire day with four of the graduates in their classrooms and schools—interspersing a formal interview protocol with classroom observations and a form of stimulated recall interviewing (e.g., "Why did you do X? Where did you learn how to do X?"). This phase also included interviews with the site administrators who hired DTE graduates.

The third site visit, in the spring of the 1995-96 academic year, focused on students' perceptions of the program. Data collection techniques included focus-group interviews with students as well as further observations of college course work and student work in schools. The author also served as a participant observer during an interview session of the admissions process for the 1996-97 cohort.

The author reviewed numerous documents about the Developmental Teacher Education Program including:

- documentation prepared for the state's accreditation visit;
- research articles written about the program (see Appendix B for complete listing);
- syllabi for all of the courses;
- program description and brochures;

- guidelines and other communications with cooperating teachers;
- a sample of student work, including 15 master's theses.

The report also used the results of a survey administered by NCREST obtaining the perceptions of graduates on the caliber of their preparation tied to INTASC-compatible knowledge, skills, and dispositions required of successful beginning teachers.

Throughout the data-collection process, the author fed notes, thoughts, and drafts to program faculty and the observed graduates. Their oral and written responses served as another essential data source and analysis technique. This ongoing feedback both affirmed the accuracy of the final document and clarified the conceptual frames used to describe and analyze the program. The author sincerely hopes the time and labor that program faculty and graduates provided to the writing of this case study benefited the informants at least partially as much as it benefited the author.

Data collection techniques are summarized in the following table.

|  | Focus Group | Individual Interview | Observations | Document Review | Survey |
|---|---|---|---|---|---|
| Current Students | X |  | X | X |  |
| Graduates |  | X | X | X | X |
| College-Based Educators |  | X | X | X |  |
| School-Based Educators |  | X | X | X | X |
| Structures Processes | X | X | X | X |  |

# APPENDIX B: 1995-1996 DEVELOPMENTAL TEACHER EDUCATION PROGRAM

In the 1995-96 university catalogue, the Developmental Teacher Education Program looked like this:

### Year One—Semester One

EP 211A: .................................Human Development and Education—Cognitive and Language Development

EMST 235: ..............................Elementary Teaching in Math and Science

ELL 158: .................................Foundations in Reading

EP 390C: .................................First Year Supervised Teaching

### Year One—Semester Two

EP 211B: .................................Human Development and Education—Individual and Social Development

SCS 283F: ...............................Education in Inner Cities

EA263A/ED 289: ...................Education and Professional-Client Law/Comprehensive

.................................................Health Education (one course for both cohorts in alternate years)

EP 390C: .................................First Year Supervised Teaching

### Year Two—Semester One

EP 211C: .................................Advanced Development and Education—Mathematics and Science

ELL 149: .................................Foundations for Teaching Language Arts and Social Science

EP 390C: .................................Second Year Supervised Teaching

### Year Two—Semester Two

EP 211D:.................................Advanced Development and Education—Language Arts

ELL 246A: ...............................Teaching Linguistic and Cultural Minority Students

EP 207D:.................................Assessment and Education of Exceptional Pupils in Regular Classes

EA263A/ED 289: ...................Education and Professional-Client Law/Comprehensive

.................................................Health Education (one course for both cohorts in alternate years)

EP 390C: .................................Second Year Supervised Teaching

# APPENDIX C: DEVELOPMENTAL TEACHER EDUCATION PUBLICATIONS, PAPERS, PRESENTATIONS, AND REPORTS

## Publications

Ammon, P. (1984). Human development, teaching, and teacher education. *Teacher Education Quarterly, 11*(4), 95-108.

Ammon, P., & Black, A. (1998). Development psychology as a guide for teaching and teacher preparation. In N. Lambert & B. L. McCombs (eds.), *Issues in school reform: A sampler of psychological perspectives on learner-centered schools.* Washington, DC: American Psychological Association.

Ammon, P., & Black, A. (1988). Response to site report on the development teacher education program. *Dialogues in teacher education.* (Issue Paper 88-4). National Center for Research in Teacher Education, Michigan State University.

Ammon, P., & Hutcheson, B. P. (1989). Promoting the development of teachers' pedagogical conceptions. *Genetic Epistemologist 17*(4), 23-29.

Ammon, P., & Peretti, D. (1998). Preparing constructivist teachers for parent involvement. The Developmental Teacher Education Program at Berkeley. In M. S. Ammon (Ed.), *Preparing teachers to make meaningful home-school connections.* Sacramento, CA: California Department of Education, California Commission on Teacher Credentialing, and University of California.

Black, A. (1990). Conditions for learning and development. In T. Stoddart (Ed.), *Perspectives on Guided Practice.* (Tech. Series 90-1). National Center for Research in Teacher Education, Michigan State University.

Black, A. (Ed.). (1989). Development teacher education [Special issue]. *Genetic Epistemologist, 17*(4).

Black, A. (1989). Developmental teacher education: Preparing teachers to apply developmental principles across the curriculum. *Genetic Epistemologist, 17*(4), 5-14.

Black, A., & Ammon, P. (1992). A developmental-constructivist approach to teacher education. *Journal of Teacher Education, 43*(5), 323-335.

Black, A., & Ammon, P. (1990). Developmental teacher education, *The Educator,* 4(1). Triannual publication of the Graduate School of Education, University of California, Berkeley.

Black, A., Ammon, P., & Kroll, L. (1987). Development, literacy and the social construction of knowledge. *Genetic Epistemologist, 15*(3/4), 13-20.

Kroll, L., & Black, A. (1993). Developmental theory and teaching methods: A pilot study of a teacher education program. *The Elementary School Journal,* 93(4), 417-441.

Kroll, L., & Black, A. (1989). Developmental principles and organization of instruction for literacy: Observations of experienced teachers. *Genetic Epistemologist,* 17(4), 15-22.

Levin, B. B., & Ammon, P. (1996). A longitudinal study of the development of teachers' pedagogical conceptions: The case of Ron. Teacher Education Quarterly, 23(4), 5-26.

Levin, B. B., & Ammon, P. (1992). The development of beginning teachers' pedagogical thinking: A longitudinal analysis of four case studies. *Teacher Education Quarterly,* 19(4), 19-37.

Peretti, D. (1997). Redesigning field experiences: From exposure to engagement. In. J. King (Ed.) *Meeting the challenge of cultural diversity in teacher preparation.* New York: Columbia Teachers College Press.

Peretti, D. (1993, Fall). Telecommunications projects in teacher education. *Kaleidoscope: Patterns of change.* CUE Conference CD-ROM (Mac version).

Peretti, D. (1991, Fall). On becoming a teacher (introduction). *California Perspectives,* 2.

Peretti, D. (1992, Spring). Student teaching in a multilingual, multicultural setting. *The Educator,* 6(1), 20-25.

Peretti, D. (1992, Spring). 12 weeks in the life of a student teacher, *The Educator* 6(1).

Tanabe W., & Alcott, A. (1991, Fall). On becoming a teacher (Introduction by Peretti, D.). *California Perspectives, 2,* 41-54.

## Papers and Presentations at Professional Meetings

Alcott, A., Ammon, P., Black, A., Peretti, D., Shaw, D., & Tanabe, W. (1991, April). *Developmental Teacher Education at age 10: The program develops in response to change in the schools.* Presentation and panel discussion organized for the California Council on the Education of Teachers Conference, Berkeley, CA.

Ammon, P. (1996, September). The importance of development for constructivist teaching and teacher education. In L. Kroll (Chair), *Applying Piaget's theory to understanding school-based domains of knowledge and teacher education.* Symposium presented at The Growing Mind, a conference on the centennial of Jean Piaget's birth, Geneva.

Ammon, P. (1996, June). The importance of development for constructivist teaching and teacher education. In L. Kroll (Chair), *Piagetian theory, learning and teaching in school-related knowledge domains.* Symposium presented at the annual meeting of the Jean Piaget Society, Philadelphia, PA.

Ammon, P., & Black, A. (1991, February). *The Developmental Teacher Education Program at Berkeley: A constructivist approach to beginning teacher education.* Presented as part of a thematic session on developmental/constructivist approaches to preservice and inservice teach education. Association of Teacher Educators Annual Meeting, New Orleans, LA.

Ammon, P., & Black, A. (1982, November). *Developmental Teacher Education.* California Council on the Education of Teachers Conference, Monterey, CA.

Ammon, P., & Hutcheson, B. P. (1988, April). *Regression and progression in teachers' pedagogical conceptions.* Paper presented at the of the American Educational Research Association Annual Meeting, New Orleans, LA.

Ammon, P., & Hutcheson, B. P. (1988, April). *Promoting the development of teachers' pedagogical conceptions.* Paper presented at the American Educational Research Association Annual Meeting, New Orleans, LA.

Ammon, P. Hutcheson, B. P., & Black, A. (1985, April). Teachers' developing conceptions about children, learning, and teaching: Observations from a clinical interview. Paper presented at the American Educational Research Association Annual Meeting, Chicago.

Ammon, P., & Levin, B. B. (1991, April). *Expertise in teaching from a developmental perspective: The Developmental Teacher Education Program at Berkeley.* Paper presented at the American Educational Research Association Annual Meeting, Chicago.

Black, A. (1991, August). *Psychology and teaching: Developmental Teacher Education at Berkeley.* With P. Ammon. Symposium, American Psychological Association, Ninety-Ninth Annual Convention, San Francisco, CA.

Black, A. (1990, February). *Conditions for Student Teacher Development.* In T. Stoddart (Organizer), Learning to teach: Perspectives on guided practice. Symposium presented by the Research and Program Evaluation SIG, Association of Teacher Educators Annual Meeting, Las Vegas, NV.

Black, A. (1989, April). *Teaching-based assessments from a cognitive-developmental (Piagetian) perspective.* With L. Kroll. 23rd Annual University of California, Berkeley, School Psychology Conference.

Black, A. (1988, April). *Developmental Teacher Education: Preparing teachers to uti-lize developmental principles across the curriculum.* In A. Black (Organizer), Developmental Psychology as core knowledge for elementary school pedagogy and teacher education. Symposium conducted at the American Educational Research Association Annual Meeting, New Orleans, LA.

Black, A. (1986, April). *Cognitive structure and structuring problems for teaching.* Paper presented at the annual meeting of the American Education Research Association, San Francisco, CA.

Black, A. (1986, March). *Developmental psychology, teachers, and teaching.* With L. Amsterdam, P. Rosenfield, M. Slakey, & L. Tempkin. Panel discussion organized for the California Association of School Psychologists Annual Convention, Oakland, CA.

Black, A. (1985, April). Structural-developmental theory and elementary school teaching. In L. Nucci (Organizer), *New developments in Piagetian theory and their implications for education.* Symposium conducted at the American Educational Research Association Annual Meeting, Chicago.

Black, A. (1985, February). *Developmental education: Students, teachers, and schools. School University Partnership Renewal (SUPER), Graduate School of Education, University of California, Berkeley.* Subsequently reproduced as a SUPER Notes and distributed to participating school personnel.

Black, A., & Ammon, P. (1982, June). *Developmental Teacher Education at Berkeley: Program design and preliminary conclusions.* Paper presented at symposium on Developmental Teacher Education at the Jean Piaget Society's Annual Symposium, Philadelphia, PA.

Black, A., Ammon, P., & Kroll, L. (1987, May). *Development and Literacy.* Paper presented at the Seventeenth Annual Symposium of the Jean Piaget Society, Philadelphia, PA.

Kroll, L., & Black, A. (1988, April). Development principles and organization of instruction literacy: Observations of experienced teachers. In A. Black (Organizer), Developmental Psychology as core knowledge for elementary school pedagogy and teacher education. Symposium conducted at the American Educational Research Association Annual Meeting, New Orleans, LA.

Kroll, L., & Black, A. (1987, April). *Cognitive developmental theory and inservice teacher education.* Paper presented at the American Educational Research Association Annual Meeting, Washington, DC.

Hutcheson, B. P., & Ammon, P. (1987). *Teachers' cognitive development in the peda-gogical domain.* Paper presented at the Seventeenth Annual Symposium of the Jean Piaget Society, Philadelphia, PA.

Hutcheson, B. P., & Ammon, P. (1986, April). *The development of teachers' conceptions as reflected in their journals.* Paper presented at the American Educational Research Association Annual Meeting, San Francisco, CA.

Peretti, D. (1994, Fall). *Computers Using Educators (CUE) "Does CUE Need a SIG for Teacher Educators?"* Paper presented at the annual meeting of Computer Using Educators, Berkley, CA.

Peretti, D. (1992, Fall). *Preparing Teacher to Work with Families of Culturally Diverse and Special Needs Children.* Panel presentation and discussion at the annual meeting of Association for Constructivist Teaching (ACT), San Francisco, CA.

## Reports

Ammon, P., & Black, A. (1984, 1983, 1982). *Progress in Developmental Teacher Education: An experimental program preparing teachers for multiple subject and learning handicapped specialists credentials.* Research reports submitted to the State of California Commission for Teacher Credentialing by the School of Education, University of California, Berkeley.

# Knitting It All Together: Collaborative Teacher Education in Southern Maine

BY BETTY LOU WHITFORD,
GORDON RUSCOE,
AND LETITIA FICKEL

# INTRODUCTION

This monograph describes a teacher education program collaboratively developed and coordinated by university and school educators in southern Maine. Known as the Extended Teacher Education Program or ETEP, the program integrates the content of professional course work with a nine-month internship. Both school-based and university-based educators comprise the program's faculty, which recommends approximately 75 postbaccalaureate students each year for initial K-8 and 7-12 certifications. The recommendations are based on satisfactory work in classes and experiences at both the University of Southern Maine (USM) and in five surrounding school district clusters: Portland; western Maine (Fryeburg, Sacopee Valley, Cornish); Yarmouth; Wells/Ogunquit and Kennebunk; and Gorham. In 1995, the National Council for Accreditation of Teacher Education (NCATE) cited the program as "representing exemplary practice in the delivery of an extended field-based model for preparing teachers for initial certification" (A. Wise, personal communication, October, 1995).

Viewed as a single program, the five sites have many features in common. We discuss these as aspects of ETEP. At the same time, to capture in detail what this collaborative program looks like day to day, we have focused on how ETEP functions in one of the sites—the Gorham School Department. We refer to the program in this site as ETEP-Gorham. We chose the Gorham site because of the degree to which ETEP is embedded in Gorham's district-wide approaches to teaching, learning, and assessment. An examination of any of the five sites would reveal the structure and substance of ETEP; ETEP-Gorham provides insight into how a university and a district with a 10-year history of restructuring are linking teacher education and district-wide reform.

Also, we focus on one phase of teacher preparation—the internship year—since it is the most distinctive program feature of ETEP. The school and university educators who designed ETEP envisioned this 33 credit-hour graduate internship as an experience which would occur between course work typically taken at the undergraduate level and the 18 credit hours of additional graduate-level work needed to complete the Master of Teaching and Learning (MTL) degree.

Students enter the ETEP internship year having completed an undergraduate degree at any of a variety of colleges and often have pursued other careers. Upon admittance to ETEP, they enter the MTL program in the graduate school at the University of Southern Maine. However, when they complete the internship year, they are eligible for initial certification; thus, the 18 hours to complete the MTL is optional to beginning a teaching career. While an increasing number of ETEP graduates complete this master's degree, for most, the internship year is how novices in this program prepare to begin a career in teaching—what an ETEP-Gorham teacher educator calls "knitting it all together."

Principals in the region agree that ETEP graduates are very competitive for job openings and are successful teachers. The ETEP-Gorham graduates feel especially well prepared in three areas stressed by the program: helping students to learn how to assess their own learning, creating interdisciplinary units, and planning and solving problems with colleagues.

In what follows, we examine the ETEP internship year in detail to discover how interns learn these and other practices and orientations toward teaching and learning. (See Appendix A for a description of the research methodology.) To personalize the experience, we followed one elementary intern, Tom Taylor, throughout the year. Tom's experiences help to substantiate how ETEP works.

The classroom depicted in the following section was the site of the first of two placements Tom experienced. One of the teachers he worked with there, Jane "Ba" Kopp, is a graduate of an earlier version of the ETEP-Gorham program who has since completed the additional 18 hours for the MTL. In her sixth year of teaching when we first observed her classroom in October, 1995, Jane was co-teaching a fourth-fifth grade class with a special-needs teacher, Peter Blackstone, a veteran with over 20 years of experience. Tom was their first intern since they began co-teaching two years earlier.

## THE ETEP INTERNSHIP YEAR
### Tom's First Internship Placement: The Classroom of an ETEP Graduate

At first glance around the room, the scene seems commonplace—a fairly typical elementary classroom. Students are seated at individual table-type desks with detached chairs; the room is lined with instructional materials; and a teacher, Mrs. Kopp, is standing by her desk holding an open book. Beth, one of the students, is at the front of the room, quietly talking about a book and occasionally referring to a diorama she has made to illustrate it. The other 25 or so students are generally attentive and quiet.

When she concludes her report, our first impression of "typical" begins to change. Without prompting, several students immediately raise their hands. Beth calls on Jeff, seated at the back of the room, and, smiling, he asks, "On a scale of one to 10, how would you rate this book?" Beth quickly replies, "10." Jeff immediately replies back: "Why?" A few students groan. (We later learn that "one-to-10-and-why" is Jeff's stock question during the monthly "book talks.") Another student asks Beth to give more detail about the plot, and she does. Referring to a half sheet of paper (see Appendix B: Oral Presentation Scoring Guide), another suggests that more eye contact with the audience would help. Still another comments that she was not loud enough to be heard at the back of the room. As she listens to these comments from her classmates, Beth seems at ease and not embarrassed.

A second adult, seated in a student-sized chair across the room, asks her what she specifically liked about the book. This is Mr. Blackstone, a special-needs teacher whose five students are part of this class. Later, we are surprised to learn that Beth is one of them. Mr. Blackstone praises her for her diorama. Several students quickly point out that the visual is really a "triorama," not a diorama. At this point, Mrs. Kopp cautions the students about talking out of turn. Beth's presentation ends with the students applauding.

Mrs. Kopp asks another student, Austin, if he is ready to give his report. Nodding "yes," Austin positions himself confidently on a stool which makes him more visible to those at the back of the room. He speaks with enthusiasm about his book in a clear, steady voice, maintaining eye contact with the audience throughout his talk. At the conclusion of his report, the hands of perhaps one-third of the students fly up. Smiling, Austin calls on Jeff, who asks his "one-to-ten-and-why" question. Then Austin calls on another student, who asks, "What genre would you place this book in?" Austin replies, "Well, it's sort of an adventure book and a thriller, too." The questioner, nodding, seems satisfied. That is when we notice that, in addition to asking questions, the children are also scoring the presentations using criteria printed on the half sheets of paper.

A third adult, who has been seated at a child's desk across the room, stands and reminds the students to be sure to turn in their "rubrics," the half sheets of paper. This is Tom Taylor, an ETEP intern, who will work with these teachers and students all day, every day, until the December holiday break. Mr. Taylor collects the scoring guides as students hold them in raised hands.

The children and teachers then move into predetermined groups for an hour of mathematics instruction. Mr. Blackstone stays in the classroom with about half the children to work on one topic. Mrs. Kopp and Mr. Taylor work with two separate groups of children on different content in a vacant room across the hall. In these small groups, the teachers use interactive strategies which encourage each child to participate.

Mrs. Kopp is seated at a table with eight children, using a textbook as the basis of a lively question and answer discussion about fractions. The children seem enthusiastic about the content, firing back responses and asking additional questions to which Mrs. Kopp sometimes responds and sometimes turns back to the group for response.

Mr. Taylor is working at another table with three boys, also on fractions. These three, he later explains, are working at a different level of knowledge of fractions than the other students in the class. He has developed an activity in which two of the students compete with each other while the third keeps score. These roles rotate during the hour. Mr. Taylor has created a set of cards, each displaying two fractions, such as 9/16 and 3/5. As he holds up a card, the competing students must say which fraction is larger. The third student decides who is correct and that student keeps the card. After going through 20 or so cards in this manner, the one with the most cards "wins" and competes with the student who had kept score in the previous round.

Perhaps two or three times in each round, all three students are stumped and need to do some calculations to figure out the answer. In these situations, Mr. Taylor queries the students about their approaches to finding the answer, has each one demonstrate his strategy, and poses questions that elicit from the boys alternative ways of determining the correct answer. Among the strategies the students offer are "estimation" and "converting the fractions to common denominators." With Mr. Taylor's prompting, they compare the strategies, describing how estimation gives them clues to the correct answer faster while finding common denominators demonstrates the correct answer but can take more time.

After lunch, the class resumes its reading of *The War with Grandpa,* a novel told from a child's point of view about his grandfather moving in and taking the grandson's bedroom as his own. Mrs. Kopp takes the lead by asking some of the students to read aloud and others to participate in a whole-class discussion. Sometimes the children respond to questions she poses, and at other times they respond to each other. The questions Mrs. Kopp poses are aimed at having the children articulate both what is happening in the story and why. She then directs the students to practice their understanding of "perspective" by making individual journal entries about what the events might mean from Grandpa's point of view rather than the grandson's.

Next, the class members, organized as small groups, take turns visiting the library to begin research for a new unit on regions of the U.S. Mr. Blackstone and Mr. Taylor accompany the groups while Mrs. Kopp stays in the room, working one-on-one with students who are engaged in different assignments—completing journal entries, organizing their groups for the upcoming research, or reviewing the assessment criteria, i.e., the rubrics, that will guide the work of the groups on this unit.

At the end of the day, the students form new small groups to work on a "challenge" from Mr. Forest's class across the hall. The challenge is to cut the longest possible strip of paper from a single 8 1/2 x 11 sheet. The students enthusiastically engage in this problem, sharing ideas about mistakes as well as strategies that work well. As strips of paper are cut, students use a meter stick to measure them, with great anticipation. The longest ones are taped to the wall in the hallway outside the classroom. Unfortunately, some of the longest strips break and are disqualified, much to the chagrin of the members of that group. Someone finally declares, "Ours is 10.7 meters!" This is slightly longer than any of the strips from Mr. Forest's class, which were already displayed in the hallway.

Mr. Blackstone and Mr. Taylor seem as excited as the children during this activity as they work with various small groups around the room. Mrs. Kopp, occasionally asking for softer voices and warning students about dashing around the room with scissors, confesses that while she agrees that such problem-solving is beneficial, she remains uncomfortable with the noise and disorderliness the activity creates.

### Discussion of Classroom Observations

This description is a composite drawn from two consecutive October days, yet it still falls short of capturing the full array of classroom life. Each day, class begins with "morning meeting." Mrs. Kopp explains that this is a time when students can talk about whatever they want: "I like it because it helps the kids settle down. It especially helps the 'gabby gazoos,' kids who like to talk a lot." Mr. Blackstone adds, "It empowers the kids." Here are excerpts from two morning meetings in mid-October. After writing TRISKAIDEKAPHOBIA on the board, Mr. Taylor turns to the class.

> Mr. T:  How do you think it's pronounced?
> (Several children speak at once.) Raise your hands, please.
> (After several children respond, he repeats the word a few
> times; the children practice saying it.)
> Mr. T:  When you break it down, you might be able to figure
> out what it means.
> A student: I think it has something to do with a disease.
> Another student: I think it has something to do with three.
> The room is silent. Then several kids figure it out all of a sud-
> den, and their hands shoot up with correct responses.
> Mr. T:  Right! Fear of the number thirteen. So when you go home
> tonight you can ask your parents if they have triskaidekphobia.
> The children and teachers talk for a few minutes about super-
> stitions, then Mr. Blackstone offers a twist.
> Mr. B:  (smiling) Friday the 13th has been very, very lucky for
> me because that's the day I met my wife.

At another morning meeting, a student talks about the commotion in her neighborhood the previous night.

> Emma: Last night about 9:30, there was something serious
> going on in my neighborhood. A boy had spilled 250 gallons of
> kerosene all over the yard. They were going crazy.
> Mrs. Kopp:  Why would that be dangerous?
> Emma:  They had to call the cops to try to clean it up.
> Mrs. Kopp:  That's a good lesson about spilling dangerous
> things. Don't try to clean it up by yourself and hide it, because
> it can be very dangerous.

Mr. Taylor later described how pleased he felt when a reticent student participated in morning meeting by sharing a personal story or idea with the class: "I loved it when Darcy talked. She rarely said anything in front of the whole class, often acting embarrassed and really shy. So that day in morning meeting when she talked, I was really excited."

During another visit to the class, Mrs. Kopp and Mr. Blackstone introduced the science textbook, explicitly teaching the class how to use this resource before continuing the unit on regions of the United States:

Mrs. Kopp: How would you go about finding information in this book?

(The class talks about the index and the glossary, as the teachers alternate asking questions of the children. They point out the bold print, the major sections of the book, and the chapter headings.)

Mrs. Kopp: What else is helpful in this textbook?

Mike: It tells you where to look up things.

Mrs. Kopp: OK, and how else is it different that helps you?

Jenny: It has summaries to help.

Mrs. Kopp: Right. It tells you the "what" and the "so what," so if you only have the "what" and don't have the "so what," you need to go back and look more.

Mr. Blackstone: Look at page 136. (pause) Turn back a few pages. The chapter is Chapter 3 and the unit is Unit 6, and they tell you, when you finish this section, there's the list of "what I need to know."

Mrs. Kopp: Mr. Blackstone, is it enough to just read about this list? When I finish reading, I should be able to. . .

Ronnie: No, it means you really have to be able to do what's there, not just read it.

Connecting this exercise to the unit on regions of the United States, Mrs. Kopp points out:

We have lots of different kinds of weather in the regions [of the United States]. We're going to study that. What do we need to be experts on before we could set up a weather lab to determine our own weather? (pause) Remember the video. Maybe you want to refer to your notes on the video. (pause) Let's not make that an option. Everyone, get out your notebooks. Good, Sally (a special needs child) has hers out.

(At this comment, Sally looks at Mrs. Kopp with just a hint of a smile showing on her face).

Joanie: Air pressure.

Mrs. Kopp: Good, what else do you need to know about?

Austin: Humidity.

Jenny: Condensation.

Mrs. Kopp: We're focusing on what we need to know that makes up weather.

(As the students continue naming elements of weather, Mr. Blackstone writes them on the board.)

Okay, you are already divided into groups. I think the fairest way to do this is just randomly. You guys are number one and you'll talk about temperature, you guys are number two and you'll study precipitation.

(She continues around the room, assigning other groups to study clouds, air pressure, humidity, and wind.)

After recess, some of you will go to the library and begin looking for information. What did the librarian tell you last year about how to get started on a topic?

(Several children mention the card catalog and taking notes from headings in books.)

Well, you are all headed in the right direction. You also need to ask yourselves some questions. Jenny, how will you get started?

(Jenny mumbles a response.)

Jenny, I don't think anyone heard you. Just belt it out.

The response doesn't satisfy Mrs. Kopp, so she instructs the students to write down the topic assigned to their group. Then, she encourages them to think about and write down questions they have about the topics. The three teachers go to different small groups of students as they begin talking among themselves about their questions.

Mrs. Kopp (getting the students' attention): At the end of this, you are going to teach this to the rest of the class.

Mr. Blackstone: So learners will become teachers.

Mrs. Kopp: That's right. You need to know it well enough to teach it to the rest of the class. So, that's what you are heading toward. Think about that as you go along with this work. One more question I have: When you are writing down your questions, do you just write down questions you already know the answers to?

Several children: No!

After recess, three groups of children go to the library armed with their questions about weather features in various regions of the United States. One child shares his questions with us as he passes by: How much moisture can air hold? What does air temperature do to moisture?

Earlier in the year, again working in groups, the students in the class had constructed a scale map of the world that nearly covered the classroom floor. They had put longitude and latitude lines on the floor, made paper cutouts of the land masses, and labeled the continents and oceans. When we stopped by to meet the teachers in September, we talked briefly with a student group who were in their words, "redoing Asia." They explained that they had previously miscalculated the map scale, a mistake they quickly discovered when they positioned their first cutout of Asia next to a much larger Europe made by another group. They explained to us what they had done wrong as well as how they had corrected their scale. They were now confident that Asia was the right size.

Later in the year, following our October visit, the small groups continued working on the unit on regions of the United States. Their culminating activity for each group was an oral presentation to the class designed to persuade Mr. Taylor, now role playing an immigrant Italian businessman, to settle and start his business in the group's region. Gorham educators call this type of culminating activity an "exhibition" since it is a way for students to demonstrate, or exhibit, what they have learned during their study of the unit.

### Student Performance Assessments

These glimpses of Tom's first placement suggest several conditions which challenged our too-quick judgment that we were observing a "typical classroom." The first unusual feature we noted was the emphasis on student performance assessment and public critique of that performance using pre-determined criteria. We later learned that this is common practice in this school district.

Two district-wide scoring guides are routinely used, one for oral presentation and one for writing (see Appendix B). These are used in classrooms by teachers and students as well as by parents and other non-school community members serving as judges during district-level exhibitions. Student exhibitions occur each spring as all third-, sixth-, eighth-, and eleventh-graders publicly demonstrate their knowledge on a predetermined district-wide topic. A goal is to have each student's exhibition judged by at least two adults from outside the school.

For example, in the spring of 1996, all sixth grade students did exhibitions on the topic "cause and effect" before a panel of adults serving as judges. The panel members were most often parents but sometimes included the superintendent, professors from USM, other community members, and even outside researchers visiting the district. The sixth graders selected a wide range of topics for their individual presentations, including drugs, AIDS, deforestation in Maine, and pollution. In their classes, each student wrote an essay relating the concept of causation to his or her selected topic. These essays became part of the students' portfolios. From the essay, each prepared an oral presentation of approximately five minutes and created a poster that visually represented the topic.

Each student was given 10 minutes to make a presentation and to answer questions posed by the adult panel. During the exhibitions, the students were expected not only to demonstrate knowledge of a broad-based concept, "cause and effect," but also to apply their understanding to a specific topic and to communicate that knowledge in an organized way that effectively informed an audience. The exhibitions we observed required a synthesis of knowledge and performance, providing an opportunity for evaluating more than the factual, discrete knowledge typically measured by more traditional teacher-made assessments or many standardized tests.

In a similar fashion, interns in the ETEP-Gorham program participate in at least three formal, public exhibitions of their knowledge: they share their "short project" from orientation called *All About Gorham* with teachers new to the district in August; they display their interdisciplinary units for teachers and administrators in April; and they formally present their portfolios to a five-member committee composed of administrators, district teachers, and ETEP instructors in May.

In this way and others, there is a parallel between what is emphasized in the Gorham school district and what is emphasized in ETEP: students demonstrating their content knowledge, applying that knowledge in specific ways, and analyzing and explaining the appropriateness of their applications.

Students and teachers also create their own scoring guides or rubrics for particular classroom projects, which they use to assess their work and the work of others. Such performance assessment is routine with Gorham students and is also a central part of the ETEP interns' experiences as they learn to assess and improve their own knowledge and practice.

### A Multidimensional Classroom

A second unusual feature of this classroom is that it is multi-grade, multi-age, and multi-ability—composed of regular-program and special-needs fourth and fifth grade students. Mrs. Kopp and Mr. Blackstone prefer this "looping" arrangement, which allows them to work with the same children for two years and to get to know each child well.

At times, every child in their classroom is expected to do the same work. For example, about once a month, each child does a book talk similar to the ones observed. At other times, the children are grouped and regrouped for different instruction and assignments, based on different needs, as with the mathematics lessons described previously.

This practice is consistent with Mrs. Kopp's beliefs about children and how they learn. Drawing a parallel between being a mother and a teacher, she compares "how we raised our children and how I treat my students and run my classroom." She talks about the individuality of each child and a teacher's need to understand students' learning styles, interests, and kinds of intelligences. She provides guidance and boundaries by being explicit about learning goals and wants children to learn to monitor their own behavior and learning. She attributes this approach to ETEP:

> Because I substituted for 10 years, I would have come in using textbooks and would have read off the questions at the bottom of the page. I still fight that. I still fight wanting things to be orderly: 'Sit down and do your pencil-and-paper work,' and I feel I still have a tremendous amount to learn in terms of the organization of hands-on, but you get better. . . . I learned through ETEP how to put out there what we're aiming for. . . [the importance of] saying 'where am I now, where are the gaps, what do I need to know.' I wouldn't have known any of that without the program.

She also talked about the importance of a safe and encouraging environment: "A student [needs to] feel safe to try new things, to venture into unknown subjects, and to hazard answers." And she stresses that to teach children how to learn and to connect what is learned "requires a cooperative venture among the classroom, the entire school community, and the larger community."

### Cooperation in the Classroom

Cooperation is the third distinguishing factor in this classroom—two teachers are routinely working with this group of children. When an intern is assigned, there are three. These adults continually interact with the students and with each other, modeling peer respect, collegial support, and collaboration—ways of working that are stressed both in ETEP and in the district.

Fourth, many of the materials displayed in the room reflect a philosophy about teaching and learning captured by the "Gorham Outcomes". These outcomes or "habits of mind," as some refer to them, state that students are expected to be self-directed learners, collaborative workers, complex thinkers, quality producers, and community contributors. (see Appendix C for detailed descriptions.)

Other materials emphasize the importance of recognizing the "multiple intelligences" of learners (Gardner, 1983). A poster drawn from the Foxfire project (Wigginton, 1985) stresses that each person in the classroom is both a teacher and a learner. Tacked above the chalkboard at the front of the room is a sign in large block letters: "What? So What? What Now?"—three questions Mrs. Kopp likes to use as major organizers to encourage children and adults, learners and teachers—to think more deeply about their work and to reflect on what they are learning.

On each student's desk is taped a set of goals toward which the student has agreed to work during the school year. These goals, set during parent-teacher-student conferences held at the beginning of the year and often led by students, are structured around the five Gorham outcomes. Throughout the year, in individual portfolios, students accumulate evidence bearing on the goals along with other examples of their work. Similar "goal-and-evidence" portfolio assessment is also required of the ETEP interns.

Moreover, some Gorham teachers and some USM faculty assemble portfolios to document their own work as part of completing the MTL degree from USM. Mrs. Kopp organized such a portfolio around the five "Gorham Outcomes." In her portfolio, she presented evidence from her teaching—curriculum materials, student work, reflections from journal entries—to show how each of the Gorham themes is addressed in her teaching. For example, for "self as learner," she included evidence of new learning from seminars and conferences as well as monitoring and evaluating her current practice by using student work to assess her teaching.

## OBSERVATIONS OF AN ETEP GRADUATE AS A FIRST-YEAR TEACHER

During the same mid-October days a few blocks away, Mr. Tim Fogg's class is underway at the district's middle school. A 1995 ETEP-Gorham graduate, Mr. Fogg teaches eighth-grade life science as part of a five-teacher "house," or team, at the middle school. His classroom is arranged so that students sit in groups of four or five at round tables. It is a comfortable setting and allows for chatting among students. The classroom has a number of visual displays, including the Gorham Outcomes, descriptions of multiple intelligences, and an exemplar project in science. In addition, the classroom has a small library of science textbooks, a blackboard containing assignments for all of Mr. Fogg's classes for the next week, and a glass cage containing a fairly large iguana.

During our observation, Mr. Fogg is showing his students how to complete self-assessments, which concern items such as attitude, attention to task, homework completion and quality, and class participation. Each student is to rate the items from "needs improvement" to "very good." Later, Mr. Fogg will review these evaluations and indicate where he disagrees with their assessments. If necessary, he will ask students for signatures from parents in order to alert them to potential problems.

After students complete and turn in their self evaluations, Mr. Fogg asks for volunteers to present their current events reports. The first report is about what Maine is doing to reduce the incidents of motorist accidents with moose on the highway. The presentation elicits a good deal of discussion, including Mr. Fogg's comments which focus the discussion on scientific information.

The second report is on a solar-powered house in California. Again, the class discussion focuses on science content, such as the amount of sunlight available in Maine, the cost of installing solar-powered equipment, and incidence of solar-powered homes in the nearby area. One student explains how her family heats with wood and relies on solar power as a backup source of energy. Another describes a home in the area that relies entirely on solar power.

By the end of the second report and discussion, the period is over. The class leaves quietly, turning in their current events homework as they go.

The fourth period, again a life science class, begins five minutes later. As soon as Mr. Fogg shuts the door, the class becomes quiet. The first task involves organizing student notebooks. He reminds the students that the three sections of the notebook—permanent, current, and past—allow them to keep track of their work. Because the class is moving to a new topic, students need to move what was current work to past work to make room for the new topic.

Once the notebooks are reorganized, Mr. Fogg turns to the subject for today's class—developing the essential criteria for distinguishing between living and non-living things. He begins with brainstorming, making it clear that each suggestion is to be listed on the board and that, afterward, each item can be disputed in order to ensure that everyone is in agreement. Tim also explains that after the dispute about criteria they will be near establishing the essential questions for their work in the unit. He calls on students as they volunteer.

After the list of suggestions is completed, Mr. Fogg points to each item in turn and asks the students to vote on whether they feel the item is truly a criterion or not. Whenever there is a division of votes or a question, Mr. Fogg initiates a question and answer period so that each student who wants to can offer their support or objections. This procedure leads to a number of lively and informative discussions, the end result of which is a tentative list of essential characteristics of living things, such as complex structure, stages of growth, and reproduction, to which all students agree.

Mr. Fogg then tells the students that he has prepared "guided reading notes" for their next assignment, a strategy he also used during his internship placement in a high school biology class. These notes are arranged on the credenza next to the door that Mr. Fogg refers to as the "paper buffet," a term which elicits several humorous remarks from students, e.g., "I don't think we're supposed to eat paper." After students collect their reading notes, they return to their tables and either prepare current events reports to turn in or begin the assigned reading in their textbooks.

When the period is about to end, the classroom gets noisier, and Mr. Fogg raises his voice several times to gain attention. But, he most effectively quiets the class when he goes to the iguana cage, takes out the iguana, and begins to pet it. Within a few seconds, the room is quieter and students are crowding around to see and touch the iguana. Mr. Fogg takes this opportunity to talk about iguanas, lizards, and animals in general, in effect, using the iguana both to control the class and to impart scientific information.

Throughout this period, a special-education teacher observes the class, assists several students with their work, and participates in the discussion about iguanas. When we ask a student who this teacher is, the student says, "Oh, she's here to do research" and seems totally unconcerned with her presence. Mr. Fogg later explains that, because the school practices "inclusion," each "house" has two special-education teachers who attend classes where special-needs students are enrolled.

### Discussion of Classroom Observations

This glimpse of Mr. Fogg's classroom illustrates several key points about the effects of the ETEP program. First, even though Mr. Fogg is only in his sixth week as a beginning teacher, he is completely in charge of his own classroom and feels quite comfortable in that situation and in being observed by outside researchers. As he explains, ETEP allowed him to get through stressful situations during his internship rather than waiting until his first year of actual teaching—to be able "to walk into teaching the first day," as he says.

Mr. Fogg is not completely new to teaching. In his undergraduate work in biology, he completed a teacher education program at another New England university. But he explains that this program was very traditional—mostly courses in the university and only nine weeks of practice teaching, mostly spent observing. He remarks that, after that experience, "I certainly [didn't] feel ready to take over a class as I did in ETEP." His four years in the Army included some time teaching and helped him plan better so as not to include too many materials for the time available. Moreover, he pointed out, the Army's "teaching to standard" was analogous to the Gorham method and, therefore, to that of ETEP.

Second, as illustrated by the student self-evaluation exercise, Mr. Fogg emphasizes the importance of students accepting responsibility for their own learning—and getting parents involved where necessary. The importance of having conferences with students had been a major point in the portfolio he assembled near the end of his ETEP internship to provide evidence about what he values in teaching and learning and what he is able to do to demonstrate those values in his practice.

Third, during the current events reports, he continually stresses the relationships among pieces of information and students' previous knowledge. In his portfolio, he called this "mental velcroing."

Fourth, Tim makes extensive use of techniques stressed in ETEP, such as the Gorham Project Design Template (see Appendix D), a curriculum planning guide that focuses attention on essential questions, exhibitions, and ongoing and final assessments as well as more common planning tasks—goals and objectives, knowledge and skills, resources, timeline, and evaluation. By helping students identify essential questions regarding living and non living criteria and by providing them with guided reading notes, he intends to promote "deep understanding," as ETEP-Gorham emphasizes. Later in this science unit, he explains, he will help students develop the criteria and standards for their projects [perhaps by providing an exemplar to also stress authenticity] and to give students public criteria against which to evaluate their work.

He adds that, whenever possible, he continues to make journal entries to reflect on his practice, much as he did during his internship. "My reflections are less formal [than during ETEP], but I still make notes on what worked and didn't immediately after a class."

Collaboration, performance assessment, reflection, active learning, exemplars, a priori public evaluation criteria, goal-directed accountability—these approaches to teaching and learning are among those we saw demonstrated in Gorham classrooms. These approaches are also modeled in teacher education courses.

## LEARNING HOW TO TEACH: AN ETEP-GORHAM LITERACY CLASS

This section describes one of the literacy classes required of all elementary interns. This course, along with the internship seminar, is cited by Gorham interns as the course where they learn the most about how to teach. As with the seminar discussed later, they note as particular strengths the blend of theory and application and the psychological, as well as substantive, support provided by peers and instructors.

We arrive about 30 minutes into the class, which is held every week at Narragansett School, Gorham's largest primary school. Instructor Susan Sedenka is seated in her rocking chair in her own elementary classroom. Ten of the 11 elementary interns at the Gorham site are seated in a rough circle, some at tables, others on a couch. The atmosphere is relaxed despite the brisk pace of activities and topics. Several students are sharing a bag of pretzels. Others talk among themselves from time to time.

Although Susan and the interns have been with children all day and many seem tired, the discussion is lively. Susan is explaining the debate between proponents of whole language and proponents of phonics as approaches to teaching reading. She emphasizes that these are not two diametrically opposed positions. Phonics need to be taught, she says, but holistically, in context. That's the approach taken at USM.

Susan has taught in ETEP before, but this time she has agreed to "blend" two ETEP courses—literacy (reading) and writing, each typically a one-semester course—into an integrated full-year unit. Although she has separate syllabi for these courses, she attempts wherever possible to combine topics from week to week. The syllabi stress expected outcomes, and particularly topics and activities for interns' practica—10 classroom experiences the interns are to try with children.

As with the math and social studies methods courses in the Gorham site, literacy is taught by a respected classroom teacher who is also a highly praised ETEP instructor. Susan appears to be able to make the switch from primary teacher to teacher educator as smoothly as if those roles had always been intertwined. She has worked with ETEP interns in the past, but not this year. As she later says, "I have interns as frequently as I can. I don't have one now because there weren't enough to go around." She explains that this is because, until recently, interns were placed only at certain schools. For the past two years, however, in part because of the superintendent's desire to emphasize the *district* nature of the program, each of the six schools in Gorham has had at least two interns.

After the discussion of whole language, Susan turns to a consideration of the reflections she has assigned the interns to write the previous week. She points out that required reflections are "richer" if they are done before class and that they should not be merely paraphrasing of assigned reading. She also distributes an intern's reflection on the previous week's reading assignment as an exemplar.

Susan then explains how to combine her next assignment with classroom work and with the case study of a child assignment in another ETEP class, life span development. As the interns are conducting their case studies for life span, she suggests that they could try various reading assessments with their students. This is what ETEP instructors call a shared assessment—where assignments from two or more ETEP courses are integrated into one project. The teacher education faculty has recently begun to stress such shared assessments for at least two reasons: They believe the assessments will help that interns to see more easily the connections across various courses and experiences and that having two or more instructors assess the same work for different purposes can reduce the number of separate assignments interns must complete. This practice also helps interns learn how to view their work from multiple perspectives.

Next, Susan turns to a discussion of the Early Literacy Assessment as a means to assess a child's reading readiness and suggests ways to use the protocol, well as the Individual Reading Inventory (IRI) in doing case studies of students with reading problems. Before we arrived, she had demonstrated an Early Literacy Assessment with a five-year-old child. She encourages the interns to try out the IRI with a student or two in their classrooms. She also cautions, "Your assessment might be a bomb, but reflect on it. I want to know what you learn from it."

The next topic is "semantic webbing." Susan explains that teachers can ask children to name five words associated with another word or concept, such as Halloween. This approach to vocabulary building is more than brainstorming, however, she warns. She explains that many teachers end the lesson after generating a list of words. However, a different level of learning is achieved if students are encouraged to sort the words into categories, or "mental file drawers," as she describes the process. To demonstrate, she has the interns construct a web of words. Using the web, she then demonstrates a classification process by using prompts such as: Which of these words seem to go together? Why? What are some things that scare you? She later explains that this process demonstrates how children can begin to develop conceptual files and to justify the appropriateness of these files. "In this way," she says, "students are building on what they already know and attaching meaning to new words."

After a break, Susan models what she terms a mini-lesson on free writing. Using the interns' assignments from the previous week as an example, she stresses the importance of working with a partner and using the partner's prompts to get ideas about how to revise a piece of writing. Such activities, she stresses, are those that ETEP interns' own students should become accustomed to because they are precisely what should become part of any elementary classroom.

She then turns to the question of conferencing techniques related to writing. She emphasizes the importance of using phrases such as "I wish I knew more about. . ., Here's what I like about. . ., But I wonder if . . .," to stimulate student to think about their writing. By using such prompts, she explains, the teacher can encourage students to develop a plan for rewriting and not to think of first drafts as all that writing entails. The interns then spend some class time doing their own free writing, either about scary stories or about their draft vision statements or other assignments they may have. They later form pairs and small groups for peer conferences on the writing.

As the class is ending, Susan reminds the interns of next week's assignment. Meanwhile, interns have begun to talk among themselves about their concern for an upcoming examination in another university course. Because several different opinions emerge about what will be covered on the exam, one intern offers to contact the instructor about the scope of the examination and to share this information with the others.

### Other ETEP Courses

In addition to the six-hour literacy course, the elementary interns take courses in exceptionality and life-span development (three hours each); math, science, and social studies methods (six hours total); and the internship seminar, which addresses learning, curriculum, and assessment (six hours). With nine hours of credit for the internship itself, these students register for a total of 33 graduate hours in nine months. These 33 credit hours of professional education courses are required by the state of Maine for initial certification.

The resulting schedule is intense and sometimes grueling, with work in schools all day, every day, followed by courses three to five afternoons each week. The course schedule can and often does vary each week, occasionally providing one or two afternoons for homework or other obligations.

For example, during the week of December 4-8, 1995, the elementary interns had literacy class from 3:30-6:30 p.m. on Tuesday, mathematics methods from 3:30-5:30 p.m. on Wednesday, life span/exceptionality (co-taught as a joint course) on Thursday from 4:00-6:30 p.m., with the seminar on Friday from 1:00-3:00 p.m., followed by the presentation of case studies for life span/exceptionality. The next week, the course schedule directed the interns to literacy on Tuesday from 3:30-6:00 p.m., life span/exceptionality case study presentations from 4:00-6:30 p.m. on Thursday, and the seminar from 3:00-5:00 p. m. on Friday, leaving Monday and Wednesday afternoons free. (See Appendix D for examples of the ETEP-Gorham schedules of classes and courses for the 1995-96 and 1996-97 cohorts.)

Assignments in the content methods classes (e.g., math, science, social studies) include learning about curriculum and content standards promulgated by various national organizations (e.g., National Council for the Social Studies, National Council for Teachers of Mathematics), developing lessons and units reflecting those standards, observing classes at grade levels other than those in the placements, assigned readings (generally textbooks and articles), and assessing work produced by children. ETEP instructors encourage the interns to develop lessons and units in the content methods classes that can become part of the larger interdisciplinary unit assigned as part of their seminar course work. For the most part, instructors have agreed to use the same criteria for judging these units.

In the life span development course, interns learn about diversity in human growth and development by reading about a wide array of theories and preparing four assignments in which they apply aspects of the theories. According to the syllabus, these four assignments are: (a) an overview of one theory of development demonstrating understanding of underlying concepts as applied to educational settings; (b) an oral presentation summarizing the research concerning an important topic or issue in child/adolescent development and applying this information to the educational environment; (c) constructing a case study through observations and interviews with one child or adolescent and demonstrating applications of theoretical concepts or relevant research findings to the child/adolescent's current developmental status; and (d) developing an authentic assessment based on one theory or several theories of development, e.g., Gardner's theory of multiple intelligences (ETEP, 1995-96, HRD 660).

In the case study, the major project in the course, each intern collects information and writes about the child in the family, the child in the school, the child as a learner, and the child in a developmental perspective (ETEP, 1995-96, HRD 660). Assignments given in other ETEP courses, such as reading assessments or developing alternative instructional approaches, can be used to learn more about the child who is the focus of the case study. This approach to intern assignments is what the ETEP instructors call shared assessment. An example of another possible shared assessment is the case study assigned in the exceptionality course: If an intern focuses on an exceptional child for the case study in the life span course, that study can be used as a major assignment in this course.

As expected, the focus for the course on exceptionality is on children with learning disabilities, behavior and emotional disorders, and mental retardation. According to the syllabus, topics include collaborative teaming, screening, referral, modification of curriculum, adaptive technologies, individual educational plans, behavior management techniques, and state and federal legislation regarding exceptional children (ETEP, 1995-96, EXE 540). In addition to the case study, and as is the case with most of the courses, interns are asked to reflect on their readings in the coordinated journal. Also called the response or dialogue journal, it is a strategy for reflection used across the program components. They also participate in micro-teaching, disability awareness activities, skits and simulations, and debates on topics such as inclusion.

Most of the courses for the Gorham interns are offered on site, held in local school buildings to provide a more authentic setting. Course instructors include both university faculty members and Gorham teachers and administrators. A course leader, either university or school staff member, is designated to help coordinate the design and content of each course and facilitate communication among the instructors across the five ETEP school district sites. In some cases, university faculty members and school district teachers and administrators co-teach a course. In Gorham, the elementary interns attend all their classes together, and the majority of their course instructors are Gorham teachers. (See Appendix F for more information concerning the content of ETEP courses.)

## THE ETEP PROGRAM

Before interns take any courses, they first must be admitted to the program. In the next sections, we describe admission to ETEP and the ETEP-Gorham orientation, which begins the year-long internship seminar.

### Admission to ETEP

Admission to the ETEP program includes one of the five school sites. The first site established in ETEP, Wells-Ogunquit (which now includes Kennebunk schools), offers preparation for certification for grades K-8 and 7-12 as well as a dual certification covering K-12. Located about 35 miles south of Portland, the site uses six schools—two high schools, one junior high school, and three elementary schools. The Yarmouth site, a suburban district 12 miles north of Portland, offers preparation for both K-8 and 7-12. Fryeburg, about 50 miles west of Portland, also offers K-8 and 7-12 and includes two public school districts as well as Fryeburg Academy, a private school that high-school students attend by means of publicly-paid tuition since there is no public high school in the community. A fourth site, Portland, offers preparation for teaching grades 7-12 only. The program takes place in two high schools and one middle school. Gorham is the fifth of these sites, and offers both K-8 and 7-12. Located 10 miles west of Portland, it is also the home of the main campus of the University of Southern Maine.

Each of the five sites admits a cohort of 15-20 students who progress through the internship as a group. In each site, a university teacher educator, known as the university site coordinator, and a teacher employed at the site, known as the school site coordinator, share responsibility for co-directing that site's program.

Applicants must first meet the basic requirements for admission: an undergraduate degree with a minimum GPA of 2.5, standardized test results with a combined GRE score minimum of 900 or 40 on the Miller Analogies Test, and three letters of recommendation.

Transcripts are then reviewed. The state of Maine requires that elementary candidates show at least six semester hours in each of four content areas—English, mathematics, science, and social sciences. Secondary candidates must show at least 36 hours in an appropriate area of concentration—English, mathematics, social studies, science, or foreign language. Content-area requirements must be completed prior to beginning the internship year. Those missing only one course may be admitted to the program but must complete the course prior to being recommended for certification. The Maine Department of Education has authorized USM to include the content-area knowledge required for elementary and secondary certification in the performance-based assessment system in use in ETEP.

Applicants submit a resume and a "catalog of experiences," the latter highlighting an applicant's development as a learner and a teacher. They also submit an essay reacting to the program's mission statement, which is reviewed for substance as well as clarity and construction. The mission statement reads in part:

> . . . the process of teaching is actually a process of learning. Effective teaching is grounded in knowledge, experience, critical reflection, and a commitment to preparing children and youth for the future. Such teaching encourages inquiry that leads to independent thinking. Teaching is a complex enterprise. It is an art, a craft, a science, a collection of skills, and common sense. Teachers and students together foster a lifelong pursuit of learning which encompasses personal growth and global awareness. (College of Education and Human Development, 1996-97, p. 4).

These admissions materials are first reviewed by a group of ETEP faculty, both from the university and from the ETEP sites. If applicants pass this initial screening, they are invited to attend open houses held at each of the ETEP sites. Site visits allow candidates to learn more about the sites and to meet key program faculty. The visits also assist ETEP site faculty in determining which candidates will be interviewed at particular sites, a decision that is based in part on the placements available in each site. These interviews are conducted by the university site coordinator, the school site coordinator, and other classroom teachers.

Following the site interviews, the 10 ETEP site coordinators (one university and one school coordinator per site) meet as a group to review all of the applicants. Here they make final decisions about admissions to particular sites. Efforts are made to match applicants' site preferences with spaces and types of certifications available. In some cases, candidates may not get their first site choice because too many are seeking places in the same site or because the candidate's area of specialization is not available, which is occasionally a problem for those in the secondary program.

## *Tom's Admission Process*

Like most ETEP interns, Tom did not apply to the program immediately after completing his undergraduate studies. After completing a degree in economics, he worked in the insurance industry for a while, played and coached professional football in Italy, and later did part-time work in special education in another Maine school district. He could have continued in that position, taking classes in the evening to gain a temporary teaching certificate. But, interestingly, he had learned about ETEP and Gorham from a fellow American player on his team in Italy and decided he wanted to try the intensive, one-year program so he could get his own classroom as quickly as possible. As Tom said, "One of the reasons I chose Gorham was because of all the things they were doing. It seemed to me they were trying new and innovative things."

In his application to ETEP the previous spring, Tom presented the required information—the transcript of his undergraduate degree in economics, his standardized test scores, and his essay about education and teaching, including his belief that he has something to contribute. After passing the initial screening, he was encouraged to visit each of the five ETEP sites before indicating his preference. He visited 3 of the 5 sites and chose Gorham because of its reputation and proximity to his home. In the next step, he successfully completed the site interview conducted by the Gorham site coordinators and several elementary teachers.

### ETEP-Gorham Orientation

In August, before either the university semester or schools have opened, each site holds its own orientation to introduce interns to the site, the program expectations, and each other. The length of these orientations varies each year from a week to two weeks depending on how well district and university calendars mesh. The orientations are designed and facilitated by the two site coordinators and actually mark the beginning of the seminar, which functions both as a course and as a way to facilitate program coordination.

One strategy used during orientation in the four sites other than Gorham is an Outward Bound experience, including a ropes course that requires on-the-spot group problem solving. The Gorham coordinators use an alternative approach to team building and problem solving based directly on the Gorham planning template, a model developed and used in the district for planning projects. (See Appendix D for an example.)

The ETEP-Gorham orientation is run by Walter Kimball and Susie Hanley, the university and school site coordinators respectively. They use a variety of activities designed with three intentions in mind. First, the coordinators want the interns to learn about Gorham and how education is practiced in the district. To this end, the interns learn about the district's approach to translating into practice such ideas as multiple intelligences and ongoing performance assessment. Orientation activities also make use of strategies developed by Gorham educators over the past 10 years as part of their restructuring efforts, such as planning templates and district-wide rubrics for evaluating writing and oral presentations.

Second, the interns are encouraged to begin to build their own community of learners that, during the year, will provide both support and critique aimed at continuous progress as they commence their formal development as teachers. Interns work together as a total team as well as in various small groups on different projects designed to facilitate their learning about key program expectations such as collaboration, ongoing assessment, and reflection. Developing a spirit of camaraderie—and using this team spirit to get them through the "hard times"—is deemed essential by the coordinators.

Third, the coordinators use the orientation to establish the routines of the internship seminar, which they will hold every Friday throughout the year. These routines are models for encouraging student-centered and learning-centered teaching. These models—such as the project-design template, reflective journals, and small group exhibitions of learning—provide the interns opportunities to experience strategies and processes contributing to building and nurturing a community of learners.

For example, at the beginning of orientation, the interns form "home groups" of four to five people; the membership is voluntary as long as each group has at least one secondary intern. Generally, there are at least twice as many elementary interns as secondary interns. These groups function throughout the year for support and critique. Each seminar session begins with the interns meeting in home groups to hear about each other's week, generate bin items, questions posted anonymously to be dealt with by the total group—and to provide peer critique as interns work on various assignments. Home groups, Ms. Hanley explains, are small clusters of interns who check in with each other and provide an audience for reviewing drafts of projects and portfolios.

Each day during orientation, Ms. Hanley, Mr. Kimball, and the interns participate in one or more inclusion activity. Through these activities, often humorous in nature, they learn the names of and some personal information about each seminar member and thus begin to build trust and cohesiveness as a group.

To create norms for the seminar, the interns spend about half a day working toward consensus on a brainstormed list. Ms. Hanley and Mr. Kimball take an active role as participants, but as the substance and wording of the norms are debated, the process is facilitated by the interns. This activity gives them initial experience as a group with managing interpersonal relations by exposing them to the range of individual values and preferred ways of working of each member of the cohort. Thus, it models consensus decision making.

Also during orientation, the interns complete what Ms. Hanley and Mr. Kimball call "the short project." For the past two years, this project has been titled, All About Gorham. Organized into voluntary small groups, the interns research various aspects of the community, put together a presentation that they rehearse and critique in the seminar and then present in a workshop for teachers new to the Gorham system toward the end of orientation, just prior to the beginning of school.

Orientation also offers the interns opportunities to meet other university and school staff who will be part of the year's program. For example, the 1995-96 ETEP-Gorham cohort had a two-week orientation with two afternoons devoted to the life span development course. Beginning one or more courses during orientation is called "front-loading" by the ETEP coordinators, a strategy used to fit the desired contact hours for each course into a very full schedule. (See Appendix H for the orientation schedule for the 1996-97 cohort.)

Orientation has a further function related to finalizing the interns' initial placements as well. Ms. Hanley, an experienced Gorham teacher, takes this time to get to know the interests, strengths, and growth areas of individual interns, knowledge which aids her in making "good" first placements, which she describes as matches between needs and interests expressed in writing by both interns and potential mentor teachers.

For example, by the end of orientation in 1995, Ms. Hanley matched Tom Taylor with Mrs. Kopp and Mr. Blackstone based on multiple factors. She considered Tom's experience with special-needs children, his preferred grade levels (four and five), his performance during orientation, and the teaching and learning interests expressed by Mrs. Kopp and Mr. Blackstone, as well as a district preference for placing interns in all schools in the district.

### The Internship Seminar

Led by the site coordinators, the internship seminar incorporates six hours of course work on learning, curriculum, and assessment with coordination of the internship which carries six hours of credit. The seminar analyzes topics such as curriculum planning, learning theory, technology in education, and classroom management as cases arising in the classroom placements (ETEP, 1995-96, EDU 541 and 542 syllabus).

Of particular importance in the seminar is the continued refinement of each intern's vision statement. First drafted during orientation, this individual statement about beliefs and practices important to effective learning communities is then revisited, critiqued, and revised throughout the year. A comment from Mr. Kimball suggests the importance of the vision statement: "If an intern says a particular practice is important, then we look for evidence of that in their work."

In regard to judging progress in developing vision, Ms. Hanley explains that the site coordinators look for evidence of thinking about the complexity of teaching and learning. As an example, she adds that at the beginning of the internship, interns generally write "the teacher will" or "the student will" but later in the year begin to talk about the community of learners and the teacher's role in developing one. Thus, both coordinators see the vision statement as a touchstone for independent reflection as well as for discussions with other interns, the coordinators, and their mentor teachers.

By May, the vision statements are used to anchor the interns' portfolios. Typically assembled in large three-ring binders, the portfolios present evidence from their year's work bearing on 11 outcomes considered criteria for certification in Maine. (See Appendix F for the full text of the outcomes.) These outcomes, revised several times since ETEP began in 1990, are based on the work of the Interstate New Teacher Assessment and Support Consortium (INTASC), an interstate group that has developed standards for beginning teachers that have been adopted by more than 20 states.

ETEP and two other teacher education programs in the state have been piloting standards-based teacher certification in Maine, and the Department of Education has established a task force that is drafting teaching standards for the state. Currently in ETEP, the outcomes are used as categories around which to collect evidence from an intern's practice during the year. Observation and evaluation instruments used by cooperating teachers are based on the outcomes, and the evidence so generated serves as the basis for formal assessment meetings held during the year by the coordinators with individual interns and their cooperating teachers.

Seminar is also one of the places where the interns and site coordinators exchange challenges and accomplishments, receiving feedback and reactions (ETEP, 1995-96, EDU 541/542 syllabus). Between the short project presented in August and the portfolio presented in May, other assignments that interns complete include: the case study of a child from the first placement classroom, presented in December; an interdisciplinary unit taught during the second placement and presented in April; an action research study; a resource file containing lesson plan ideas, lists of resources and bibliographies; and coordinated journaling, and a response journal in which interns are expected to link their experiences across classrooms and courses with their developing ideas about teaching and learning. Interns make entries in their journals about what they are learning and observing. Cooperating teachers and site coordinators read the journals and respond to the comments. The journals can also be shared in the home groups in the seminar. For example, one of Tom's journal entries described how Mrs. Kopp and Mr. Blackstone introduced the science book to their students, an idea he plans to use in his own teaching.

As mentioned earlier, the ETEP faculty calls these assignments shared assessments because they link course and classroom experiences, reflections on readings, observations of students, and emerging questions, making the interns' work more focused, cohesive, and programmatic rather than fragmented, discrete, and disjointed. As one teacher educator explains, "We have worked hard to coordinate the assignments and assessments so that the literacy practica, for example, connect well with the action research study and the interdisciplinary unit."

A good deal of program coordination also occurs in the seminar. Here, interns sign up for time with the site coordinators each week, indicating a specific purpose for the visit—observation of teaching, review of materials developed, or discussion of a particular question or idea. Interns also write weekly one-page action plans, briefly describing what they did the week before, what they intend to do the next week, and a problem or question encountered needing attention. These plans are also a useful record of what each intern is doing each week and help Mr. Kimball and Ms. Hanley to coordinate their visits so that specific needs are addressed. Other types of coordination are needed at times because of the schedule. Since the course schedule can, and often does, vary from week to week, conflicts with district committee meetings or parent conferences or the Maine weather sometimes arise. Questions and emerging problems about such conflicts are raised and dealt with in the seminar.

The emphasis on continuous improvement throughout the seminar and during visits with interns is not without problems, of course. As the site coordinators themselves point out, they are responsible both for evaluating intern progress and providing support. Following the suggestion of a university school counseling faculty member experienced in clinical supervision, the site coordinators talk directly with the interns about the coordinators' roles as educator, consultant, counselor, and evaluator, since these roles are potentially in conflict. As Ms. Hanley explains, occasionally interns see the coordinators as "evil evaluators" rather than "buddies" as they discuss an intern's standing in the program. Over time, as the seminar and weekly visits focus on constructive, positive feedback, the coordinators believe any initial tension among the roles generally disappears.

## ETEP-GORHAM INTERNSHIP PLACEMENTS

The specific requirements of the internship—daily practice with cooperating teachers in Gorham classrooms—are described in ETEP-Gorham guidelines as two separate semester-long placements, each with requirements and expectations for interns and cooperating teachers. These include the degree to which interns take lead responsibility for the classroom; the ongoing dialogue journal which each intern keeps and in which cooperating teachers and site coordinators write comments or questions; expectations for the interns' role in instructional planning; how interns' work is assessed; required videotaping of teaching episodes; and cooperating teacher participation in the intern's portfolio presentation and recommendation for certification.

These requirements are also discussed and coordinated during weekly visits to each intern by the site coordinators. The weekly meetings with a coordinator, critical to documenting each intern's progress, are informed by the interns' action plans, both coordinators' previous observations of interns' teaching, reports from cooperating teachers, the dialogue journals, and materials interns have developed during the week, either for the classroom or for their courses.

A larger purpose of the weekly visits and meetings is to help interns learn to identify evidence of continuous improvement from their work. During both semester-long placements, the 11 ETEP outcomes serve to organize the evidence. They are introduced during orientation and reviewed during the seminar and the weekly visits as needed. As the coordinators explained, "We talk about the planning template and outcomes and other expectations during orientation and then again and again as needed during the seminar. It is too much to take in all at once." Later they added, "The outcomes are the criteria used to organize and judge evidence regarding recommending [an intern] for Maine's initial teaching certificate."

Each intern is involved in two conferences associated with each semester-long placement—a mid-point conference and an exit conference. During each mid-point conference, the cooperating teacher and the coordinators review the intern's performance in terms of the 11 outcomes. Each outcome is judged as developing satisfactorily or needing attention. In effect, the mid-point conference is intended to help interns examine their progress. The site coordinators and the cooperating teachers complete evaluation forms and use these forms to make suggestions as to how improvement could be accomplished. There is also space on the forms to cite specific evidence from the intern's practice related to each outcome. (See Appendix G for an example of the evaluation form.)

During each exit conference, the interns take the lead in presenting the evidence that they have worked toward the 11 outcomes. While the cooperating teacher and the coordinators can make suggestions during this meeting, the intern is in effect rehearsing what will later become a critical assessment: the portfolio presentation.

During the first placement, interns are not expected to take full responsibility for the classroom. They do take the lead with segments of a day, perhaps starting with leading the morning meeting, as did Tom. Many interns do complete, in November or December, a week of lead teaching, or partner-teaching with the cooperating teacher. This week of teaching, near the end of the first placement, will be expected of all interns in the 1996-97 cohort. The specific set of responsibilities to be taken by an intern is an individual decision made by the cooperating teachers and the interns, in consultation with the coordinators as needed.

By the time we first observed Tom in mid-October, he had already developed and presented lessons in partnership with Mrs. Kopp and Mr. Blackstone, worked with students individually and in small groups, attended curriculum planning meetings in the school, and cooperated with Mrs. Kopp and Mr. Blackstone on classroom management and organization. He had, in effect, been immersed in the life of the classroom since the students arrived for the first day of school.

Later in the semester, he co-taught the unit of regions of the United States, playing a central role in the students' culminating activity; completed a case study of a special needs child for Life Span Development and Exceptionality; worked on his resource file; made daily entries in his dialogue journal; designed and led a field trip; met with the coordinators during weekly visits; and attended ETEP courses three to five afternoons each week.

After the first placement, Tom met with the coordinators for his mid-year review. This review, which did not include the cooperating teachers, examined, as one coordinator explained, ". . .the evidence we see that supports [Tom's] performance around quality outcomes and some suggestions that we may have, holes that we see, things that we really want [him] to do. . . ."

### Tom's Second Internship Placement:
### Development of an Interdisciplinary Unit

Early in January, Tom Taylor began his second placement, this time at Gorham's White Rock School, one of two primary schools enrolling children in grades 1-3. Tom's placement is in a multi-age first- and second-grade classroom, and the transition from fourth and fifth graders to younger children is initially problematic for him. He has not anticipated the shorter attention spans he encounters, and he has difficulty explaining his expectations and assignments in terms the younger children readily understand. He finds he often loses the attention of most of the children before he finishes explaining an activity. As his cooperating teacher later shares, "He would plan something, and six-year-olds' attention spans are so short they would be doing somersaults on the floor just as he was just getting into it." Tom feels he is out of his "comfort zone" with younger children, later commenting, "It was a struggle for me, using the appropriate language, being able to speak to their level to where it made sense to them." He later adds, "I sat for four hours just trying to do one lesson because I didn't know what to include—is this too little, is this too much, am I over their heads?"

His cooperating teacher and Ms. Hanley, herself an experienced kindergarten teacher, help him learn to make appropriate adjustments by suggesting that he create shorter, more focused assignments with fewer components and have more of them. They also suggested that his explanations be more concrete. For example, one assignment in his interdisciplinary unit on weather requires the children to count air molecules and record their measurements on a chart. Part of what they need to do involves copying words like pressure onto the blank chart. Many of the children, being unfamiliar with some of the words they were to put on the chart, use most of the time trying to accurately copy the words rather than counting and recording the number of molecules. Later, Tom reworks the assignment by giving the children a chart with the words already printed in the appropriate places. This time, the children are able to focus on the measurements, the real purpose of the lesson.

Tom's experiences are illustrative of the purpose and process of ETEP-Gorham's second placement in three ways. First, arrangements for this placement begin toward the end of the first semester, when Mr. Kimball and Ms. Hanley invite the interns to write proposals for their second placements. The intent of this second placement is to broaden the interns' experiences within the school system, even if it disrupts their "comfort zones." For elementary interns in Gorham, placements are possible in five of the district's six schools; they can work at Little Falls (the kindergarten center), Narragansett or White Rock (grades 1-3), Village School (grades 4-6), or Shaw School (7-8), since their certificates will be for grades K-8. Secondary interns, however, are usually limited to one subject and therefore have fewer choices, since there is only one high school and one middle school in the district. As a result, sometimes the coordinators, as Ms.

Hanley explains, have to "craft an appropriate experience at a high school or middle school in another nearby district."

Second, during this placement, Tom continues to take program courses after school. Recognizing that the internship year requires an enormous amount of time from the interns, the coordinators from all of the sites work to stagger the courses so that some are front-loaded, as we have seen. Still, the requirements of the immersion in classrooms along with course work means that the Gorham interns continue to attend classes most afternoons.

Third, during this second placement, the role of the intern grows to that of the primary leader of instruction in the classroom. This is when Ms. Hanley and Mr. Kimball emphasize that teaching has to be seen as more than just the 11 outcomes. As Ms. Hanley explains, "This is where the interns have to knit it all together." The development of an interdisciplinary unit, fondly referred to as "the Big Kahuna," provides the opportunity for this process. To successfully develop and teach the unit, interns have to integrate what they have learned from both their course work and previous placement experiences.

The interdisciplinary unit originates in the seminar and is a major focus of that class during the spring. The criteria and unit assessment rubric reflect the program's focus on continuous improvement, feedback, and reflection. The five criteria include: use of templates with explanations; infusion and explanation of local, state, and national standards; inclusion of a time line and assessment system; interdisciplinary lesson plans with documentation and evidence of student work; and intern reflection and analysis, including an analysis of student work. Early in the spring semester, the interns bring their developing units to the seminar for an evaluation of progress by both peers and coordinators. Mr. Kimball, Ms. Hanley, and the interns use feedback sheets which outline specific items of evidence for each of the five criteria to assess the unit in progress. They also provide suggestions for how the interns can strengthen their units.

The interns then begin teaching the unit in their classrooms. Each week during the seminar, they can share and discuss how the unit is going and continue to receive support and suggestions from the seminar members. Ms. Hanley and Mr. Kimball have the opportunity to provide their feedback during observations and individual meetings. Toward the end of the semester, the interns present their final products to the seminar, and turn in the units for evaluation. Once again, the notion of continuous improvement is honored. Interns can use the feedback from the assessment to change and amend the document and resubmit it. This process of reflection and reevaluation allows the interns to improve their work as well as their final grade on the project. During one afternoon in April, the units from all of the ETEP-Gorham interns K-12 are put on display for review by Gorham and USM faculty and administrators. Echoing the sentiments of many Gorham faculty who saw the units, Mr. Kimball states "[they] are the best ever. They are also models for Gorham teachers, who are now expected to create at least one such unit or project each year [by district policy.]"

The interdisciplinary unit can also serve as one of the assessments shared across ETEP courses. For example, in 1995-96 the social studies methods course syllabus listed the unit as one of the assignments (ETEP, 1995-96). While the instructor honored the design and criteria laid out for the unit in the seminar, course-specific criteria, such as incorporating children's literature into specific lessons, were added.

With the interdisciplinary unit assignment, the interns do the work of being a teacher; they decide on specific learning goals; collect, evaluate, and alter materials; develop and implement lessons and embedded assessments; and continually assess student learning and make appropriate adjustments according to student needs. As one intern saw it, the purpose of the unit was for interns to "see how all the pieces go together."

During interviews, the interns generally spoke of the unit as an important learning experience. One intern reported that it helped him better understand the workload of teachers because "it helped us see what a long process it is to develop a unit. It's not an easy job." Another shared the same sentiments: "One thing I learned was that it was a lot more involved, and it took a lot more time to pull together than I ever imagined—and a lot more work. [It took] hours every night in planning and getting things ready." Others commented on the importance of creating a unit with embedded assessments of students' learning. One shared that his unit had convinced him that students could and would improve their work based on feedback from teachers: "[The unit] opened my eyes to see that [students] can see where they made errors and fix them." For the 1995-96 cohort, then, this unit provided an important window into the complexity of teaching as well as serving as a key tool for assessing whether interns had indeed "learned to knit."

# THE PORTFOLIO PRESENTATION

Early one Wednesday morning in mid-May, in a corner of the Gorham High School auditorium, Tom presents his ETEP portfolio. His three cooperating teachers (two from his first placement, one from his second), the principal from his first placement, and the two site coordinators are present and form his review committee. Tom is given 45 minutes to present his beliefs about education and school in general and the evidence of his work in instruction, curriculum, and assessment in particular. He is expected to reference the 11 ETEP outcomes, preferably in an integrated fashion, but the list is not intended to drive the presentation. The presentation, which is akin to a dissertation defense, is videotaped. The tone remains relaxed and collegial throughout.

Using his portfolio notebook, Tom begins by reading his vision statement, which he drafted the previous fall during orientation and has refined during the year based on his classroom and course experiences and on reactions from other interns. He then gives examples of lessons and units he has prepared during his internship, accompanied by samples of student work, photographs, and his reflections on his work.

Because of his case study assignment in the fall semester, Tom has developed heightened awareness of special-needs students and of multiple intelligences. This awareness is reflected in his comments about the activities he has planned and carried out. At one point he recounts a story about one of his students who had been reluctant to talk in class but had been drawn out when, at his suggestion, her desk-mate read her comments to the class. As Tom remarked, "Her smile lit up the whole room. It made her day. And it made mine."

In his second placement, as Tom explains, his unit on weather was the result of his second-semester interdisciplinary unit assignment. The weather unit allowed him to relate science, math, and music (songs about weather and an original blues number performed by students on harmonicas). During the development of this unit, he invited student suggestions for other topics and, based on their suggestions, added activities involving sundials and air pressure, including having the students themselves act like air molecules under different temperature conditions.

When Tom finishes his presentation, the audience applauds and then Ms. Hanley invites questions. Tom responds to questions about how he approaches planning, how his activities exemplify the ETEP outcomes, and how he uses his frequent note-taking about students to inform his teaching and assessment. As the intermediate school principal comments, "He is such a tremendous kid watcher . . . He's got such a solid base and cares so much about the kids."

Tom is asked to leave the room so that the committee can discuss confirming and disconfirming evidence affecting its recommendation concerning his certification. The group engages in about 10 minutes of frank conversation. Particularly central is Tom's initial difficulty in his second placement. The committee discusses the fact that he has learned to work well with young children and, especially, that he chose to remain in the placement and work on improving his performance. Following the discussion, Tom is invited back into the room and is informed that he is being recommended for Maine's two-year provisional teaching certificate. After applause and congratulations, the session participants debriefed.

As the coordinators later explain, Tom could have asked for a placement change because of the difficulties he initially experienced. His decision to stay and try to improve was viewed by the committee as strong evidence of his willingness and ability to learn and grow in difficult situations with appropriate support from more experienced educators. As one of his cooperating teachers observed, "In essence, he was starting over in January, but he didn't come away from this year with two separate experiences. He was able to link them and learn from them."

Successful completion of his course work also earns him 33 credits toward the master's degree. He has completed the internship year of ETEP and is ready to enter the teaching profession.

At the writing of this report, Tom was teaching fourth grade in a near-by Maine school district. In looking back over his ETEP experiences, he commented: "I worked my tail off last year. I kind of pushed my own limits and realized what I could do—which is going to help me this year because I know I'm going to have to do it again."

## ASSESSMENT OF THE ETEP PROGRAM
### Survey Results and Follow-up Interviews

"Pushing one's limits" may be a key to the success of the ETEP program and its graduates. This success may be observed in several ways—ETEP graduates' perceptions of their preparation, how they organize and implement teaching and learning, and their employers' perceptions of their preparation.

In 1996, NCREST surveyed ETEP graduates and their employers as well as a random sample of beginning teachers nationwide garnered from a list provided by the National Education Association (Silvernail, 1997). Both sets of graduates responded to questions about their preparation and about how they approach teaching and learning; employers responded only to items about ETEP graduates' preparation relative to that of other beginning teachers.

Eighty-four ETEP graduates, 18 of whom interned in Gorham, responded to the survey. Of these 18, three graduated in 1993, seven in 1994, and eight in 1995. Sixteen were women, most between the ages of 25 and 45. Seventeen ETEP-Gorham graduates were teaching at the time of the survey, typically in suburban or rural public elementary schools. Asked if they would become teachers if they had it to do over again, 12 said "certainly," five said "probably," and one said "chances are about even." In the same vein, asked if they would choose the same preparation program again, six said "definitely" and 12 said "probably." Respondents indicated several reasons for choosing the ETEP-Gorham program: "fit my teaching philosophy" (13 respondents), "geographical convenience" (12 respondents), and "reputation of the program" (9 respondents).

Asked to consider 41 items about how well their program prepared them for teaching, both the ETEP-Gorham and comparison groups generally reported that they feel either "well" or "very well" prepared. Overall, 76 percent of ETEP-Gorham graduates and 66 percent of the comparison group feel quite prepared. Significantly, the ETEP-Gorham graduates see themselves as especially well prepared in three areas stressed in the ETEP-Gorham program: creating interdisciplinary curricula, helping students to learn how to assess their own learning, and planning and solving problems with colleagues. Interestingly, both groups report feeling relatively less well prepared in these areas: identifying special learning needs, teaching to support new English learners, using technology in the classroom, working with parents and families, and resolving interpersonal conflict.

The ETEP-Gorham and comparison group respondents also reported how frequently 16 aspects of teaching and learning occur in their classrooms. Differences on five items are striking. ETEP-Gorham graduates much more frequently feel that they "often" or "nearly always" emphasize student participation in the assessment of their own work, complete portfolios or projects to show their learning, and revise their work for re-evaluation. In contrast to the comparison sample, ETEP-Gorham graduates reported that they seldom punish students for misbehavior or have students regularly take written tests and quizzes.

In the same survey, 18 principals rated ETEP graduates employed in their schools. The principals were not asked to indicate particular ETEP sites, such as Gorham or Portland, where their teachers had interned. Thus, these data apply to ETEP generally. Overall, 87 percent of principals rated ETEP graduates as "well" or "very well" prepared—a higher evaluation than graduates gave themselves. Moreover, this higher evaluation by principals held true across virtually all of the items. That graduates rated themselves lower perhaps suggests that they continue to be reflective and self-critical, striving for continuous improvement in their employment, as was the expectation in ETEP.

The principals' comments are also instructive. The principals have, as a group, employed a total of 42 ETEP graduates over the past several years, compared with 59 non-ETEP graduates. Representing urban, suburban, and rural elementary, middle, and high schools, the principals consistently used such phrases as "excellent" and "outstanding" to describe the ETEP program and "committed," "superior," "dedicated," and "mature" to describe its graduates. Only three ETEP graduates were considered to be problems, two because they were seen as not well-prepared, and one because of a lack of interpersonal skill.

Especially illuminating are several more detailed comments from the principals about employability and performance. Regarding *employability*, one principal noted, "We know that we can assume that an ETEP candidate will be in the top five percent of candidates for a position." Another commented, "ETEP graduates are sought and are readily invited for interviews. Program graduates have [an] excellent success rate in our district."

Comments about the *performance* of ETEP graduates in their teaching positions are similarly positive. Several principals observed that ETEP graduates are "reflective," "professional," and "learner-centered." In another vein, one principal called ETEP graduates "team players," and another said, "They induct quickly into our school culture." Another pointed to the graduates' leadership ability, saying, "I look to ETEP grads to help change the culture of this school. They have the big picture. . . ."

While graduates from 1993 to 1995 gave themselves lower ratings than the principals gave them, in follow-up interviews with the 1995-96 cohort, several echoed the sentiments of these principals. In their first year of teaching, these graduates are active members of their faculties, particularly when asked to provide expertise gained from ETEP. The experiences in portfolio development, cited by teachers and principals in praising interns, have carried through into current teaching and school-wide leadership. As one graduate explained, "I can help teachers who really don't know that much about portfolios. . . . I have teachers coming to me to ask advice on [such] topics." More generally, another graduate explained, "I just jumped into the group" on assessment in preparation for the 10-year accreditation visit.

The 1996 NCREST survey results augment and substantiate an earlier survey conducted by USM's placement office (Howe, 1994). This five-year follow-up study traced graduates of ETEP at all sites from 1989 through 1993. Of the 130 respondents (a 57 percent response rate), 87 percent were employed in education, two-thirds of those were teaching full-time, mostly in Maine, and an additional five percent were employed in teaching-related positions such a child-care and adult services. Moreover, nearly one-half said they were actively involved in school reform efforts.

Nearly three-fourths of respondents rated their preparation as "superior" or "above average," and 90 percent planned to stay in—or return to—teaching. Respondents particularly saw their internships as the most helpful aspect of their program. In contrast, many saw their courses as the least useful aspect, and some did feel that their prior preparation in content areas was somewhat weak.

## KEY COMPONENTS OF THE ETEP PROGRAM: PROMOTING LEARNER-CENTERED PRACTICE

How does teacher education promote learner-centered—and learning-centered—practice? How are novices socialized to be reflective and committed to continuous improvement? What conditions are present? With ETEP-Gorham, three features are key: institutionally supported *collaboration* among university and school educators, program *"embeddedness"* in a progressive school district, and intern *immersion* in progressive classroom practice.

### School-University Collaboration

One of the distinctive features of ETEP is that it was conceived from the beginning as a collaboration among public school and university educators who had already established a history of trust and mutual respect through the Southern Maine Partnership (SMP). The SMP and the leadership of the current executive director and the former and current Gorham superintendents were repeatedly cited by many respondents as significant to the shaping of school reform, teacher education reform, and the substantial intertwining of the two. As one respondent noted, referring to these leaders, "[They have] kept us centered and remind us of the important values concerning collaboration and reform."

Due to the high degree of collaboration, ETEP functions within and across the variety of organizational structures comprising schools, districts, and the university. A result has been new organizational roles, arrangements, and distributions of responsibility and resources (including time) related to teacher preparation, bringing in new practices as well as new tensions.

For example, unlike other graduate-level programs offered by the College of Education and Human Development, ETEP is unique in that it serves cohorts of students admitted both to a master's program and to a particular school district site. The program is also largely self-contained. That is, ETEP maintains its own standards and expectations, its own admission procedures, its own sequence of courses and assessments, and its own rhythm of program activities and events to celebrate. Sometimes these do not coincide well with established university calendars or all aspects of the schools' calendars. Intern cohorts begin work in the summer a week or more before schools open; thus they are able to participate in the opening of school. However, they officially complete the internship prior to the closing of school in late June. Many interns continue on their own volition to visit their placement classrooms even into June.

As part of the department of teacher education, the program is overseen by the director of the department and the dean of the college. But the details of daily management are handled in the five sites by pairs of university and school site coordinators and through regular meetings of all site coordinators and other teacher education faculty. The role of coordinator includes administrative and teaching responsibilities: managing and allocating the site budget, coordinating calendars and courses within and across sites; admitting, placing, mentoring, observing, and evaluating interns; and leading the year-long, weekly internship seminar.

### *Financial Arrangements of the Collaboration*

ETEP is, of course, financially part of the larger structure of the college of education and human development. The college includes 37 full-time professors, seven professors with joint appointments, and 50 part-time faculty. Nearly all full-time faculty hold doctorate degrees from institutions throughout the United States, and nearly one-third of part-time faculty also hold doctorates.

The college, with a yearly budget of approximately $2,500,000 (about 10.5 percent of the total university budget), funds ETEP within the regular university budget system, based on projected enrollments in and tuition generated from the program. This method of financing is relatively recent, however. Prior to 1995, the financing of ETEP depended on what Dean Richard Barnes terms "a continuing education model." That is, ETEP finances depended on tuition generated, thereby creating an account that varied as enrollment ebbed and flowed but had the advantage of being separate from the university's base budget.

Based on ETEP's revenue history, however, the college and the university negotiated to make ETEP a part of the regular university budget system. In effect, ETEP moved from a soft-money to a base-budget account. Each year, ETEP enrollments are projected, usually based on the assumption of about 15 interns per site. The tuition generated by these projected enrollments then becomes the budget for the program. If ETEP enrollments are lower than anticipated, the University receives tuition income lower than the established budget. Conversely, higher enrollments lead to University income greater than projected.

Because ETEP is a graduate-level program, its finances are enhanced by receiving higher tuition per credit hour than would be the case in undergraduate courses. Also, because ETEP is so closely connected to its sites, it has created something of a captive market for further graduate-level course work of teachers, thereby generating additional revenues for the University.

This system of financing, while helping to stabilize ETEP budgetary planning, is not without problems, however. Because it is a one-year program, ETEP must be able to offer all required courses each year, regardless of class size. While the college's rule of thumb is to have a minimum of 10 students in graduate-level courses, ETEP course enrollments often drop to eight or lower, with the class sometimes even becoming a one-on-one tutorial. The salaries needed to pay the university and school personnel teaching these courses thus become a major unknown until the year's course offerings are established. For example, while each site receives $500 per intern in stipends for district cooperating teachers, the number of such teachers needed may vary considerably from year-to-year as course offerings and class size vary.

To manage and teach in the program, each university coordinator receives six hours of course credit each semester—that is, one-half of a normal semester load. The school coordinator receives at least one-half of her/his salary from the school district. In return, the school district receives a stipend of $15,000 yearly to help defray these costs. Additional costs are covered by the district, thus promoting the "shared funding" characteristic of the program. Moreover, the school coordinators are considered members of the department of teacher education and recently were given voting rights in the department.

In ETEP-Gorham, the school site coordinator holds a teacher-leader position in the district; as such, it is on an elevated district salary scale. Despite recent budget cuts that eliminated several other teacher-leader positions, however, Gorham has not only kept this position but has designated it a full-time position focused on ETEP for the past two years, 1994 to 1996.

Just as Gorham teachers have new responsibilities and authority for teacher education, the university site coordinator for ETEP-Gorham now helps make decisions in the school district as a member of the district's leadership team. This policy-making body is led by the superintendent and composed of central office administrators, principals, teacher-leaders, and the ETEP-Gorham university coordinator. Discussing this relationship, the superintendent commented, "They [USM faculty] are a tremendous resource for us. They have been so supportive of our work. I sometimes feel that they're part of our organization and we're part of theirs."

The high level of collaboration between USM and Gorham has expanded over time, despite turnover in many key leadership roles— dean, superintendent, teacher education department head, Southern Maine Partnership director, school site coordinator. The partnership is now clearly district-wide, symbolized by the fact that in the fall 1995-96 placements, ETEP interns were working in every school in the district.

To be sure, other collaborative teacher education programs have developed strong ties with schools (see Darling-Hammond, 1994). Few, however, have maintained strong partnerships between a higher education institution and a *school district* over time, as is the case with ETEP in Gorham. The collaboration we observed goes well beyond cooperation among like-minded individuals working at different institutions and advising one another about the work in their home institutions. Rather, it is characterized by what Schlechty and Whitford (1988) have called "organic collaboration," in which the partners are institutionally supported for working on a shared, jointly-developed agenda.

In part, this mature level of collaboration may be a function of Gorham's relative stability and small size (2,300 students and 120 teachers in six schools), which reduces the complexity of developing relationships. It also grows out of prior connections forged within the Southern Maine Partnership and is strengthened by affiliations with national reform-minded groups.

### Gorham School Department

Located 10 miles west of Portland, the Gorham schools have had a reputation for innovative practice for at least the past decade. During much of the 1980s, elementary educators, especially, engaged in restructuring efforts promoting reflective practice and inquiry. Gorham was also one of the original members of the Southern Maine Partnership, begun in 1984, which brought together superintendents of several school districts with the University of Southern Maine to discuss educational issues and district initiatives to address them. Two years later, this collaborative work led southern Maine educators to join John Goodlad's National Network for Educational Renewal. A few years after that, they became active in the Professional Development Schools network established by NCREST. Interest in reform, especially at the elementary level, was often spurred by external grants and the network of educators established by the Southern Maine Partnership. (For example, Lieberman and Grolnick, 1996.)

When the current superintendent assumed leadership in 1990, he began promoting reform across all levels in the district. Important in this regard was Gorham's participation in the Authentic Teaching, Learning, and Assessment for all Students (ATLAS) Project, begun in 1993. ATLAS was consistent with Gorham's previous work on inquiry and reflective practice and prompted Gorham educators to focus on performance assessment, developing rubrics and templates by which to guide teaching and assessment of student work district wide.

Building on these reforms in 1995-96, the Gorham leadership adopted five areas of concentration designed to address continuous progress and public accountability. Four of these areas—compulsory performances, portfolios, projects, and conferences—culminate in the fifth area: exhibitions for all students in grades 3, 6, 8, and 11. As Kimball and Hanley (n.d.) report,

> The emphasis is on educating students in a way where each year builds on the individual's previous work—student goals will provide the threads of improvement across his/her school career. The district is developing systems where portfolios follow the students throughout their school careers; where exhibitions are displayed and evaluated every three years; where every student is expected to demonstrate competent performance in reading, writing, data analysis, oral presentation, and visual representation; and where parent conferences involve students presenting their portfolios to the parents and teacher (p. 1).

In Gorham, compulsories or "comps" are defined as "what all students must be able to do to express or show what they know and understand" (Gorham School Department, 1996). At present, the comps focus on written and oral communication while developmental work is underway for a third compulsory—data analysis. Teachers are expected to engage students frequently in producing written work and oral presentations which are then assessed by both students and teachers using district rubrics (see Appendix B).

Introduced in 1990, student portfolios are a key to accomplishing these goals. Portfolios are a tool for reflection and assessment, not merely collections illustrating students' work. Written pieces from the compulsory performances form the core of the portfolio, and at least one piece of writing included in the portfolio is scored using the district's rubric, the "Writing Process Inventory."

The importance of the portfolio is particularly clear in the third area of concentration—student-parent-teacher conferences. These conferences have become a system-wide event where students' progress and goals for the year are discussed. Often, students are expected to lead the conferences, using the portfolio to guide the discussion. The priority of the conferences is indicated by the fact that the district has added four days to the school year to accommodate them.

With project design, the fourth area of concentration, teachers are expected to use a standard planning template (see Appendix D) to design at least one unit during the year. Curriculum planned in this way requires students and teachers to focus on an identified theme, essential questions, compulsories, on-going assessment, and a final exhibition—a culminating performance which demonstrates learning.

Each year, students in the third, sixth, eighth, and eleventh grade also participate in "benchmark exhibitions," the fifth area of concentration. These exhibitions have been held for two years and are assessed by at least two adults outside the school. According to the superintendent, the inclusion of community members in the assessment process is typical of the Gorham restructuring effort.

### Embedding ETEP in Gorham

With ETEP-Gorham, the effect of the school-university collaboration has been to embed the program in the practices of the district. Thus, interns in Gorham learn how to use performance assessments and portfolios as ongoing assessment tools, how to plan curricula using the district's template, and how to reflect on their practice using evidence from their work and the work of their students. Program embedding is supported by several perspectives held by both USM and Gorham educators.

First, and perhaps most important, practitioner knowledge is valued. A USM professor and a Gorham teacher share much of the responsibility for the internship and the seminar—maintaining contact two to three times a week with each intern. This intensive interaction also serves to integrate the various program components. Gorham teachers become involved in ETEP by interviewing possible interns, recommending them for admission, mentoring them, and serving, along with district administrators, as members of the portfolio committees which make certification recommendations. As the university site coordinator points out, ". . . in this [intern] assessment process, we're banking on diverse points of view and different sources of evidence, and the system has to be built that way."

Further, teachers often serve as ETEP course instructors, an arrangement held in high regard by the interns. As one principal stressed, however, "This arrangement does not mean that teachers teach practice and professors teach theory. It doesn't mean professors versus teachers. It may be risky at first, but it is working." Both principals and cooperating teachers see their involvement in ETEP as enhancing their own professional development. One principal observed, "When teachers serve as instructors for interns' courses, their own teaching improves. Others learn from them, and they learn from others." A teacher, commenting on her role as an ETEP instructor, reported:

> It's a nice professional development opportunity for people in Gorham, but it's also very beneficial for the [interns], because they get to see what happens in the classroom and to hear from people who know the pitfalls. It's not just the theory. It's also a lot of the practical, day to day: here's what [the theory] says should happen, and here's what it looks like.

Second, knowledge brought into the Gorham schools from the university is valued. One principal, admitting that his school is behind others in using portfolios, said that ETEP interns are "models for portfolio development." A similar opinion is offered by another principal, who reported that interns bring in new skills and experiences that existing staff do not have—again citing portfolio development as the example. In considering how Gorham educators view the university, this principal commented:

> Both parties have an interest in getting better—because no matter what we [in schools] do that we think is good, we always have a long way to go to get better at it, and universities can be a great help in that—their access to research and information, the kinds of studies they want and need to do all those things can really help school systems.

Third, the ETEP interns themselves are seen as valued members of the school district. As one cooperating teacher said:

> The benefit that I have seen really is that it gives the teacher a partner to talk to, someone to talk about their work with. You don't always have that, even if you say you want to team with so and so who's next door, you never have the time. [With an intern,] someone's in the room watching you teach. So the ben-

efits of the team teaching, the collaboration, the conversations for the practicing teacher are wonderful. Also, it keeps the practicing teachers current on research, and the interns help the practicing teachers learn about the new documents that are out there, such as the new state learning goals or the social studies standards. . . .

And, as another cooperating teacher observed:

I know that we need to teach people how to teach—that's a mission that I have. But I also do it because I learn from them. Five years ago, I took the first [intern]. I hadn't been in school in 30 years, for goodness sakes. Anyway, when I took the first one, I realized there's a source of knowledge for me right there because they were getting knowledge. . . and coming right into my classroom.

Yet another cooperating teacher perhaps best captured the views of many when she observed, "Interns are another warm body. But they come with a brain, too!" A principal commented, "After an intern left our school for his second placement, the kids asked, 'What happened to the teacher? Where did the teacher go?'"

Cooperating teachers see benefits for their students as well. As one teacher says, "An intern supplies an extra facet to the classroom. I would never have tried a poetry unit, but our intern did, and it was wonderful for the children. . . . You learn, but the kids learn, too." She goes on:

What I also think is very important is that [the interns'] whole process is modeled after what we expect kids to do here. . . . So when I can say, "Hey, kids, Ms. Jones' big portfolio presentation is next week, we've got to make a card for her," they know what we're talking about. They know she has to stand up and go through this whole thing, just as they do in their conferences, just as they have to do for their unit project.

Part and parcel of the collaboration and embedding is the high degree of trust within ETEP-Gorham. This trust is especially evidenced in joint responsibility: the university coordinator's membership in the district's leadership team, teachers having voting rights in ETEP program meetings, and the lack of differentiation between university and school coordinators in terms of responsibility and voice in describing and determining ETEP directions.

Another indicator of the embedded nature of the program is the extent to which both university and school personnel use the same language to describe teacher education and teaching. This language is not merely jargon or a collection of the current education reform buzz words. Rather, it indicates thoughtful commitment to similar conceptions and norms of teaching and learning. For example, rubrics and portfolios are used for performance assessment of Gorham students and ETEP interns. The program coordinators use the Gorham planning template with its focus on essential questions, rubrics, and ongoing assessment in their work with interns and to describe ETEP to others; they require the interns to develop their units using this template and the Gorham outcomes. Moreover, at least one USM faculty member not involved in the ETEP internship year is using the Gorham planning template to organize an assessment course for the MTL program.

## UNRESOLVED PROGRAM ISSUES

Even with the trust, common norms, and authentic partnership, embedding a teacher education program in a school district is not unproblematic. A simple issue as the calendar is a case in point. In their first placement, interns follow the school district calendar and are in the schools at virtually the same time as the classroom teachers with whom they work. One reason the program is designed this way is so that interns can experience the beginning of school and see firsthand how teachers set norms with new groups of learners. About half way through the second placement, interns begin taking lead responsibility for teaching and are at the same time preparing for their portfolio presentations. To provide time for this latter task, however, interns begin to remove themselves from their classrooms by late April. The classroom, of course, continues. Several cooperating teachers expressed concern about this lack of synchronicity between school and university calendars. As one commented:

> We had our parent-teacher-student conferences last week—a wonderful place for [the interns] to be sitting. And they were released from their duties here to get their portfolios together

and so forth. So that's poor timing for that critical piece.

Additionally, teachers' curriculum plans and interns' course assignments are not always in synch. As another teacher pointed out:

> On a second placement, in the spring, you need to know in January of the teaching year that you will have an intern who needs to focus on math and science and so plan your year accordingly so they can have that focus. I think that's disruptive for some placements. [The classroom teachers] already know what they're doing, and they have this person who has an agenda they have to be able to carry out. I think that's been problematic.

Another issue concerns a long-standing problem with teacher induction—what might be called the "wash-out" effect. In essence, the problem is that regardless of what is learned in a teacher education program, it is the school culture that most determines how a teacher will practice over time. In other words, the type of teaching and learning valued and rewarded in a particular school tends to overwhelm or "wash out" the values and practices inherent in teacher preparation programs.

Clearly, the experiences interns get during their year in Gorham are strikingly different from what has typically been the approach to teacher preparation. Gorham schools are on the forefront of school restructuring and would seem to be an ideal situation into which to place interns. The innovations aimed at continuous improvement and public accountability have strong district support. Interns whose practice is dependent on the support of what we might call " the Gorham way," however, may have problems accommodating themselves to working conditions in districts that do not prize the kind of work which has become commonplace in Gorham and in ETEP.

Moreover, while Gorham administrators indicate they are very impressed with the interns, they can hire only a few of the ETEP graduates each year. Problems with the Gorham tax base and with voter reluctance to increase tax rates suggest that the market for ETEP graduates in Gorham will remain small for the coming years. Moreover, Gorham is a small district with economic diversity but not much cultural or ethnic diversity. As such, the district obviously does not reflect the conditions found in large, urban, multi-ethnic school systems which hire interns.

When asked about these conditions last May, Tom Taylor indicated that, while he would prefer to teach in a district that supports ETEP practices, he anticipated working outside Gorham. In that case, he argued, he would start introducing new practices, especially the use of portfolios. Further, he expressed confidence that he would be able to provide such leadership based on what he has learned and the commitments he has developed during ETEP. Data from principals who have ETEP graduates in their schools indicate that Tom's confidence is not misplaced.

## Immersion: Juxtaposing Theory and Practice

Another set of issues is related to what in ETEP-Gorham is called immersion in classroom practice. How time is allocated between course work and classroom experiences is a factor that varies by site. The Portland site, for example, has alternated supervised teaching and the university courses on a bi-weekly basis; the Wells site has used a "six-four" plan whereby interns are in schools six days and then attend university courses for four days. Compared with interns in other sites, the ETEP-Gorham interns spend more time immersed in classrooms—virtually all day, every day for two semester-long placements—leaving only late afternoons for their course work.

As described previously, with ETEP-Gorham, interns are immediately incorporated into the classroom life that becomes their first placement. As one of the site coordinators pointed out:

> [After orientation] they have two days prior to school officially starting, where they can pretty much bet that teachers are going to be in fixing their rooms, looking at cumulative folders or something like that so they can drop by school—or at least contact [teachers] by phone or whatever and say, "I'm with you and you're with me." The first two weeks [of school], there are no [university] classes. [The interns'] only job is to be there every day, all day long, doing, helping, observing, connecting with kids, that kind of thing. We don't have seminar; there aren't any courses going on. They just have an opportunity to settle in.

Teacher education courses, where possible, are arranged to enhance the immersion. Over time, course work and classroom experience have been increasingly integrated and courses are scheduled to minimize taking time away from working directly in classrooms. In fact, in interviews, the ETEP-Gorham coordinators repeatedly stressed the importance of basing program courses on the interns' work in classrooms, which, in turn, should be determined by, as Mr. Kimball put it, "what first year teachers should be expected to be able to do."

The attempt to link course content directly to daily practice also means that theory and practice are juxtaposed almost daily. On the one hand, this puts pressure on interns to find a means of integration. The theoretical work of the previous afternoon is to find application in this morning's practical classroom experience. On the other hand, the juxtaposition highlights course content and assignments which do not find immediate application—or at least are not often taught in such a way as to make this application apparent. This can result in intense intern criticism of such courses and assignments.

These problems are played out in several ways. The ETEP-Gorham immersion approach has recently been at the center of debates, sometimes heated, among the teacher education faculty. Those most closely associated with the Gorham site find great value in immersion, while some other ETEP instructors believe the Gorham interns spend too much time in schools, leaving too little time for sustained, thoughtful attention to course work. Some university-based course instructors also worry about having sufficient contact hours to cover what they consider essential.

Central to this question of essential knowledge and disposition is the practical problem of determining how time should be allocated within the extremely full nine-month schedule. In that time, the program cannot develop specialists in all facets of an elementary teacher's work.

The Gorham coordinators, while very committed to immersion, are working to make adjustments in the interns' schedule to provide more "quality time" for course work. As Mr. Kimball put it to his colleagues during one contentious faculty meeting, "For a long time, we held the courses sacrosanct. We cannot now hold classroom time sacrosanct." So, for the fall of the 1996-97 year, planning provided the Gorham interns with Wednesday afternoons for program course work in addition to their seminar time on Fridays. Strategies for teaching science were to be addressed during several full-day workshops rather than two-and-one-half-hour weekly sessions. While this move may relieve the time pressures somewhat, the questions regarding essential content and academic credit structured as contact hours remain unresolved.

A second facet of the debate seems related not so much to immersion per se but to the site-based nature of ETEP. As one professor commented:

> Not all the knowledge that we have about teaching is in any one given place. The work that's done by researchers, by people working on language development, [the] work of Vygotsky—all of this work has been critical in terms of expanding our knowledge. Gardner's work came from working with people who had severe injuries to the brain. It doesn't only come out of the schools. So you've got to have a bigger catch. You've got to have a bigger place to say what counts as knowledge. I think there is room for that understanding that moves in and out between the places where the kids are working—you can take things, but you also need the time to kind of mull through what the heck is really known about development.

Another professor expressed concern about the relative course credit allocated to literacy (six hours) versus math, science, and social studies (six hours total) in the elementary program. A cooperating teacher responded to this concern this way:

> Almost everything you do [in the elementary school] in science and social studies is literacy. So [the interns] have to have those strong foundations. But they have to have those other pieces, too, that are really important. They have to understand classroom climate, they have to understand how important the social piece is. . . .

A third part of the debate concerns how to maintain a balance between high standards and a reasonable work load. As one cooperating teacher said:

> I don't want to make the program [an] easier [way into teaching]. I think we need to have the rigid standards and the integrity of our program, but I'm not sure we're not asking too much in one year. I know that the literacy department [at USM] is very concerned that we don't water down the content of those two courses, because

they feel that they are so important. And I feel we haven't done that. . . . We've dignified the true six-credit nature of that work.

A fourth issue identified by some education faculty is the stress caused by the intensity of immersion along with taking 33 graduate credits in nine months. One commented, "How can they possibly attend well to courses and readings and assignments at a graduate level when they are in classrooms all day?" Mr. Kimball later added these comments while reviewing this part of a draft of the case study:

> Bingo! That's the heart of the stress question—especially if we're still looking for solutions grounded in a course mode. That way of thinking reflects an assumed dichotomy of classroom practice and graduate study that courses are for readings and assignments and the province of the university on top of and separate from classroom experience.—Can interns think about theory and practice both while in the classroom and in seminars/course sessions? Can we use the principles [of] clarity of criteria or standards, teaching necessary skills and tools, ongoing feedback, opportunities for improvement, student presentation and explanations, and relevant and meaningful exercises, projects, exhibitions as the basis for looking at university teaching?—These issues are directly related to the stress question. We are not sure the answer has to be less of "this" so we can make room for "that."

The ETEP-Gorham interns have responded to the stress by developing a variety of ways to cope. Seminar and the support of particular cohort members were often cited as invaluable. Also, in early May, the 1995-96 interns designed and printed T-shirts for the cohort depicting "The Twelfth Outcome" as an intern diving unscathed through a ring of fire. At the graduation celebration, they proudly presented Mr. Kimball and Ms. Hanley with the shirts they had ordered for them as gifts. Despite the stress of the year's experiences, the interns had maintained a sense of humor—and perhaps increased their cohesiveness as well.

Several cooperating teachers acknowledged the presence of stress but did not view the workload as all that much out of line from what is routinely expected of teachers. This comment about stress is illustrative:

That's a reality, but I try to equate it to what it's like to be a teacher in Gorham because we have—certainly we're getting paid for our work, which is a huge difference—but for people who are taking courses and who are involved in district work and all the things that are asked of us—you have a little more stress but [it's] not unlike your job, the real world.

And another pointed out:

The things that they are expected to do are hard. It's time consuming to take those classes and do your internship in school. And while that's the biggest complaint they have during course work, they're always reminded that that's the real life of a teacher. A lot of people in this building have courses, so it's real life.

## CONCLUDING COMMENTS

ETEP-Gorham—much like Gorham itself—stresses ongoing assessment with the understanding that, when evidence is reflected upon, performance can always improve. The emphasis is on linking beliefs, goals, and evidence of progress as explicitly as possible. This notion of continuous progress has programmatic as well as individual connotations. Just as students in Gorham and interns in ETEP are expected to improve continuously, the program itself changes over time, as this comment from a cooperating teacher illustrates:

I think it's kind of unnerving—each year they change what they do, but it's usually for the better. There are times when I whine about all the work. But, I've got to tell you, I went to that [intern portfolio] presentation this morning, and then I knew why I was doing what I was doing. If we're going to continue to get products like that, then we've got to continue to do what we're doing.

Part of continuing to "do what they are doing" is about making collaborative teacher education a deliberate, reflective process. Debating how to address what teacher educators believe is essential preservice knowledge and discussing evidence bearing on these issues will likely continue to motivate ETEP educators to improve the way they prepare interns to enter teaching. The process of embedding a teacher education program into a school district and immersing program students into that district's classrooms requires continuous—and honest—conversation. The collaboration between the University of Southern Maine and the Gorham School Department indeed illustrates how teacher education can profit from such conversation.

# REFERENCES

College of Education and Human Development. (1995). *A report to the National Council for Accreditation of Teacher Education and the Maine Department of Education.* University of Southern Maine: Author.

College of Education and Human Development. (1996-97). *Extended Teacher Education Program booklet.* University of Southern Maine: Author.

Darling-Hammond, L. (Ed.). (1994). *Professional Development Schools: Schools for developing a profession.* New York: Teachers College Press.

Gardner, H. (1983). *Frames of mind: The theory of multiple intelligences.* New York: Basic Books.

Extended Teacher Education Program. (1995-96). *Course handout for EDU 660: Life Span Development.* University of Southern Maine: Author.

Extended Teacher Education Program. (1995-96). *Course syllabi for EDU 541/542.* University of Southern Maine: Author.

Extended Teacher Education Program. (1995-96). *Course syllabi for EDU 540: Exceptionality.* University of Southern Maine: Author.

Extended Teacher Education Program. (1995-96). *Course syllabi for HRD 660: Life Span Development.* University of Southern Maine: Author.

Extended Teacher Education Program. (1995-96). *Social studies methods course syllabus.* University of Southern Maine: Author.

Gorham School Department. (June 11, 1996). Handout. Gorham, Maine: Author.

Howe, E. (1994). *Five year follow-up study of interns from the University of Southern Maine Extended Teacher Education Programs 1989 through 1993.* University of Southern Maine, Department of Career Services and Cooperative Education. Gorham, Maine: University of Southern Maine.

Kimball, W. H., & Hanley, S. (n.d.). *A case study of intertwined P-12 school renewal and teacher education redesign.* Gorham, Maine: Gorham School Department, Gorham ETEP Professional Development Site.

Lieberman, A. & Grolnick, M. (1996). Networks and reform in American education. *Teachers College Record, 98* (1), 7-45.

Schlechty, P. C., & Whitford, B. L. (1988). Shared problems and shared vision: Organic collaboration. In K. A. Sirotnik and J. I. Goodlad (Eds.), *School-university partnerships in action: Concepts, cases, and concerns* (pp. 191-204). New York: Teachers College Press.

Silvernail, D. (1997). *Results from surveys of graduates of exemplary teacher education programs and the employers of their graduates*. Gorham, Maine: Center for Educational Policy, Applied Research, and Evaluation.

Wigginton, E. (1985). *Sometimes a shining moment: The Foxfire experience*. New York: Doubleday.

## ACKNOWLEDGMENTS

We thank the many people at the University of Southern Maine, the Gorham School Department, and the Southern Maine Partnership who, without exception, responded generously to our many requests for assistance in helping us understand the Extended Teacher Education Program (ETEP) generally and ETEP-Gorham, particularly. We are grateful to them for their hospitality, their willingness to share their work, their cooperation in helping us schedule interviews and observations, and their openness even though we were "from away." Teachers, professors, students, staff, and administrators shared not only their understandings of the program but also unfailingly directed us to their favorite lobster shacks. We are very grateful.

We also express special appreciation to Walter Kimball and Susie Hanley for their untiring efforts in explaining the complexities of the program, sharing their many program documents, alerting us to additional sources of data, and reacting thoroughly and constructively to drafts of our work as it progressed. Their assistance was invaluable and their generosity much appreciated.

Primary funding for the study was provided through grants secured by Linda Darling-Hammond, co-director of the National Center for Restructuring Education, Schools, and Teaching (NCREST). Additional support was provided by the Offutt Fund, awarded by the Research and Faculty Development Committee, University of Louisville. Without this support, the study would not have been possible.

Linda Darling-Hammond provided several detailed reviews of drafts along the way. The study is clearer and more detailed because of her assistance and insights. However, the interpretations expressed here and any errors are our own.

## APPENDIX A: RESEARCH METHODOLOGY

The data for this study were collected by three researchers who spent a total of 37 person days on site from August 1995 to August 1996. During this time, we reviewed program documents, observed university and school classes and meetings, and interviewed school teachers, university teacher educators and administrators, and ETEP interns and graduates. In addition, we met with key program instructors and administrators and attended sessions conducted by them at professional meetings both in Gorham and at national conferences.

Specifically, we interviewed all ETEP-Gorham course instructors and reviewed their course syllabi. The interviews, lasting from 45 minutes to two hours each, were audiotaped and transcribed. Additional interviews, lasting from forty-five minutes to three hours, were conducted with the dean of the college of education and human development, the director of teacher education, the Gorham superintendent of schools, and the director of the Southern Maine Partnership. Since each of the six schools in the Gorham School Department—a kindergarten center, two primary schools, and an intermediate, a middle, and a high school— serve as sites for ETEP interns, we met with each principal individually, toured each school, and interviewed these administrators for thirty to forty-five minutes each.

We met with 15 mentor teachers in four of the schools, sometimes in small groups and sometimes individually, to query them about the program and the effects of having interns in their schools. Since some of the mentor teachers and school administrators also serve as ETEP course instructors, we interviewed them in that capacity separately. Two staff development specialists in the district met with us on two occasions to describe Gorham curriculum reforms at the elementary and secondary levels.

We met with the 1995-1996 ETEP-Gorham interns twice in focus group sessions and a third time during their graduation ceremony and dinner in May 1996. The first focus group session, conducted in October 1995, was approximately 90 minutes, the second, in May 1996, lasted approximately one hour. We also followed one intern throughout the year. We observed him in his first placement classroom for two full days; interviewed him twice in person, with several follow-up telephone conversations; and observed his portfolio presentation at the end of the program in May 1996. We selected this intern primarily because his first placement was in the classroom of an ETEP-Gorham graduate. We reasoned that we could best observe the effects of the program in such a setting. The mentor teacher who had graduated from ETEP was also well positioned to explain changes in the program over time and the effects of those changes on how a novice in the program learns to work with children.

We also observed the classroom of a second ETEP graduate for three-fourths of a day and interviewed him about the program and his teaching experiences. Since ETEP-Gorham is very embedded in the Gorham School Department s educational program, we wanted to see how a graduate of ETEP began working on his own in Gorham. We also viewed the videotape of his portfolio presentation, the final exhibition of his work in ETEP, filmed in May 1995.

Most ETEP graduates from Gorham and other sites in the program are teaching in districts other than Gorham. We interviewed four ETEP-Gorham graduates who are currently teaching in other districts and met with a group of 12 ETEP graduates from all sites for three hours during a graduate class on assessment. This class completed their Master of Teaching and Learning degree, begun when they entered ETEP several years previously. The day we visited the class, the graduates were presenting projects from their classrooms demonstrating how they had used performance assessment in a curriculum unit. We observed four such presentations and also had an opportunity to speak with these students informally about their experiences in ETEP.

Our most extensive interviews were with the two ETEP-Gorham site coordinators. Formal interview time on site totaled 10 hours. In addition, we had numerous follow-up conversations by telephone and e-mail. One of the coordinators accompanied us on the initial visits to each school. They provided us with many program documents which we reviewed independently and, on occasion, with their assistance. These documents included course syllabi and evaluations, program planning documents, intern portfolios—hard copies and videotaped portfolio presentations, coordinators intern observation notes, curriculum units developed by interns, accreditation reports, program-relevant videos from both the university and the school system, and school system documents related to the district's reforms.

We also attended several professional presentations by the ETEP-Gorham coordinators: an hour-long workshop for about 15 USM faculty on using portfolios to assess teaching, a three-hour invited pre-session on ETEP at the annual meeting of the 1996 American Association of Colleges for Teacher Education in Chicago, and a two-day workshop in the summer of 1996 for approximately 50 teachers and teacher educators involved in the University of Louisville's early grades MAT program.

We observed the ETEP-Gorham class on literacy, required for elementary interns, for two hours in fall 1995 and the intern seminar for a total of three hours on two occasions, one in the fall and again in the spring 1996. As mentioned previously, we also observed a class for ETEP graduates from all sites finishing the Master of Teaching and Learning degree for three hours in May 1996. In August 1996, we observed two full days of the orientation for the 1996-97 ETEP-Gorham cohort. During each observation, we had limited time to talk informally with ETEP interns or graduates. At the end of each observation, we talked informally with the instructors about what we had observed.

We also observed several key meetings in the Gorham school district and at the university. With the coordinators for all five sites, we attended two ETEP program-wide meetings, one in which curriculum content, contact hours with interns, and program planning were debated by the program instructors and another in which ETEP instructors discussed progress on an intern video portfolio project. We met with the entire teacher education faculty for two hours during a visit in October 1995, to explain our research project and hear about several others that were being conducted on ETEP. We sat in on a two-hour Gorham Extended Leadership Team meeting where district reforms and their connections with ETEP were discussed. The National Network for Educational Renewal, a reform network to which USM and the Gorham School Department belong, held several meetings while we were on site. We attended two of these meetings, both focused on financing professional development schools. The Gorham superintendent and the dean of the college of education and human development were active participants in these meetings, sharing information about the effects of ETEP and how the program is financed.

The data from several surveys sponsored by NCREST were included in our analysis of the program. These surveys provided data from ETEP graduates, their employers, and a comparable group of graduates of teachers education programs nationally. The survey of employers also included open-ended comments from principals. We also reviewed another survey of graduates conducted by the USM placement office.

All interview transcriptions, observation notes, notes from reviewing videos, and curriculum materials were read by each of the three members of the research team. We discussed the notes numerous times and wrote drafts describing emerging themes. These drafts were reviewed by the two ETEP-Gorham sites coordinators for accuracy of information and logic of interpretation. Several inaccuracies concerning load credit and financing were corrected in this manner. Differences in interpretations were included as additional data. Also, each vignette focusing on a specific classroom or instructor was reviewed for accuracy by the teachers involved. Direct quotes from individuals were also reviewed by them for accuracy. All of the adults named in the study agreed to have their real names used in the publication. All names of children are pseudonyms.

# APPENDIX B: ORAL PRESENTATION SCORING GUIDE AND WRITING PROCESS INVENTORY, GORHAM SCHOOL DEVELOPMENT

## ORAL PRESENTATION SCORING GUIDE
### (DRAFT)

| Process | very little | | sometimes | | most of the time |
|---|---|---|---|---|---|
| Spoke clearly, used appropriate speed and was easily heard. | 1 | 2 | 3 | 4 | 5 |
| Spoke with appropriate expression to keep audience interested. | 1 | 2 | 3 | 4 | 5 |
| Maintained eye contact with audience. | 1 | 2 | 3 | 4 | 5 |
| Speaker's face was clearly seen by audience. | 1 | 2 | 3 | 4 | 5 |
| Speaker used appropriate posture. | 1 | 2 | 3 | 4 | 5 |
| Shared information with audience, rather than reading from paper. | 1 | 2 | 3 | 4 | 5 |
| If visual was used, it was shared in a way that could be clearly seen by audience. | 1 | 2 | 3 | 4 | 5 |
| **Content** Speaker presented information sequentially. (logical beginning, middle, end) | 1 | 2 | 3 | 4 | 5 |
| Speaker stayed focused on topic. | 1 | 2 | 3 | 4 | 5 |
| Speaker included main ideas that were supported with details. | 1 | 2 | 3 | 4 | 5 |

**Comments:**

Name _____  Date _____

Gorham School Department, draft 8/1/95, contact:

Student: _____

Title: _____

Date: _____

## Conference Notes

## Student Goal

Teacher _____

Gorham School Department, Adopted 8/29/95, contact: Debbie Lovett or Stephanie McLaughlin

## GORHAM SCHOOLS
## WRITING PROCESS INVENTORY

This tool is based on one originally developed by Hillsboro School District in Beaverton, Oregon, modified by Northwest Regional Educational Laboratory, and further refined by the Gorham Literacy Committee.

## IDEAS/CONTENT

1 - 2 The piece does not convey a central idea or purpose.

3 - 4 The reader can figure out what the writer is trying to say but the piece may not fully answer the prompt or may lack depth.

5 - 6 The piece fully answers the prompt in a clear, compelling way, and holds the reader's attention all the way through.

## VOICE

1 - 2 The writer's voice lacks involvement, passion or sincerity.

3 - 4 The writer seems sincere but is less engaging. The result is pleasant, acceptable, sometimes personable, but not compelling.

5 - 6 The writer speaks directly to the reader in a way that is individualistic, expressive, and engaging. Clearly, the writer is involved in the text and is aware of the audience.

## SENTENCE STRUCTURE

1 - 2 Sentence flaws make this paper hard to read and understand.

3 - 4 Most sentences are well formed and understandable but tend to be mechanical.

5 - 6 Sentences are consistently well formed, have varied structure, and enhance the writer's meaning.

## ORGANIZATION

1 - 2 The writing lacks direction and the ideas are out of sequence.

3 - 4 The reader can readily follow what is being said, but the overall organization may sometimes be ineffective or too obvious.

5 - 6 The organization enhances the central idea or theme. The piece is compelling and moves the reader through the text

## WORD CHOICE

1 - 2 Words reflect the writer's struggle with vocabulary.

3 - 4 Words convey the message but only in an ordinary way.

5 - 6 Words reflect appropriate developmental level and convey the intended message in a compelling, precise, and natural way.

## WRITING CONVENTIONS

1 - 2 Numerous errors in conventions distract reader and make text difficult to read.

3 - 4 Errors in writing conventions are distracting, although they do not block meaning.

5 - 6 The writer demonstrates a good grasp of standard writing conventions, and uses them effectively to enhance readability.

## GORHAM SCHOOLS
## WRITING PROCESS INVENTORY

| | 1 - 2 ABSENT/EMERGING | 3 - 4 DEVELOPING | 5 - 6 WELL DEVELOPED |
|---|---|---|---|
| **IDEAS & CONTENT** | • Ideas need to be more thoughtfully explored or presented.<br>• Ideas seem very limited or go off in several directions.<br>• Topic needs to be developed in a meaningful way. | • Some ideas may be clear, while others may be fuzzy or may not seem to fit.<br>• The writer may spend too much time on main ideas.<br>• Extra, unneeded information may get in the way of important ideas. | • Writer knows the topic well, and chooses details that help make the subject clear and interesting.<br>• Topic is controlled and focused.<br>• Writing is balanced. Important ideas stand out. Details support the topic. |
| **ORGANIZATION** | • Ideas, paragraphs, and sentences need to be tied together or related.<br>• Transitions are missing. | • Beginning, middle, and ending are there, but one or two may be weak.<br>• Placement or relevance of some details leaves the reader occasionally confused.<br>• Ideas, paragraphs, and sentences are not always tied together; transitions may be awkward or missing. | • Details seem to fit where they are placed; sequencing is logical and effective.<br>• Ideas, paragraphs, and sentences are tied together; transitions are smooth.<br>• An inviting lead draws the reader in, and a satisfying conclusion leaves the reader with a sense of resolution. |
| **VOICE** | • The writer's voice needs to be evident.<br>• Writing communicates on a functional level without moving or involving the reader. | • Avoids risks and uses predictable language.<br>• Communicates earnestly but routinely; occasionally amuses, surprises, delights or moves reader.<br>• Voice may occasionally engage the reader. | • Paper is honest; written from the heart.<br>• Language is natural, provocative, and vigorous.<br>• Projected tone and voice enhance message.<br>• Writer's voice amuses, surprises, delights, or moves reader. |
| **WORD CHOICE** | • Words are vague and flat.<br>• Writer may use words incorrectly.<br>• Words create no clear images.<br>• Writer may repeat words or phrases. | • Words are more general and less precise.<br>• Language communicates but rarely captures the reader's imagination.<br>• Settles for common, clichéd words and phrases.<br>• May use some words inappropriately. | • Words are specific and accurate.<br>• Imagery is strong.<br>• Powerful verbs give the writing energy.<br>• Expression is fresh and appealing. |
| **SENTENCE STRUCTURE** | • Sentences are often awkward, rambling, and/or confusing.<br>• Sentences are generally short and choppy.<br>• Run-ons or fragments are distracting. | • The reader may have to reread sometimes to follow meaning.<br>• The writer shows good control over simple sentence structure but has trouble with more complex patterns.<br>• The writer starts many sentences the same way.<br>• Run-ons or fragments, if present, may be confusing.<br>• The writing may be wordy. | • The sentences sound natural, not choppy or forced.<br>• The writer controls sentence structure. Risks, such as run-ons and fragments, are effective.<br>• The writing is concise (not wordy).<br>• Dialogue, if used, sounds natural. |
| **WRITING CONVENTIONS** | • No evidence of editing.<br>• Writer shows limited skill in standard writing usage.<br>• Punctuation tends to be omitted or incorrect.<br>• Spelling errors are frequent, even on common words.<br>• Paragraphing may be absent. May be only one paragraph with almost every sentence. or may contain a new paragraph with almost every sentence. | • Noticeable lapses in editing; text may be too simple or short to reflect mastery of conventions.<br>• Terminal punctuation is almost always correct; internal punctuation may be incorrect or missing.<br>• Spelling is usually correct, or phonetic, on common words.<br>• Errors in usage do not distract meaning.<br>• Paragraphs sometimes run together or begin in incorrect places. | • Few lapses in editing.<br>• Punctuation is appropriate and helps reader understand the text.<br>• Spelling is generally correct, even on more difficult words.<br>• No major errors in grammar and usage.<br>• Writing shows mastery in use of wide range of conventions.<br>• Paragraphs reinforce organizational structure. |

Gorham School Department, Adopted 8/29/95, contact: Debbie Lovelitt or Stephanie McLaughlin

# APPENDIX C: GORHAM SCHOOLS
# FIVE ESSENTIAL OUTCOMES

Gorham's Essential Outcomes are derived from the community's Vision and Values and Beliefs, and are intended to support the accomplishment of our identified goals. These outcomes are based on a system that encourages continuous individualized learning.

These outcomes are dynamic in that we see them as a work in progress framework. We accept the responsibility of continuing to examine, adapt, and strengthen them as we continue to learn more about the variety of needs, skills and abilities of learners.

In addition to establishing outcomes, we recognize the need to maintain a climate, a culture, and a professional staff that enable and support learners in order to successfully demonstrate these outcomes.

## 1. Self-directed Learner

In Gorham, we value the development of habits of mind, heart and work conducive to self-directed learning. A self-directed learner:
   a. Demonstrates a positive attitude towards learning
   b. Sets priorities and goals
   c. Used curiosity, inquiry, reflection, and research to extend learning
   d. Uses creative thinking to generate new ways of viewing situations and to push the limits of knowledge and ability
   e. Monitors, evaluates, and annotates work and progress

## 2. Collaborative Worker

In Gorham, we value and respect people as individuals as well as collaborative workers. An individual capable of collaboration:
   a. Demonstrates acceptance and respect for diversity
   b. Monitors and controls one's own behavior
   c. Demonstrates an ability to participate in group problem solving situations
   d. Demonstrates interactive participation
   e. Honors personal freedom, choice, and the democratic process

### 3. Complex Thinker
In Gorham, we value a dynamic core of knowledge and abilities. A complex thinker:
  a. Accesses and uses topic relevant knowledge and skills
  b. Can define essential questions necessary to problem solving
  c. Selects strategies appropriate to the resolution of complex issues and applies strategies with accuracy and thoroughness
  d. Uses a variety of strategies for managing complex issues, including critical and creative thinking

### 4. Quality Producer
In Gorham, we value purposeful high quality work. A quality producer:
  a. Creates products and services done in context
  b. Creates products and services appropriate to the intended audience
  c. Creates products and services that reflect thoughtfulness, attention to detail, creativity, and craftsmanship
  d. Uses appropriate resources and technologies

### 5. Community Contributor
In Gorham, we value active community participation in the learning process. A community contributor:
  a. Demonstrates knowledge of one's community and other diverse communities
  b. Demonstrates a service to one's community
  c. Shares in the celebration of ideas
  d. Shares responsibility and accountability with others
  e. Demonstrates compassion and respect for other community members

# APPENDIX D: ETEP SCHEDULE OF COURSES
# ELEMENTARY INTERNS, PROPOSED FOR 1996-97

## FALL SEMESTER:

| Monday | Tuesday | Wednesday | Thursday | Friday |
|--------|---------|-----------|----------|--------|
| Math & Social Studies periodic sessions 3:30-5:30 p.m. Narragansett School | Literacy & Writing 4-6:30 p.m. Narragansett School | | Life Span & Exceptionality 4-6:30 p.m. 404 Bailey | Seminar 3-5:30 p.m. 102 Bailey |

## SPRING SEMESTER

| Monday | Tuesday | Wednesday | Thursday | Friday |
|--------|---------|-----------|----------|--------|
| Math 3:30-5:30 p.m. Narragansett School | Science 3-4:30 p.m. 110 Bailey | | Social Studies 4-6:30 p.m. Narragansett | Seminar 3-5:30 p.m. 102 Bailey |

# December 1995

1995-96 Gorham ETEP

| S | M | T | W | T | F | S |
|---|---|---|---|---|---|---|
| 3 | 4<br>SEC: Content Methods | 5<br>Literacy 3:30 - 6:00 P.M.<br>Narragansett | 6<br>Math 3:30-5:30 P.M.<br>Narragansett | 7<br>Lifespan/Except.<br>4:00 - 6:30 P.M.<br>404 Bailey | 8<br>Seminar 1:00 - 3:00 P.M.<br>102 Bailey<br>Lifespan/Exception. Cases | 2<br><br>9 |
| 10 | 11<br>SEC: Content Methods | 12<br>SEC: Curriculum Dvlpt.<br>3:00-5:00 P.M. High School<br><br>ELEM: Literacy<br>3:30-6:00 P.M. Narragansett | 13<br>"Unofficial" last day of fall<br>placement- classroom work<br>still encouraged.<br>(Tom N. and Mike R. stay<br>until end of semester in Jan) | 14<br>Lifespan/Except.<br>4:00 - 6:30 P.M.<br>404 Bailey<br>Presentations | 15<br>Seminar 3:00 - 5:00 P.M.<br>102 Bailey<br>Holiday Celebration | 16 |
| 17 | 18<br>SEC: Content Methods | 19<br>Literacy 3:30 - 6:00 P.M.<br>Narragansett | 20 | 21<br>Lifespan/Except.<br>4:00 - 6:30 P.M.<br>404 Bailey<br>Final School Day of 1995 | 22 | 23 |
| 24 | 25 | 26 | 27 | 28 | 29 | 30 |
| 31 | | | | | | |

EXIT CONF.

12/11 - 12/21

# January 1996   1995-96 Gorham ETEP

| S | M | T | W | T | F | S |
|---|---|---|---|---|---|---|
| | 1 | 2 Literacy 3:30 - 6:00 P.M. Narragansett | 3 Curric. Design 3:00-5:30 P.M. High School | 4 Literacy 3:30 - 6:00 P.M. Narragansett | 5 Seminar 3:00-5:00 P.M. 102 Bailey | 6 |
| 7 | 8 SEC: Content Methods Lab; ELEM: Math 3:30 - 6:00 P.M. Narragansett | 9 Literacy 3:30 - 6:00 P.M. Narragansett | 10 Curric. Design 3:00-5:30P.M. High School | 11 | 12 Seminar 3:00 - 5:00 P.M. 102 Bailey | 13 |
| 14 | 15 No school | 16 SEC: Curric. Design 3:00-5:30 P.M. High Sch. ELEM: Literacy 3:30-6:00P.M. Narragan. | 17 | 18 Math 3:30 - 6:00 P.M. Narragansett | 19 Math 1:00 - 5:00 P.M. Narragansett | 20 |
| 21 | 22 Content Methods Lab | 23 SEC: Curric. Design 3:00-5:30 P.M. High School; ELEM: Science 3:00-5:30 P.M. Bailey 110 | 24 SEC: Diversity 3:30-5:30 P.M. Bailey; ELEM: Literacy 3:30-6:00 P.M. Narragan. | 25 Math 3:30-6:00 P.M. Narragansett | 26 Seminar 3:00 - 5:00 P.M. 102 Bailey | 27 |
| 28 | 29 SEC: Content Methods Lab; ELEM: Math 3:30 - 6:00 P.M. Narragansett | 30 SEC: Curric. Design 3:00-5:30 P.M. High School; ELEM: Science 3:00 - 5:30 P.M. 110 Bailey | 31 Literacy 3:30 - 6:00 P.M. Narragansett | | | |

Annotations: ----- K-8 Conferences ----- ; ----- Diversity Workshop 1/16 - 1/18 -------

## February 1996 — 1995-96 Gorham ETEP

| S | M | T | W | T | F | S |
|---|---|---|---|---|---|---|
| 4 | | | | 1<br>Soc. Studies 3:30 -6:00 P.M.<br>White Rock | 2<br>K-12 Inter-disciplinary Teaching<br>1:00 - 5:00 P.M.<br>High School | 3 |
| 11 | 5<br>SEC: Content Methods Lab<br>ELEM: Math 3:30 - 6:00 P.M. Narragansett | 6<br>SEC: Curric. Design 3:00-5:30P.M. High School<br>ELEM: Science 3:00 - 5:30 P.M. 110 Bailey | 7<br>SEC: Diversity 2:30-5:00 P.M. Bailey<br>ELEM: Literacy 3:3 -6:00 P.M. Narragan. | 8<br>Soc. Studies 3:30-6:00 P.M.<br>White Rock | 9<br>Seminar 3:00 - 5:00 P.M.<br>102 Bailey | 10 |
| 18 | 12<br>SEC: Content Methods Lab<br>ELEM: Math 3:30 - 6:00 P.M. Narragansett | 13<br>SEC: Curric. Design 3:00-5:30 P.M. High School<br>ELEM: Science 3:00 - 5:30 P.M. 110 Bailey | 14<br>Literacy 3:30 - 6:00 P.M. Narragansett | 15<br>Soc. Studies 3:30-6:00 P.M.<br>White Rock | 16<br>No Seminar<br><br>Early Release K-8 | 17 |
| 25 | 19 | 20 | 21 | 22 | 23 | 24 |
| | 26<br>Content Methods Lab | 27<br>SEC: Curric. Design 3:00-5:30 P.M. High School<br>ELEM: Science 3:00 - 5:30 P.M. 110 Bailey | 28<br>SEC: Diversity 2:30-5:00 P.M. Bailey<br>ELEM: Literacy 3:30-6:00 P.M. Narragan. | 29<br>Soc. Studies 3:30 - 6:00 P.M.<br>White Rock | | |

- - - - - B R E A K - - - - - -

# March 1996

## 1995-96 Gorham ETEP

| S | M | T | W | T | F | S |
|---|---|---|---|---|---|---|
| | | | | | 1<br>K-12 Inter-disciplinary Teaching 1:00 - 5:00 P.M. High School | 2 |
| 3 | 4<br>Content Methods Lab | 5<br>SEC: Curric. Design 3:00-5:30 P.M. High School<br>ELEM: Science 3:00 - 5:30 P.M. 110 Bailey | 6<br>Literacy 3:30 - 6:00 P.M. Narragansett | 7<br>Soc. Studies 3:30-6:00 P.M. White Rock | 8<br>Seminar 3:00 - 5:00 P.M. 102 Bailey | 9 |
| 10 | 11<br>Content Methods Lab | 12<br>SEC: Diversity 2:30-5:00 P.M. Bailey<br>ELEM: Science 3:00-5:30 P.M. 110 Bailey | 13<br>Literacy 3:30 - 6:00 P.M. Narragansett | 14<br>Soc. Studies 3:30-6:00 P.M. White Rock | 15<br>No Seminar<br>7-12 Inservice | 16 |
| | | | ------- 7 -12 Conferences 3/13, 14, 15 -------- | | | |
| 17 | 18<br>Content Methods Lab | 19<br>Science 3:00 - 5:30 P.M. 110 Bailey | 20 | 21<br>Soc. Studies 3:30 - 6:00 P.M. White Rock | 22<br>Seminar 3:00 - 5:00 P.M. 102 Bailey | 23 |
| 24 | 25<br>Content Methods Lab | 26<br>Math 3:30-6:00 P.M. Narragansett | 27<br>Diversity 2:30 - 5:00 P.M. Bailey | 28<br>Soc. Studies 3:30 - 6:00 P.M. White Rock | 29<br>Seminar 3:00 - 5:00 P.M. 102 Bailey | 30 |
| 31 | | | | | | |

# April 1996

1995-96 Gorham ETEP

| S | M | T | W | T | F | S |
|---|---|---|---|---|---|---|
| | 1 | 2 SEC: Diversity 2:30-5:00 P.M. Bailey / ELEM: Science 3:00-5:30 P.M. 110 Bailey | 3 | 4 Soc. Studies 3:30-6:00 P.M. White Rock | 5 Seminar 3:00-5:00 P.M. 102 Bailey | 6 |
| 7 | 8 Content Methods Lab | 9 | 10 | 11 Soc. Studies 3:30-6:00 P.M. White Rock | 12 Seminar 3:00-5:00 P.M. 102 Bailey / Early Release K-8 | 13 |
| 14 | 15 | 16 — — — B | 17 R E | 18 A | 19 K — — — — — — | 20 |
| 21 | 22 Content Methods Lab | 23 | 24 Diversity 2:30-5:00 P.M. Bailey | 25 Soc. Studies 3:30-6:00 P.M. White Rock | 26 K-12 Inter-disciplinary Teaching 1:00-5:00 P.M. High School | 27 |
| 28 | 29 Content Methods Lab | 30 | | | | |

# May 1996

## 1995-96 Gorham ETEP

| S | M | T | W | T | F | S |
|---|---|---|---|---|---|---|
| | | | 1 | 2<br>Soc. Studies 3:30 - 6:00 P.M.<br>White Rock | 3<br>Seminar 3:00 - 5:00 P.M.<br>102 Bailey<br><br>Final day of spring placement | 4 |
| 5 | 6 | 7 | 8 | 9 | 10 | 11 |
| | EXIT CONFERENCES AND PRESENTATION PREPARATION | | | | | |
| 12 | 13 | 14 | 15 | 16 | 17<br>Conferences K-8 | 18 |
| | INTERN | | PORTFOLIO | | | |
| 19 | 20 | 21 | 22 | 23 | 24 | 25 |
| | | | | PRESENTATIONS | | |
| 26 | 27 | 28 | 29 | 30 | 31 | |

# APPENDIX D, continued

## Gorham ETEP 1996-97 Internship Year Curriculum Calendar

| | August | September | October | November | December | January | February | March | April | May |
|---|---|---|---|---|---|---|---|---|---|---|
| | Introduce Outcomes | Intro. Lessons | content area lesson planning | series of lessons or short units of study | extended teaching | entering new placement repeat Sept. (Independently) | courses end, all assignments due | Interdisciplinary Unit | Full Time Teaching | |
| | Gorham Context-5 Concentration areas | Review school / classroom curriculum | content standards Introduced | content area teaching and assessments | content area templates | preparing for interdisciplinary planning and teaching | extended teaching | Extended to Full Time Teaching | Synthesis | |
| | Project Design-Short Project | observing preassessment and conferencing | differentiated Instruction | classroom profile | Case study well underway | finishing up case study | planning the Interdisciplinary unit | Awareness or Involvement Exhibition Process Work | Preparing for Student Teacher Parent Conferences | |
| | All About Gorham Project | establishing classroom community | content area documentation toward goals and standards | prep. & rehearsals for conferencing | Action research project | analyzing student work for content understanding | | | | |
| | Course Frontloading | Goal Setting | running small groups / skill boosting lessons | Case Study info. gathering | content area assessments | | | | | |

**School Year Milestones**

| | August | September | October | November | December | January | February | March | April | May |
|---|---|---|---|---|---|---|---|---|---|---|
| | Opening Day Inservice | Entry Conferences | Open House | Parent Conferences | Progress Reports | | Progress Reports | Exhibitions | | |

**Internship Year Milestones**

| | August | September | October | November | December | January | February | March | April | May |
|---|---|---|---|---|---|---|---|---|---|---|
| | Introduce Outcomes | Entry Conference w/ Cooperating teachers | Mid-Placement Outcomes Review | Involved in parent conferencing | Placement Wrap-up | Mid-Year Reviews | Mid-Placement Outcome Review | Full-Time Teaching | Placement Ends | Portfolio Presentation |
| | Full-Time Teaching Guidelines | Courses Begin | Goal Setting | Reporting on the work of Subject Area Committee | Exit Conferences | 2nd Placements Begin with Entry Conference | Portfolio Building continues and Presentation Discussions Begin | Interdisciplinary Unit Teaching | Professional Development Plan | |
| | First-Placement Set-up | Action Planning | Shared Assessments defined and underway | Building of process folio | 2nd Placement Proposals | Finish All About Gorham | Seminar coordinates Interdisciplinary unit | | Full-Time Teaching | |
| | | | | | Vision Statement due | | | | | |

# APPENDIX E: PROJECT DESIGN TEMPLATE MODEL, GORHAM SCHOOL DEPARTMENT

Gorham ETEP Professional Development Site
1995-96 Internship
Project Design Template

TOPIC=
OR
THEME=

## CONTENT AND SKILLS

### CONTENT

- Specific concepts, facts, processes

### SKILLS

- Compulsory Performances
  (reading, writing, data analysis, visual representations, oral)

## ASSESSMENTS

- Criteria for product forms and performances
- Rubrics utilized
- Varied Modes:
  journals (on-going)
  quizzes (one shot)
  KWL (processes)
  conferences (formal, informal)
- Reflections of student and teacher

## ESSENTIAL QUESTION(S)

- Cut across disciplines
- Drives teaching and requires inquiry
- Is relevant to students
- No one right answer

## EXHIBITION

- Culminating performance(s)

## GOALS AND UNDERSTANDINGS

- Guiding questions related to content
- Outcomes for theme or topic that will be assessed
- Understandings students should retain (a year from now)

## TOOLS AND RESOURCES

- Materials needed
- References
- Consultants
- Models
- Technology (Internet)

Gorham ETEP Professional Development Site

1995-96 Internship

Project Design Template

**TOPIC= BOSNIA**
**OR**
**THEME=**

## GOALS AND UNDERSTANDINGS

Political ideologies of parties
Conflict resolution
Understanding of the conflict
Roles of the major powers in the conflict
Religious differences
What turned situation violent?
Why turn to violence?
Roles of the major parties in the conflict
How does media affect the outcomes of conflicts?
Difference between U.S. and
Bosnian/Serb/Croatian culture and government

## ESSENTIAL QUESTION(S)

Why do people hate?
What is a country?
How involved should the U.S.
 be in peacekeeping efforts
 around the world?
Why do differences cause conflicts?
What is peacekeeping?
What is the role of a peacekeeper?
How do people of different religions
 live together?

## CONTENT AND SKILLS

Religions in Bosnia- features/background
Ethnic cleansing
Location of Bosnia and Balkan countries on map
History of Christian/Muslim conflicts
Basic differences of parties involved
News bias/reporting

SKILLS

Reading articles for essential information
Improvement in oral presentation
Mapping

## EXHIBITION

Diary/Family Story
Establish "pen-pal" system where
 peacekeeping soldiers and
 citizens respond to essential
 questions
Proposed resolution to conflict

## TOOLS AND RESOURCES

Christian Science Monitor
Geopol Newsgroup
Internet
Guest speakers: Bosnian refugees, Bosnian
heritage, Portland Hate Crime Task Force

## ASSESSMENTS

Pre/post concept map
Quizzes on geography, history demographics
Essay
Draw a map of the region showing ethnic historical
areas of conflict
Position papers, briefs, presentations

# APPENDIX F: ETEP OUTCOMES, CONTENT AND SKILLS, AND CLASSROOM KEY LEARNING

In 1993, many of the faculty's statements and beliefs about teaching were delineated as 11 outcomes, or standards. This delineation resulted from a project sponsored by the Maine State Education Department and the National Association of State Boards of Education. The outcomes (revised 1/95) in use during this study are:

1. **Knowledge of Child/Adolescent Development and Principles of Learning.** The teacher demonstrates respect, concern for children, and an understanding of how they continue to develop and learn. S/he uses this knowledge to plan and guide instruction and create a supportive learning environment for all students.

2. **Knowledge of Subject Matter and Inquiry.** The teacher understands the framework of the subject matter(s) s/he teachers and makes accessible to students the discipline's tools of inquiry, central concepts, internal structure, and connects to other domains of knowledge, in a manner that promotes the learners' independent inquiry.

3. **Instructional Planning.** The teacher consistently plans and evaluates instruction based on knowledge of the learner, the subject matter, the community, the intended student outcomes, and the curriculum.

4. **Instructional Strategies and Technology.** The teacher understands and uses a variety of teaching strategies, including appropriate technology, to promote learning and independent inquiry for all students.

5. **Assessment.** The teacher enhances and documents learning through continuing use of formal and informal assessment strategies, communicates feedback, and promotes guided self-evaluation in learners.

6. **Diversity.** The teacher models respect for individual differences among students and co-workers. S/he plans and creates instructional opportunities with sensitivity to individual learners.

7. **Beliefs about Teaching and Learning.** The teacher clearly communicates his/her beliefs about teaching, learning, assessment, and the role of education in society and demonstrates practices that support those beliefs.

8. **Citizenship.** The teacher understands principles of democratic community and plans instruction to promote ideals, values, and practices of citizenship.

9. **Collaboration and Professionalism.** The teacher demonstrates professional responsibility to school and community. S/he works collaboratively with colleagues, parents, and community members to improve the conditions of learning for all students and adults.

10. **Professional Development.** The teacher recognizes that s/he is, above all, a learner. S/he continually reflects on and evaluates choices and actions, and seeks out opportunities for professional development as well as ways to improve teaching and learning.

11. **Classroom Management.** The teacher understands and implements classroom management techniques that support individual responsibility and the principles of democratic community.

# APPENDIX F, continued

Gorham ETEP Professional Development Site
PROGRAM TEMPLATE CONTENT & SKILLS
November 27, 1995

## LITERACY
*Reading and Writing theory, development,
    teaching strategies
*Inter-disciplinary (joint with content areas)

## LIFESPAN/EXCEPTIONALITY/
DIVERSITY: Knowing students, their
    schools and their community

*Theorists
*School/community demographics, services,
    and programs
*Rules and regulations
*Case study/child study
*Individual student characteristics and
    development
*Reviewing student records
*Analyzing student work
*Cultural and diversity issues

## CONTENT AREA TEACHING:
Differentiating instruction and
assessment for all students

*Standards
*Content specific teaching strategies
*Issues and research
*Curriculum/Instruction/Assessment process
*Inter-disciplinary (joint with content areas)

## SEMINAR: Professional growth and
classroom and school culture

*Intern assessment process (vision and
    outcomes, portfolio)
*Cohort Group
*Planning
*Classroom Community
*Culture of Schools
*Professional behavior, collegiality, career
    issues (hiring,...)
*Organizing tasks and responsibilities
*Managing stress and change
*District and school program development
*Technology series
*Mutual influences of society and schools
    (Inquiry Project)

## CLASSROOM/SCHOOL PLACEMENT:
Complex system of continuous
group and individualized learning.

*Reflective language
*Shared language
*Establishing relationships with cooperating
    teachers and students
*Assessment practices
*Knowing children individually-
    developmentally, academically
*Science process skills
*Research models/project models
*Relationships outside the classroom- school-
    wide, community, parents
*Establishing classroom community
*Classroom organization- layout, materials,
    schedule
*Personalization
*Behavior and Group Management tricks;
    crisis intervention
*Maintaining professional language and
    behavior
*Adaptability and Flexibility

## SUPPORT SYSTEM

*Journal writing
*Documenting evidence of performance and
    understanding
*Reviewing student work
*Coordinated planning and scheduling
    between team members
*Evaluating performance and understanding
    in outcome areas
*Giving, receiving and using feedback
*Organizing time and tasks
*Professional goal setting

# APPENDIX F, continued

Gorham ETEP Professional Development Site
May, 1994

## Classroom Key Learnings

The attached ETEP outcomes represent areas which need to be addressed during the interns' work in their classroom placements. The following items represent a continuing sampling of areas considered important by a group of cooperating teachers.

*reflective language
*assessment practices
*where are the children developmentally as individuals?
*science process skills
*research models/project models
*relationships outside the classroom- school-wide, community, parents
*establishing classroom community
*shared language
*classroom organizational tricks
*establishing relationships with cooperating teachers and students
*personalization
*management tricks; crisis intervention

# APPENDIX G: EXTENDED TEACHER EDUCATION PROGRAM OUTCOMES, PERFORMANCE REVIEW AND FEEDBACK FORM

INTERN: _____

DATE: _____

## EXTENDED TEACHER EDUCATION PROGRAM OUTCOMES
## PERFORMANCE REVIEW AND FEEDBACK FORM

ASSESSOR: _____

_____ Developing Satisfactorily

_____ Needs Attention

### 1. Knowledge of Child/Adolescent Development and Principles of Learning:

The teacher demonstrates respect, concern for children, and an understanding of how they continue to develop and learn. S/he uses this knowledge to plan and guide instruction and to create a challenging, supportive learning environment.

*Engages supportively with children; uses appropriate body language and verbal language; listens to students and plans/modifies instruction based on individual needs...*

EVIDENCE:

### 2. Knowledge of Subject Matter and Inquiry

_____ Developing Satisfactorily

_____ Needs Attention

The teacher understands the framework of the subject matter(s) s/he teaches and makes accessible to students the discipline's tools of inquiry, central concepts, internal structure, and connections to other domains of knowledge, in a manner that promotes the learner's independent inquiry.

*Engages students in activities that highlight key concepts in content area(s); engages learners in generating concepts and testing ideas and knowledge pertinent to the content area(s); creates interdisciplinary learning experiences*

EVIDENCE:

### 3. Instructional Planning

_____ Developing Satisfactorily

_____ Needs Attention

The teacher consistently plans and evaluates instruction based on knowledge of the learner, the subject matter, the community, the intended student outcomes, and the curriculum.

*Assesses students' prior knowledge and adapts instruction; considers students' needs, capabilities, interests , and intended outcomes when planning instruction; plans thoroughly, incorporating clear knowledge and skill goals with thoughtful selection of tools, resources and design of activities and assessment*

EVIDENCE:

**4. INSTRUCTIONAL STRATEGIES AND TECHNOLOGY**

The teacher understands and uses a variety of teaching strategies, including appropriate technology, to promote learning and independent inquiry for all students.

*Uses strategies and resources , including technology, to stimulate  critical/creative thinking; problem solving, inquiry, knowledge and concept acquisition....*

EVIDENCE:

INTERN:

_____ Developing Satisfactorily

_____ Needs Attention

**5. ASSESSMENT**

The teacher enhances and documents learning through continuing use of formal and informal assessment strategies, communicates feedback, and promotes guided self-evaluation in learners.

*Encourages student goal setting and self-appraisal;  keeps accurate records; uses a variety of assessment strategies; uses assessment  data to make instructional decisions*

EVIDENCE:

_____ Developing Satisfactorily

_____ Needs Attention

**6. DIVERSITY**

The teacher models respect for individual differences among students and co-workers.  S/he plans and creates instructional opportunities with sensitivity to individual learners.

*Equitable and fair with all students; uses multi-cultural materials  when possible; avoids and discourages ridicule and stereotyping....*

EVIDENCE:

_____ Developing Satisfactorily

_____ Needs Attention

**7. BELIEFS ABOUT TEACHING AND LEARNING**

The teacher clearly communicates his/her beliefs about learning, teaching, assessment, and the role of education in society; and demonstrates practices that support those beliefs.

*Communicates and demonstrates a clear and realistic vision of teaching and learning*

EVIDENCE:

_____ Developing Satisfactorily

_____ Needs Attention

INTERN: _____

## 8. CITIZENSHIP
The teacher understands principles of democratic community and plans instruction to promote ideals, values, and practices of citizenship.

*Implements strategies for democratic decision making in classroom; uses strategies to develop student responsibility for learning and behavior; engages student participation in classroom, school and community*

**EVIDENCE:**

_____ Developing Satisfactorily

_____ Needs Attention

## 9. COLLABORATION AND PROFESSIONALISM
The teacher demonstrates professional responsibility to school and community. S/he works collaboratively with colleagues, parents, and community members to improve the conditions of learning for all students and adults.

*Receptive to feedback from peers and supervisors; works collaboratively in teaching and professional responsibilities*

**EVIDENCE:**

_____ Developing Satisfactorily

_____ Needs Attention

## 10. PROFESSIONAL DEVELOPMENT
The teacher recognizes that s/he is, above all, a learner. S/he continually reflects on and evaluates choices and actions, and seeks out opportunities for professional development as well as ways to improve teaching and learning.

*Participates in professional development opportunities; solicits and uses feedback from students, peers and supervisors .....*

**EVIDENCE:**

_____ Developing Satisfactorily

_____ Needs Attention

## 11. CLASSROOM MANAGEMENT
The teacher understands and implements classroom management techniques that support individual responsibility and the principles of democratic community.

*Has clear expectations and respect for all students; uses time effectively; establishes clear routines and procedures; promotes student responsibility...*

**EVIDENCE:**

_____ Developing Satisfactorily

_____ Needs Attention

# APPENDIX H: ETEP-GORHAM ORIENTATION SCHEDULE FOR 1996-97

Gorham ETEP Professional Development Site
Walter H. Kimball and Susie Hanley
August 14- Sept 1 ETEP Orientation Schedule

| Monday | Tuesday | Wednesday | Thursday | Friday |
|---|---|---|---|---|
| LITTLE FALLS Kindergarten Center (8:30-3:00) Daily throughout first week | | | | |
| ---opening------concensus------(cohort 2 day short project)------sharing--- | | | | |
| 14 | 15 | 16 | 17 | 18 |
| K-12 Exceptionality (tentative) 21 | English Content Methods 9-12  Math 8:30-11:30  Lifespan 1-4  22 | 23 | ALL ABOUT GORHAM  24 | K-12 Planning  25 |
| Reading and Writing in Content Area    Everyday this week | | | | |
| Gorham New Staff/Intern Orientation 28 | Final Preparations 29 | 30 | 31 | 3:30- 5:30  1 |

# ABOUT THE AUTHORS

**Letitia Hochstrasser Fickel** is Assistant Professor of education at the University of Alaska-Anchorage, where she is involved in the collaborative redesign of the teacher education program and continuing her research on teacher professional development and learning. She is the author of a book chapter titled, "Teacher Community and Commitment: A Case Study of a High School Social Studies Department," in B. L. Whitford and K. Jones (Eds.)., *Assessment, Accountability and Teacher Commitment: Lessons from Kentucky,* published by SUNY Press. She completed her doctorate at the University of Louisville in 1998 with a speciality in teaching and learning.

**Linda Darling-Hammond** is the Editor of the three volumes of *Studies in Excellence in Teacher Education.* Her biographical information is included in About the Editor.

**Maritza B. McDonald** is the Director of Professional Development and Evaluation at the American Museum of Natural History in New York. Her professional experiences in research and evaluation, program design and administration, and graduate school teaching include positions as the Senior Researcher and Evaluator for NCREST at the Teachers College, Columbia University and as the Director, Advisor, and Instructor of the preservice teacher education program at the Bank Street College of Education. She holds a doctorate in education with specialization in teacher education and curriculum development from Teachers College, Columbia University.

**Gordon Ruscoe** is Professor Emeritus at the University of Louisville, Kentucky. After more than 30 years as a professor of education at the University of California-Los Angeles, Syracuse University, and the University of Louisville, he retired to Florida in 1998.

**Jon Snyder** is currently the Director of Teacher Education and a faculty member in the Graduate School of Education at the University of California at Santa Barbara. He is also a Senior Researcher for the National Commission on Teaching and America's Future. He has interned as an elementary school principal and served as a staff and curriculum developer. Upon receipt of his doctorate at Teachers College Columbia University, Snyder worked in the teacher education program at Teachers College. Immediately prior to his move to Santa Barbara, Snyder was the Associate Director of Research for the National Center for the Restructuring of Education, Schools, and Teaching.

**Betty Lou Whitford** is Professor of Education in the Department of Curriculum and Teaching and Director of the National Center for Restructuring Education, Schools, and Teaching (NCREST) at Teachers College, Columbia University. From 1981-1999, she was a professor at the University of Louisville where, with Gordon Ruscoe and Letitia Fickel, she co-authored *Knitting It All Together: Collaborative Teacher Education in Southern Maine,* the monograph from which the chapter in this book is drawn. Her research focuses on education reform, including case studies of school restructuring and the work of school-university partnerships. Her recent book is *Accountability, Assessment, and Teacher Commitment: Lessons from Kentucky's Reform Efforts* (with Ken Jones) available from SUNY Press.

## ABOUT THE EDITOR

**Linda Darling-Hammond** is currently Charles E. Ducommun Professor of Teaching and Teacher Education at Stanford University. Her research, teaching, and policy work focus on issues of school restructuring, teacher education, and educational equity. She is also executive director of the National Commission on Teaching & America's Future, a blue-ribbon panel whose 1996 report, *What Matters Most: Teaching for America's Future,* has been widely acclaimed as a major blueprint for transforming education so that all children are guaranteed access to high quality teaching.

Prior to her appointment at Stanford, Darling-Hammond was William F. Russell Professor in the Foundations of Education at Teachers College, Columbia University, where she was also Co-Director of the National Center for Restructuring Education, Schools, and Teaching (NCREST). Darling-Hammond is past president of the American Educational Research Association, a two-term member of the National Board for Professional Teaching Standards, and a member of the National Academy of Education and has served on many national advisory boards.

She is the author or editor of seven books, including *The Right to Learn: A Blueprint for Creating Schools that Work,* which was awarded the Outstanding Book Award from the American Educational Research Association in 1998, and more than 200 journal articles, book chapters, and monographs on issues of policy and practice. Among her other recent books are *Professional Development Schools: Schools for Developing a Profession, A License to Teach: Building a Profession for 21st Century Schools,* and *Authentic Assessment in Action.*

*In 1996,* the National Commission on Teaching and America's Future (NCTAF) under-took a research project to document teacher education programs that successfully prepare teachers to teach diverse learners to high standards. The study documented the successes and strategies of teacher education programs that have reputations for preparing teachers to teach in ways that are learner- and learning-centered; that is, they prepare teachers who are responsive to individual students' intelligences, talents, cultural backgrounds, needs, and interests. These programs also prepare teachers for understanding, teachers who support active in-depth learning for powerful thinking and flexible, proficient student performances. The study produced seven case studies that provide detailed descriptive evidence about the outcomes of the programs, the content they engage, and the processes they employ.

Those seven case studies are presented here. Edited by Linda Darling-Hammond, executive director of the National Commission, this three-volume series includes:

**STUDIES OF EXCELLENCE IN TEACHER EDUCATION: PREPARATION AT THE GRADUATE LEVEL**

**Where There is Learning There is Hope: The Preparation of Preservice Teachers at Bank Street College of Education,** *by Linda Darling-Hammond, Stanford University and Maritza B. Macdonald, Teachers College, Columbia University*

**Knowing Children—Understanding Teaching: The Developmental Teacher Education Program at the University of California-Berkeley,** *by Jon Snyder, University of California-Santa Barbara*

**Knitting it All Together: Collaborative Teacher Education in Southern Maine,** *by Betty Lou Whitford, Gordon Ruscoe, and Letitia Fickel, University of Louisville (KY)*

**STUDIES OF EXCELLENCE IN TEACHER EDUCATION: PREPARATION IN A FIVE-YEAR PROGRAM**

**Teacher Education at the University of Virginia: A Study of English and Mathematics Preparation,** *by Katherine K. Merseth, Harvard Project on Schooling and Children (Cambridge, MA) and Julia Koppich, Management Analysis and Planning Associates, San Francisco, (CA)*

**Trinity University: Preparing Teachers for Tomorrow's Schools,** *by Julia Koppich, Management Analysis and Planning Associates, San Francisco (CA)*

**STUDIES OF EXCELLENCE IN TEACHER EDUCATION: PREPARATION IN THE UNDERGRADUATE YEARS**

**Ability-Based Teacher Education: Elementary Teacher Education at Alverno College,** *by Kenneth Zeichner, University of Wisconsin-Madison*

**Learning to Become a Teacher: The Wheelock Way,** *by Lynne Miller and David Silvernail, University of Southern Maine*

AACTE

National Commission
on Teaching & America's Future